What Your Colleagues Are Saying

"No one combines novel insights and precise ideas like Viviane Robinson. Robinson is as comfortable around the details of the trees as she is in stepping back to take in the forest. You won't find a more unique and powerful book on leadership—one suited exactly for our times—than *Virtuous Educational Leadership*."

Michael Fullan
Professor Emeritus, OISE/University of Toronto
Toronto, Ontario, Canada

"In *Virtuous Educational Leadership*, Viviane Robinson has made explicit what I have often described as an X factor in leadership—something that distinguishes excellent leaders from the rest. Her description and portrayal of virtuous leadership provides insights into the dispositions that underpin wise leadership."

Anne Berit Emstad
Professor, Norwegian University of Science and Technology
Trondheim, Norway

"Viviane Robinson is one of my favorite educational leadership researchers and writers, and this book illustrates so well why that is so. The school leader plays an essential role in engaging students in deep learning. Robinson offers invaluable insights for how to foster this type of learning through virtuous leadership."

Peter DeWitt
Author, Leadership Coach, Education Week Blogger
Albany, NY

"Viviane Robinson takes us out of our comfort zone to challenge how we think about the true purpose of educational leadership. Full of insight and analysis combined with rich examples, this book shows us that when school leaders not only do the right things but do them in the right way, it is the students themselves who benefit the most."

Steve Munby
Visiting Professor, Centre for Educational Leadership, University College London
Cumbria, UK

"*Virtuous Educational Leadership* is a gift for all of us searching for guidance in school leadership development. It is both inspiring and practical. Viviane Robinson promotes leadership excellence by showing how virtues are at the very core of leadership and how crucial they are in the face of today's educational challenges."

Anna Jolonch
Director of LID Barcelona, Educational Leadership Centre
Barcelona, Catalonia, Spain

"Making a positive change in any role, from teacher to principal, requires both a 'what' and a 'how.' *Virtuous Educational Leadership* provides a framework for identifying the 'what' (collaborative complex problem-solving) and approaching the 'how' (virtuous leadership). With Viviane Robinson's characteristic depth and rigor, the ideas hidden in these pages will empower leaders worldwide."

Oliver Lovell
Author of *Tools for Teachers* and *Cognitive Load Theory in Action* and host of the Education Research Reading Room Podcast
Victoria, Australia

"*Virtuous Educational Leadership* is a comprehensive examination of the complex world of school leadership. It draws upon research from a wide range of disciplines, supported by rich analysis, of examples of the work of leaders. Voices from the front lines are expertly interwoven throughout. I highly recommend it."

Tom Rees
Executive Director, Programmes, Ambition Institute
Manchester, UK

"Educational leaders inhabit a world that expects simplicity to be curated from complexity, certainty from unpredictability, coherence from chaos. And, while the existing literature on educational leadership contains plenty of advice and its recommendations seem intuitively compelling, it is, ultimately, lacking in actionable specificity. Thankfully, *Virtuous Educational Leadership* is a work of deep practical wisdom that is anchored in theory, acknowledges the critical importance of context, and illustrates clearly how educational leadership is not simply about doing the right work of leadership but also about doing it in the right way."

Stuart Kime
Director of Education, Evidence Based Education
Sunderland, UK

Virtuous Educational Leadership

Virtuous Educational Leadership

Doing the Right Work the Right Way

Viviane Robinson

FOR INFORMATION

Corwin
A SAGE Company
2455 Teller Road
Thousand Oaks, California 91320
(800) 233-9936
www.corwin.com

SAGE Publications Ltd.
1 Oliver's Yard
55 City Road
London EC1Y 1SP
United Kingdom

SAGE Publications India Pvt. Ltd.
B 1/I 1 Mohan Cooperative Industrial Area
Mathura Road, New Delhi 110 044
India

SAGE Publications Asia-Pacific Pte. Ltd.
18 Cross Street #10-10/11/12
China Square Central
Singapore 048423

President: Mike Soules
Vice President and
Editorial Director: Monica Eckman
Senior Acquisitions Editor: Tanya Ghans
Content Development Manager: Desirée A. Bartlett
Editorial Assistant: Nyle De Leon
Production Editor: Tori Mirsadjadi
Copy Editor: Rachel Keith
Typesetter: Hurix Digital
Cover Designer: Janet Kiesel
Marketing Manager: Morgan Fox

Printed and bound by CPI Group (UK) Ltd, Croydon, CR0 4YY

Library of Congress Cataloging-in-Publication Data

Names: Robinson, V. M. (Viviane M.), author.

Title: Virtuous educational leadership : doing the right work the right way / Viviane Robinson.

Description: Thousand Oaks, California : Corwin, 2023. | Includes bibliographical references and index.

Identifiers: LCCN 2022022662 | ISBN 9781071803721 (paperback) | ISBN 9781071803738 (epub) | ISBN 9781071803776 (epub) | ISBN 9781071803752 (ebook)

Subjects: LCSH: Educational leadership–Moral and ethical aspects. | School management and organization–Moral and ethical aspects.

Classification: LCC LB2806 .R569 2023 | DDC 371.2/011–dc23/eng/20220706 LC record available at https://lccn.loc.gov/2022022662

This book is printed on acid-free paper.

22 23 24 25 26 10 9 8 7 6 5 4 3 2 1

Contents

Preface

Educational leadership matters. We know that the excellence of a school's leadership is linked to the learning and achievement of its students. We also know that without it, school improvement is impossible, or at least impossible to sustain. Until we solve the problem of developing and retaining more excellent educational leaders, we will struggle to reduce the long-standing disparities in student outcomes that plague many Western education systems.

But what is excellent educational leadership? Is it possible to specify it in ways that do justice to the complexity and diversity of the role? Is it possible to specify it in ways that go beyond theoretical abstraction and offer practical guidance to policy makers and practitioners who seek to develop leadership excellence in themselves and others?

The Story in the Title

The purpose of this book is to answer those questions. Since the essence of my answers is captured in the title of this book, it is worth unpacking what I mean by "virtuous educational leadership" and "doing the right work the right way."

Virtuous Educational Leadership

While I was writing this book, people frequently asked why I was using virtue theory. My short answer was that I wanted to give more attention to the ethical dimensions of educational leadership, and virtue theory, with its emphasis on character, enabled me to do that. I had become increasingly aware that the language of capabilities, which I had used in my previous writing, did not afford me the tools to discuss what constituted doing the right work in the right way, because it lacked an ethical dimension. Educational leaders are very powerful people, for their decisions influence the lives and learning of hundreds of students and teachers. I am concerned, therefore, not only with what educational leaders should know and do but additionally with how to ensure their capabilities are used for worthy purposes and in worthy ways. It is that concern that led me to virtue theory.

A virtue is a desirable quality of character—evident in a reliable tendency to respond to situations in excellent ways. Virtues are deep-seated personal qualities that are central to the way of being of the virtuous leader. A leader demonstrates the virtue of respect, for example, by acting in a respectful way not only with powerful parents and administrators but in all interactions, including with students. Furthermore, the virtue of respect is evident not just in face-to-face interactions. The respectful leader *characteristically reasons, acts, and reacts in respectful ways* (Annas, 2011).

In short, virtue theory requires us to consider not only what our leaders should know and do but also what type of person they should be. Since virtues are rich concepts that include all these aspects, I no longer needed separate consideration of leadership capabilities, which in my previous writing I had understood as knowledge and skills. Virtues could express what educational leaders need to know, do, and be, all in one integrated package.

Doing the Right Work the Right Way

Since the virtues I concentrate on are those that are of particular relevance to the work of educational leadership, it is time to turn to the subtitle of this book and explain my argument about the nature of the right work and what it means to do it the right way. I argue that the right work is the dedicated pursuit of the proper purposes of education. After a brief discussion of the debates among philosophers of education, I settle on three proper purposes: **preparation** of children and young people through mastery of the competencies they require to lead fulfilling and productive lives; **socialisation** into particular cultures and communities; and the development of **autonomy** by enabling children and young persons to exercise choice without surrendering to the will of others or to uncontrolled inner drives. Since these purposes are distinctive, the practical wisdom that is central to virtuous educational leadership requires substantial educational knowledge and teaching experience. Generic leadership knowledge and experience will not build the virtues that are required for excellent educational leadership.

In modern curricula the three purposes are pursued through the development of students' competencies—clusters of knowledge and skills that can be applied to the analysis of real-world problems. Developing such competencies requires students, teachers, and leaders to embrace what has been called deep or deeper learning—terms that I use interchangeably throughout this book. Through deep learning, students become experts in a particular knowledge or skill domain and know when, why, and how to apply that knowledge in solving newly encountered problems within that domain.

If the right work for educational leaders is the dedicated pursuit of the three purposes by ensuring deep learning for all students, then my next challenge was to identify the virtues that leaders needed to do that work. My approach was to backwards map by arguing that, if the purpose is to ensure deep learning, then leaders need to know the science of deep learning and of teaching for deep learning (see Figure 0.1). From this science, I then derive, through logical argument and reference to empirical research, broad descriptions of the right leadership work.

In leadership, context is critical. Leaders need to do the right work guided by the science and adapting to the requirements of every situation in which they are making decisions. Those requirements are not adequately specified by the usual categorical accounts of context—size of school, urban versus rural, and so forth. Instead, I argue that context is everything that needs to be taken into account in solving particular problems, and that context shifts every time something new or different has to be taken into account. I then explain what problems are, how

Figure 0.1 A Process for Determining the Right Leadership Work

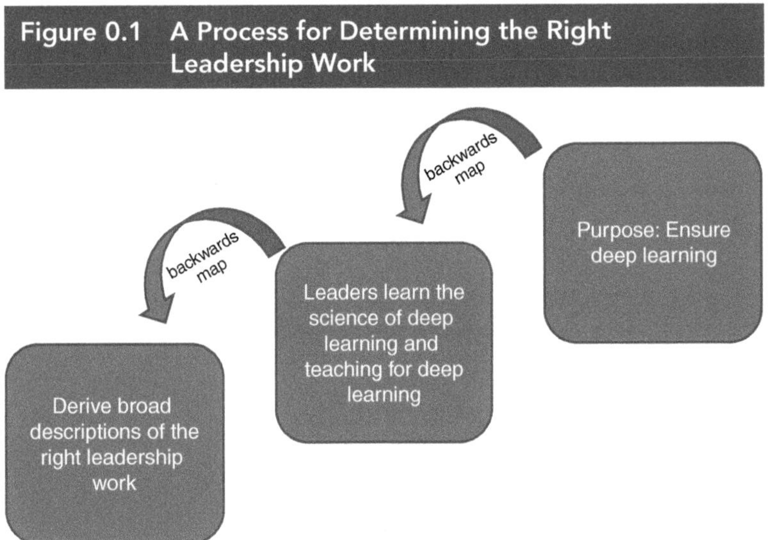

they are solved, and illustrate the process with real school examples. Leaders do the right work by solving or re-solving problems that prevent pursuit or achievement of the purposes. They also do the right work by ensuring the smooth operation of the hundreds of routines that are the result of prior problem-solving efforts.

Having identified the right work, I then identified virtues that are required to do that work the right way. I propose three clusters of virtues that have particular relevance to the work of educational leaders (see Figure 0.2). In the first cluster are leadership virtues. Leadership virtues are evident in the worthiness of the educational purposes being pursued and in the sources of influence that are employed in their pursuit. Virtuous leaders recognise that leadership rests on fundamentally consensual rather than coerced influence processes and, therefore, that the sources of their influence lie in their knowledge and ideas, their admirable personal qualities, and in the reasonable exercise of any authority that their role accords them.

The problem-solving virtues that constitute the second cluster comprise strategic, analytic, and imaginative virtues. Strategic virtues are applicable to every problem, not just to those described as "strategic" in strategic and annual plans. Strategic virtues shape how leaders think about all their work because they are continually asking, "How does this meeting, activity, project, or resource add value to the most important goals we are pursuing?"

Analytic virtues are apparent in leaders who are motivated to test rather than assume the validity of their own and others' key beliefs, who are skilled in doing so, and who can explain why such testing is important to them. Virtuous leaders are very aware of the ethical dimensions of their decision-making—that mistaken assumptions and taken-for-granted beliefs can produce poor-quality decisions that waste resources, do not solve the problem, and may have negative impacts on students. The stance of leaders with strong analytic virtues is that of truth-seeking rather than truth-claiming.

Figure 0.2 A Taxonomy of Virtues

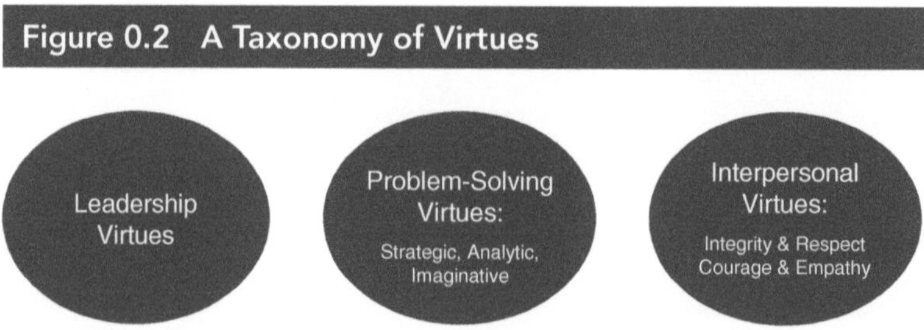

While analytic virtues are required to gain an accurate understanding of the elements of a problem and their interrelationships, imaginative virtues are required to reconfigure and integrate those elements in ways that suggest how the problem could be solved. Imaginative virtues are seen in the creativity with which some educational leaders are able to reimagine apparently conflicting solution requirements so that they can be integrated in ways that advance multiple educational purposes. Such creativity requires a foundation of deep knowledge of the relevant concepts, because such knowledge enables flexible yet principled interpretations of solution requirements.

Doing the right work the right way nearly always requires productive collaboration with others. The challenge for educational leaders is to develop the types of relationships that advance the proper purposes by addressing the complex problems that stand in the way of achieving them. What must be avoided are good relationships with teachers that do not serve students well because the adult relationships are not sufficiently focused on achieving the purposes.

In the third cluster of interpersonal virtues, I have highlighted two virtues that build trust—integrity and respect—for without trust it is difficult to resolve the problems that prevent achievement of the purposes. Leaders with integrity can be relied on to tell the truth, not only about external situations but also about their own thoughts and feelings. For educational leaders, integrity requires not only congruence between words and actions but also that their words and actions be educationally worthy because they serve the interests of students.

Respect is evident in the way leaders treat others as having goals and interests of their own, and as entitled to pursue them in an autonomous and self-directed manner, as long as such autonomy is compatible with the pursuit of agreed educational purposes and role responsibilities. Virtuous educational leaders strive to be respected rather than liked, and their respect is evident in the way they pay attention and listen, especially to views that differ from their own.

Two additional interpersonal virtues, courage and empathy, are essential to addressing the problems that prevent achieving the purposes. Courage is needed to overcome the fear and anxiety that may be experienced when giving or receiving negative feedback, facing opponents, or challenging the status quo. But leaders also need empathy to deeply understand why others disagree, or why their expectations have not been met.

Since interpersonal vices, of which we all have plenty, prevent the consistent exercise of interpersonal virtues and their deployment in collaborative problem-solving, I give considerable attention to how such vices can be overcome, and the learning involved in doing so. I explain how various vices contribute to the dilemma that so many leaders experience between addressing the quality of teaching and learning and maintaining the trust of their staff. Leaders with strong problem-solving and interpersonal virtues are able to avoid this task-relationship dilemma by treating their opinions as fallible rather than as truth and by treating others as people with whom they can inquire and learn rather than as objects of persuasion.

I have learned from my experience in leading hundreds of workshops for educational leaders that there are situations in which being virtuous is particularly challenging. That is why I have included a chapter on being virtuous in tough situations (Chapter 12), including a nine-step guide to more virtuous communication of critical evaluations.

The Scope and Organisation of the Book

It is unusual for a book on educational leadership to range so widely across disciplines. Despite its wide range, it is tightly structured and organised. I draw on the philosophy of education, the science of teaching and learning, and the philosophy and psychology of virtues to develop an argument about what constitutes the right work and how to do it in the right way. The tight structure and argument mean that this book is best read from start to finish. For those readers who are short on time, I suggest they read the summaries in chapter order first, for that will give them the essence of the argument and enable them to decide which chapters to study in more depth.

In Part A I draw on the philosophy of education to identify the proper purposes of education and note how these purposes are represented or not in modern curricula (Chapter 2). Since achieving the purposes requires learning to apply well-organised bodies of knowledge to real-world problems (deep learning), Chapter 2 summarises the science of deep learning and its implications for classroom teaching. This knowledge is critical, for the right work of educational leadership is that which the science of learning and teaching suggests is needed to achieve the purposes of educational institutions—ensuring the development of self-directed and well-prepared students.

In Part B, I spell out what doing the right leadership work involves. My account of this work in Chapter 3 is organised under five dimensions of leadership practice that are included in the frameworks that guide leadership development and policy in many jurisdictions. The description of each dimension emphasises the work that is required to ensure that students have high-quality opportunities for deep learning. Guidance about how to tailor that work to different contexts is provided in Chapter 4.

Part C enriches the story with eight chapters devoted to describing and illustrating how to do the right work the right way. In Chapter 5, I provide an accessible explanation of virtues and explain how they are learnable despite their deep-seated personal quality. I then explain my selection of three clusters of virtue as being of particular relevance to the role of educational leaders—leadership, problem-solving, and interpersonal virtues. In Chapter 6, I discuss the first cluster, which is largely concerned with more and less virtuous leadership motivations. I also explain the sources of leadership influence and how leadership is not confined to those with positional authority.

The second cluster, problem-solving virtues, comprises strategic (Chapter 7), analytic (Chapter 8), and imaginative (Chapter 9) virtues. I explain how all three categories are essential to solving the problems that prevent achievement of the proper purposes of education. At least half of each chapter shows the application of the virtues, often in combination with one another, to the real work of educational leaders. Since virtuous leadership requires virtuous thinking and action, many of the excerpts, from meetings and conversations, include leaders' thoughts as well as their speech. In addition, I have included detailed annotations and commentary to make explicit how virtues and vices are shaping the problem-solving.

I take the same approach in the chapter on the third cluster of interpersonal virtues (Chapter 10), and in the subsequent two chapters, I show how situationally relevant interpersonal and problem-solving virtues are integrated in excellent ways (Chapter 11), even in tough spots (Chapter 12).

The case of complex collaborative problem-solving in Chapter 13 brings all the strands together to show how the collective virtues of high school leaders resolved a long-standing attendance problem. The leaders were not perfect—they made some mistakes by succumbing to their vices on occasion—but they were collectively sufficiently strong in their leadership, problem-solving, and interpersonal virtues to analyse the complexity of the attendance problem and craft and sustain a solution.

Despite the considerable scope of this volume, there are many further questions to be answered. In my view, one of the more important ones is the role of institutional (education) and organisational (schools and school districts) cultures in enabling and inhibiting virtuous leadership. Individually virtuous leaders are not the whole answer, for in too many contexts it is too hard to be virtuous while swimming against a virtue-inhibiting tide. Virtue-inhibiting educational cultures include those in which a tight focus on educational purposes is hindered by constantly shifting and distracting policy priorities; those in which there are too many undiscussables except in the car park; those where too much weight is given to the "optics"; and those where there is too little understanding of and respect for the depth of educational knowledge and experience that is required to do the right work the right way.

While the creation of more virtuous institutional and organisational cultures is not the focus of this book, suffice it to say that such an endeavour requires leaders who have a deep practical understanding of relevant virtues, a strong personal motivation to be virtuous, and at least moderate skill in doing so. Without such knowledge and commitments, those leading cultural reform are unlikely to know what a virtuous institution looks like, let alone know how to design the structures and processes that would make it a practical reality.

The Book's Features and Benefits

Several features of this book are designed to ensure that readers will see strong connections between its theoretical content and their own leadership challenges:

- Strong connections are made between relevant published research and practical implications.
- Numerous examples of leaders' thinking and action are provided, so readers can see what virtuous practice looks like.
- Examples of leadership practice are analysed to show how theoretical concepts are evident in practice.

Additional features help readers understand, remember, and use the book in their own contexts:

- A detailed table of contents helps readers see the sequence of ideas and how the argument unfolds.

- Summaries at the end of each chapter assist recall and review.
- Reflection questions at the end of each chapter support individual or group book study.
- Readers can select those leadership conversations and meetings that have particular relevance to their current challenges and use them to practise more virtuous approaches. Since many excerpts include leaders' thoughts as well as their speech, readers can identify and practise the type of thinking and talking that will help them to be more virtuous.

Acknowledgments

My inspiration comes from practitioners, and it is to the many hundreds who have done me the privilege of sharing their challenges with me that I owe the greatest debt. In particular, I thank those leaders who gave me permission to use excerpts of their speech, whether real or role-played, to illustrate the points I make in the text. As a student of Chris Argyris at Harvard University, I was held to a tough standard—"If you can't illustrate your advice, don't give it." By giving permission to use excerpts from audio and video recordings we have made over the years, these practitioners enabled me to bridge the enormous gulf between giving abstract advice and showing leaders what that advice could look like in practice.

I am grateful to the organisations and individuals who have encouraged and supported my new venture into virtuous educational leadership. The Melbourne-based Bastow Institute of Education Leadership, now integrated into the Victorian Academy of Teaching and Leadership, gave me my first opportunity to write about those virtues that were critical for school leaders, and after presentations to and feedback from school leaders, those virtues are now included in the Victorian Leadership Framework that guides the statewide leadership development curriculum.

The New Zealand–based company Evaluation Associates gave permission to use excerpts from audio and video transcripts that we made during the development of Leading by Learning—a series of workshops that build capability in building trust while tackling complex problems. In particular, I thank the CEO of Evaluation Associates, Anna Sullivan, and staff members Jacqui Patuawa, Allan Powell, and Cleve Shearer for permission to use speech excerpts. Permission was also granted by Jodi Devine, Siliva Gaugatao, and Margaret Palmer.

This book has taken me into new philosophical territory, and I am deeply grateful to Christine Swanton for being my guide through the minefield of virtue theory and virtue ethics. It was a pleasure to discover in doing so that Aristotelian virtues are deeply practical, flexible, and context sensitive. Christine helped me to appreciate how virtue theory could provide a rich framework for meeting my goal of giving more emphasis to leadership character. Her critique and support have been invaluable.

My research and development on complex collaborative problem-solving would not have been possible without my long-standing collaboration with my friend and colleague Jacqui Patuawa. While Jacqui was completing her doctoral thesis, I worked with her and her cosupervisor, Claire Sinnema, on early versions of Table 13.1 and on resources to teach leaders how to be more systematic in solving the complex problems that have been barriers to the achievement of their improvement goals. The case study in Chapter 13 had its origins in a course Jacqui and I taught Victorian system leaders, and that course, and the subsequent case, would not have been possible without our collaboration.

Rachel Cann, my research assistant on this project, saved me hours of work by completing literature searches, checking references, and helping with diagrams. Her speed, accuracy, and research skills are greatly appreciated. Finally, I thank the team at Corwin, who have been infinitely patient and supportive of this project. Feedback from Desirée Bartlett made this a better manuscript, and Nyle De Leon helped me obtain the many permissions that were required.

I am fortunate to live in a family where spending hours thinking and writing about tough stuff is accepted and encouraged. My husband David encouraged me in multiple ways—by understanding how important this work is to me, by helping me to get through the blockages right to the finish, by listening, never pressuring, and being patient. Virtues indeed!

About the Author

Viviane Robinson is a distinguished professor emeritus at the University of Auckland, New Zealand, and visiting professor at University College London. She completed her doctorate with Chris Argyris and Donald Schon at Harvard University and then dedicated her career to improving educational leadership policy and practice through a programme of research and development focused on the impact of educational leaders on the learning and well-being of their students.

Viviane's academic research programme on how leaders build trust while attempting to improve teaching and learning has informed the profession through her numerous academic articles and widely translated books (*Student-Centered Leadership*, Jossey Bass/Wiley; *Reduce Change to Increase Improvement*, Corwin) and professional development resources (Leading by Learning).

Viviane remains closely connected to the realities of educational leadership by working as a leadership facilitator and coach and by consulting on leadership policy and development for professional and government bodies in England, Norway, Singapore, Chile, Israel, Canada, Australia, and New Zealand.

She has received awards from national and international professional and academic organisations. In 2011 she was made a fellow of the American Educational Research Association for sustained excellence in educational research. In 2017 she was elected as a fellow of the Royal Society of New Zealand and awarded its Mason Durie Medal in recognition of the international impact of her leadership research.

PART A

Identifying the Proper Purpose of Leadership Work

Three Proper Purposes of Education[1]

1

In a world where the responsibilities of educational leaders are constantly expanding, where today's to-do list is displaced by unanticipated crises, interruptions, and new external demands, it is easy for educational leaders to lose sight of what, among all the important things they could be doing, is more important than the rest. How can they, in this complex, uncertain, and even chaotic environment, develop and sustain a sense of coherent purpose—a sense of purpose that will guide their decisions about what constitutes the right work?

In this chapter I argue that the right leadership work is that which achieves the proper purposes of educational institutions. I refer to proper purpose because for the last 50 years at least, sociologists of education have identified the numerous ways in which education has served improper purposes, such as perpetuation of social and racial inequalities through policies and practices like tracking, streaming, and disproportionate suspension and exclusion of certain student groups. My aim, as is appropriate for a book on virtuous educational leadership, is to identify the proper purposes of educational institutions so their leaders can steer a course towards the ideal.

Since it is the proper purpose of education as an institution that should shape leaders' role-related responsibilities, my first step in arriving at the right work of educational leadership is to settle on the proper purposes. That is the subject of this chapter. Once some clarity is gained about purposes, I examine the evidence (Chapter 2) about how students learn and how teachers foster that learning, because leaders' pursuit of the purposes should be strongly informed by the science of teaching and learning. It is from that evidence that I then derive the implications for the right work of educational leaders (Chapter 3).

---

[1] Portions of Chapters 1 and 2 are a slightly revised version of Robinson, V. (2022). What is distinctive about educational leadership? In R. Tierney, F. Rizvi, E. Kadriye, & G. H. Smith (Eds.), *International encyclopedia of education* (4th ed.). Elsevier.

The Proper Purposes of Educational Institutions

So, what are the proper purposes of educational institutions? I tackle this question with a brief foray into philosophical writing on the proper functions, or purposes, of educational institutions. I then check the extent to which the three broad purposes derived from this philosophical analysis are reflected in the statements of purpose found in the policy and curriculum documents of seven educational jurisdictions. Next, I argue that at least one of the three broad purposes is unique to education, and that since the role obligations of educational leaders are derived from institutional purposes, educational leadership itself is distinctive from leadership in other domains.

Philosophical Accounts of Purpose

Over many decades, philosophers of education have debated the proper purpose of educational institutions (Hand, 2014). Those debates, which are never finally resolved, have traversed such issues as the relative importance of vocational preparation and broader civic education (Winch, 2002).

The stance I take with respect to these debates is that educational institutions have three purposes and that a crucial role of leaders is to make decisions that integrate rather than set up an opposition between them. Such integration requires not only the right philosophical commitments but also knowledge and skill in formulating curricula and pedagogies that enable integration of purposes that are too readily set in opposition to one another.

I call the three broad purposes of education:

- Preparation
- Socialisation
- Autonomy

Purposes related to **preparation** are focused on the acquisition of knowledge and skills that enable children and young persons to lead satisfying and productive lives, including enabling them to make choices about the type of paid employment they desire (MacAllister, 2016; Winch, 2002). The valued knowledge and skills range from various forms of literacy and numeracy to the specialist skills required for particular trades and professions. The importance of preparation is justified in terms of individual fulfilment (Winch, 2002), the relationship between a strong national economy and a skilled workforce (Biesta, 2009; Winch, 2002), and the strong expectation of young people themselves that their schooling will prepare them for the pursuit of fulfilling paid employment (Winch, 2002).

Purposes related to **socialisation** are concerned with the initiation of students into particular cultures and communities, which may be associated with subject disciplines, professional groups, or political, social, religious, and ethnic traditions (Biesta, 2009). In democratic societies, socialisation includes providing students with the experiences and critical abilities that enable them to participate freely in community and civic life at school and beyond.

Some philosophers of education see it as critical that students are exposed over extended periods of time to members of different traditions, so they are equipped to engage in the type of debate that characterises an educated public (MacIntyre & Dunne, 2002). The choices educators make about socialisation contribute to the formation of students' identity and to the historical continuity and renewal of cultures and traditions.

While the socialisation purpose is more obviously pursued in religious or special character schools, socialisation is involved in the way in which any knowledge and skills are represented. In teaching math, for example, the subject can be taught in ways that, wittingly or unwittingly, communicate to students that the purpose of their maths lessons is fluency—that is, to get the right answer as reliably and quickly as possible. Alternatively, math can be taught in ways that induct students into a mathematical community of practice through explicit teaching of mathematical ways of thinking and problem-solving. In making these choices, educators are socialising students into very different ways of doing math and being mathematicians.

This socialisation purpose is an inevitable concomitant of pursuing the first "preparation" purpose. It is the worth of what students are being socialised into and the mode of that socialisation that needs explicit debate. For example, it could be argued that student management practices such as detentions, lining up, and hall passes constitute an improper form of socialisation if they unnecessarily limit student autonomy.

My third set of purposes is the development of autonomous persons, with **autonomy** understood as the ability to manage one's life. This purpose provides a counterpoint to socialisation, for it involves the freedom to make choices about how to live in the world—choices that might question or even reject the cultures and traditions into which one has been socialised (Biesta, 2009).

The development of autonomy requires educators to focus on three personal attributes (Winch, 2002). First, as students grow older, they begin to get a sense of the kind of life they would like to lead, and so the development of autonomy involves exercising choice about how they can achieve the fulfilment they envisage.

Second, students need sufficient knowledge, including self-knowledge, to make informed choices. Autonomy, in this educational sense, requires the development of a critical capacity to examine one's life so that judgment is not surrendered to the will of others or to uncontrolled inner drives. Third, students "need to be equipped with the self-mastery to pursue projects to a successful conclusion in the face of doubts and difficulties" (Winch, 2002, p. 103).

Teaching knowledge and skills (preparation) must be integrated with the deliberate development of autonomous persons so that students can lead lives that are personally meaningful and socially worthwhile. American philosopher of education Hugh Sockett explains the importance of integrating these two purposes as follows:

> There is little point in business and industry's demanding people with knowledge and skills from the schools, if graduates lack integrity, are closed-minded, lack judgment, are not prepared to take risks intellectually, and have little self-understanding. Required, are not people with critical thinking "skills" but people who are critical thinkers. . . . Education's primary emphasis must be on those moral and intellectual dispositions that characterize the free, autonomous individual in a democratic society, developed through content embedded in official educational standards. (Sockett, 2012, pp. xi–xii)

In an era of fake news, science denial, and siloed social discourse, there has never been a greater need for educators to focus on how schools can strengthen the development of moral and intellectual dispositions.

In an era of fake news, science denial, and siloed social discourse, there has never been a greater need for educators to focus on how schools can strengthen the development of the moral and intellectual dispositions to which Sockett refers.

Official Statements of Purpose

To what extent are each of these three purposes (preparation, socialisation, and autonomy) enshrined in the official statements of educational purpose in Western democracies? This question is important because it does not make any sense to anchor the work of educational leadership in purposes derived from a philosophical analysis if there is little relationship between those purposes and curriculum policy.

While school districts and individual schools have some discretion about how they tailor policy to their local context, official statements of purpose are powerful because they signal what is valued by governing authorities and, in democratic societies, by those who elect them. In addition, such statements shape the frameworks against which local curricula are developed, schools are evaluated, and their leaders are selected and appraised.

I reviewed the official curriculum documents of seven jurisdictions (New Zealand; Victoria, Australia; California, United States; Ontario, Canada; England; Scotland; and Norway), paying particular attention to explicit or implicit statements of purpose. Since all seven jurisdictions have strong democratic and liberal traditions, I recognise that other purposes may be more relevant in countries with different political and cultural traditions.

Unsurprisingly, the first preparation purpose was the most salient. More surprising, perhaps, was the ambitiousness and richness of the nature of the preparation that was envisaged. Preparation was much more than the mastery of curriculum content in a range of subjects. Rather, it involved the development of students' competencies, requiring the integration of the knowledge, skills, and attitudes required to meet complex demands.

> A competency is more than just knowledge and skills. It involves the ability to meet complex demands, by drawing on and mobilising psychosocial resources (including skills and attitudes) in a particular context. For example, the ability to communicate effectively is a competency that may draw on an individual's knowledge of language, practical IT skills and attitudes towards those with whom he or she is communicating. (OECD, 2005, p. 4)

The documents reviewed refer to such competencies as collaboration, creativity, critical thinking, adaptability, taking responsibility, and a strong sense of agency—competencies that are thought essential to living a fulfilling and productive life in the complex and uncertain world of the 21st century.

The more specific curriculum objectives that follow from the high-level purposes describe the knowledge, skills, attitudes, and values that learners require to understand their world, analyse and solve problems in collaboration with others, transfer their learning to new contexts, and manage their own learning. The proper purpose of teaching history, for example, is not for students to learn screeds of facts but to understand the structure of a discipline in which facts are organised into bodies of knowledge and to engage in the forms of historical inquiry that are particular to the discipline (Bransford et al., 2000; OECD, 2019a).

Developing such competencies requires students, teachers, and leaders to embrace what has been called deep or deeper learning—terms I use interchangeably throughout this book. The U.S.–based National Research Council defines deeper learning as "the process through which an individual becomes capable of taking what was learned in one situation and applying it to new situations (i.e., transfer)" (National Research Council, 2012, p. 5). The individual becomes expert in a particular knowledge or skill domain and knows when, why, and how to apply that knowledge in solving newly encountered problems within that domain.

For many educators there is nothing new about deep learning. The goals of teaching transferable knowledge and of having students analyse and solve real-world problems, both independently and in collaboration with others, are articulated in the local curricula of many school districts. Similarly, there is already a great deal of research evidence about how students acquire and how teachers can foster the competencies involved in deep learning (Bransford et al., 2000; National Research Council, 2012). What is much more problematic is creating the conditions that make it happen in every class and in every school. My assumption is that if leaders understand that the preparation purpose of education requires deep learning and they have access to the research evidence on how it happens, they will be in much better position to pursue the purpose and responsibilities of their role.

The official documents I reviewed gave less explicit emphasis to socialisation and autonomy than to the preparation purpose. For example, official documents from California, Victoria, and Ontario all refer to the acquisition of knowledge and skills needed to contribute to society but make little reference to the role of educational institutions in socialisation. In contrast, the English national curriculum document states that the English curriculum introduces students to "the best of what has been thought and said" (Department for Education, 2014, p. 6), and the New Zealand Ministry of Education makes the socialisation purpose explicit in its vision that every New Zealander "is strong in their national and cultural identity" (Ministry of Education, 2018).

The Norwegian Ministry of Education and Research goes further by making explicit the values into which students shall be socialised in such statements as:

> Education and training shall be based on fundamental values in Christian and humanist heritage and traditions, such as respect for human dignity and nature, and on intellectual freedom, charity, forgiveness, equality, and solidarity, values that also appear in different religions and beliefs and are rooted in human rights. (Ministry of Education and Research, 2019, p. 5)

Norway also stood out in its explicit reference to autonomy in such statements as "pupils and apprentices shall develop knowledge skills and attitudes so they can master their lives . . ." (Ministry of Education and Research, 2019, p. 5), and "[educators] should stimulate pupils and apprentices/trainees to develop their own learning strategies and critical-thinking abilities" (Utdanningsdirektoratet, n.d., p. 2).

In summary, both philosophical writings and official statements suggest that educational institutions are charged with multiple complex purposes. While it is tempting to assume from these abstract formulations that there is tension between them (e.g., between socialisation and autonomy), the actual degree of tension will depend on their precise specification and on how they are pursued. For example, the pursuit of knowledge may be done in ways that indoctrinate, in which case there is considerable tension between the preparation and autonomy purposes, or there may be little tension, if preparation is pursued through a pedagogy that is educational in the sense of cultivating reason and independent thought.

The Distinctiveness of the Purposes

I turn now to the question of the distinctiveness of these three purposes. A great deal turns on that question, for if the purposes of educational institutions are not distinctive, then neither is the role of educational leadership. Educational authorities would be justified in recruiting and appointing school leaders from noneducational organisations, because leadership skills and knowledge would be treated as largely generic; that is, as readily transferable from one type of organisation to another (Shamir, 2013).

In other words, if the knowledge and skills needed to lead a school were the same as those required to lead a hospital or a business, then authorities could legitimately waive requirements that principals be registered teachers. They could also justify the inclusion of business and management courses in preparation and development programmes for senior educational leaders. If, on the other hand, the skills and knowledge required to lead educational organisations are seen as particular to those organisations, then generic approaches will be found wanting, and more emphasis will be given to such things as how adult relationships in a school are conditioned by the requirement to achieve excellence in learning and teaching (Robinson, 2006).

European philosopher of education Gert Biesta argues that "what is special and most likely unique about education is that it is not orientated to *one* purpose . . . but actually is orientated to three purposes or, as I prefer to call it, three domains of purpose" (2020, p. 92).

For Biesta, the complexity and distinctiveness of education lie in the need for leaders to think about the implications of every decision for the quality of students' preparation, socialisation, and opportunity to think and act autonomously. Educational leaders need to think in this three-dimensional space because students learn not only from content and how it is represented but also from the quality of their interactions with their teachers. That is why Biesta and other philosophers of education are calling for more attention to the values that leaders and teachers espouse and enact in pursuit of the three purposes.

My own view is that it is the substance of the purposes, rather than their number, that provides the stronger ground for claiming that the purposes of education are distinctive. While it could be argued that educational, religious, and cultural institutions all share a socialisation purpose, only education has preparation as a major purpose. Preparation involves developing the distinctively human qualities and abilities, such as reasoning, wisdom, and understanding, that enable people to manage their lives more intelligently and to appreciate the world in which they live (Pring, 2014). Only education is charged with developing students' competencies by teaching the knowledge, skills, and dispositions that are valued by a particular society and that can, at least at the secondary level, be accessed only at school.

Some may object that I have exaggerated the distinctiveness of educational institutions by overlooking the ways in which running a school is like running a business. That similarity is seen in the increasing intrusion of the language of business (e.g., *inputs*, *outputs*, *targets*, *performance indicators*, *chief executives*, and *clients*) into education and in calls for principals and other senior leaders to be trained in business management (Pring, 2014). Such intrusion is undeniable, particularly in those jurisdictions where decisions about budgets, staffing, property, and health and safety are devolved to the local or school level.

The necessity for some managerial work in any organisation, including schools, does not undermine my claim about the distinctiveness of the purposes of education. The proper function of business, subject to relevant ethical constraints, is to produce "goods and services in such a way as to increase owner value . . ." (Swanton, 2016, p. 689). The proper function of education is to educate students in ways that achieve the three purposes.

The danger is not only that managing the school diverts leaders' attention from pursuit of its educational purposes but also that its language and activities so infect the educational activities that they undermine or displace the pursuit of the educational purposes. Such displacement occurs, for example, when, in pursuit of exam targets, teachers are pressured to concentrate on those students who are achieving just below the required standard and to reduce their attention to those who are well below it (Pring, 2014).

In such examples, the proper purpose of preparing all students with valued knowledge and skills is displaced by an improper purpose—increasing the school's ranking and reputation. One of the contributions of the philosophers of education discussed earlier is their call for constant vigilance in ensuring that the necessary management aspects of schooling serve rather than displace educational purposes (Pring, 2014; MacIntyre & Dunne, 2002). Such vigilance can be fostered by making certain that leaders have a deep understanding of the purposes and a strong commitment to achieving them.

The proper function of education is to educate students in ways that achieve the three purposes: preparation, socialisation, and autonomy.

The position I take is that the distinctive purposes of educational institutions lead to the unique role-related responsibilities of educational leaders and the unique core technologies required to achieve them. Although there are commonalities across educational and noneducational leadership, the unique purposes of the former, and the distinctive knowledge and skills required to pursue them, have been given far too little emphasis. It is these distinctive purposes that should shape the work of educational leaders.

Less Satisfactory Approaches to Identifying the Right Work

It is unusual in a book on educational leadership to devote a chapter to discussion of educational purposes. I have done so because

I am anchoring my account of the work of educational leadership in the distinctive nature of the purposes of educational institutions and in the consequent distinctiveness of the work of its leaders. Since this approach is quite different from more typical strategies for identifying the right work of educational leadership, I conclude this chapter with a brief discussion of these more typical approaches and why I have found them wanting.

One typical approach to identifying the right work is to use descriptive research on what educational leaders currently do in order to build frameworks for recruiting, identifying, and developing educational leaders. The qualitative and quantitative methods involved include field observations, diaries, logs, and surveys of leaders' involvement in various activities (Grissom et al., 2013; Sebastian et al., 2018; Spillane et al., 2008).

The classic example of such descriptive research is Wolcott's (1973/2003) anthropological study of the school life of one elementary school principal. It resulted in a view of the work of principals as comprising fragmented and short activity sequences in which there was little time for reflection. Wolcott also noted the frequent political intrusions and, in comparison to other higher-status professions, the lack of technical expertise that characterises the role.

Such descriptive research provides important information about how the role is currently enacted and, as such, offers an important reality check on those who promote a radically different vision for the role. For example, descriptive research on the time principals spend being instructional leaders has prompted important questions about why, despite the espousal by most principals of this type of leadership, it is so difficult for them to make the shifts that they desire (Hallinger, 2005; Shaked, 2019).

But while utopian visions for educational leadership are to be avoided, the reification of the status quo is equally undesirable. Descriptions of how educational leaders currently do their work should not be interpreted as setting the standard for how they should work. Nor should such descriptions be used uncritically when formulating policies and procedures for identifying, preparing, and inducting the next generation of educational leaders. Rather, we need a normative standard for how educational leaders should work and detailed descriptive research that enables us to identify the gap between that standard and current leadership practice. I am suggesting that the standard should be derived from the work required to achieve the distinctive and proper purposes of educational institutions.

A second typical approach to determining the right work of educational leaders is based on evidence of the differential impact of different types of leadership on valued student outcomes. In this approach, tighter links are made between leadership work and educational purposes because student outcomes are used as a standard for what counts as the right leadership work.

Sufficient research on the relationship between different types of leadership and student outcomes has now been published to warrant the conduct of several meta-analyses (Marzano et al., 2005; Robinson et al., 2008; Witziers et al., 2003). Despite the considerable theoretical and methodological challenges involved in tracing causal paths between leadership and student outcomes, the overall conclusion from this research is that "the more leaders focus their relationships, their work and their learning on the core business of teaching and learning, the greater their influence on student outcomes" (Robinson et al., 2008, p. 636).

While the current focus on the links between educational leadership and student outcomes has brought us closer to identifying the nature of the work involved in achieving the purpose of educational institutions, it still falls short of enabling us to precisely identify the nature of that work. It falls short because the standardised tests of student achievement that are typically used do not capture the richness and ambitiousness of the three educational purposes. Preparation is no longer only about promoting student achievement in literacy and numeracy and gaining qualifications—important as those are—but about all students achieving the competencies associated with deeper learning. The purpose of schooling is now specified more precisely as the development of learners who understand their world and are able to collaboratively analyse important problems, transfer their learning, and be self-managing (Graesser et al., 2018). The autonomy purpose is now strongly shaping how the preparation purpose is to be understood.

The standardised assessments used in the great majority of research on the impact of school leadership on student achievement (Marzano et al., 2005; Robinson et al., 2008; Sun & Leithwood, 2015; Witziers et al., 2003) do not capture the complexity of the deeper learning competencies described by Graesser et al. (2018). While a programme of research and development for the assessment of key competencies is underway (OECD, 2019b), it will be a long time before research will provide reliable evidence about the relationships between various types of leadership practice and the development of those competencies.

When leaders are knowledgeable about the science of deep learning and its implications for teaching, they can lead in ways that are more likely to be successful in achieving the distinctive purposes of schooling.

That is why we need to be cautious in how we use the current evidence about the impact of leadership on student outcomes to determine the right work for school leaders. Even if we had a strong evidence base describing the links between leadership and measures of deeper learning, a great deal of wisdom would be needed to identify how leaders ensure that teachers provide high-quality opportunities for deeper learning.

The position I take is that an important starting point for gaining such wisdom is the science of how students learn. When leaders are knowledgeable about the science of deep learning and its implications for teaching, they can lead in ways that are more likely to be successful in achieving the distinctive purposes of schooling. In the following two chapters, I summarise what I think leaders should know about how students learn for understanding, and about how to teach for such deep learning, before discussing some of the implications of that body of research for the distinctive work of educational leaders.

SUMMARY

The right work for educational leaders is the dedicated pursuit of the distinctive purposes of educational institutions. Drawing on recent debates in the philosophy of education, I argue that those purposes are preparation, socialisation, and the development of autonomy.

Purposes related to preparation are focused on the acquisition of knowledge and skills that enable children and young persons to lead satisfying and productive lives, including enabling them to make choices about the type of paid employment they desire. Purposes related to socialisation are concerned with the initiation of students into particular cultures and communities, which may be associated with subject disciplines, professional groups, or political, social, religious, and ethnic traditions (Biesta, 2009). Purposes related to the development of autonomy foster increased student choice about the type of life they wish to lead and how to pursue it. It is the duty of educators to develop students' knowledge, skills, and critical capacities so they can exercise their autonomy without surrendering to the will of others or to uncontrolled inner drives.

The challenge for educational leaders is to make decisions that integrate these three purposes rather than set up oppositions between them. Such integration is promoted by the emphasis on competencies in many modern curricula, for they require that students be increasingly self-directed in their application of their knowledge and skills to real-world challenges.

Educational institutions are distinctive because their purposes are distinctive. While educational, religious, and cultural institutions all share a socialisation purpose, only educational institutions have preparation as their major purpose. The distinctive purposes of educational institutions lead to the unique role-related responsibilities of educational leaders and the unique core technologies required to achieve them. Although there are commonalities across educational and noneducational leadership, the unique purposes of the former, and the distinctive knowledge and skills required to pursue them, mean that deep educational knowledge and experience are critical to performing the role of a school leader.

REFLECTION AND ACTION

1. In your context, how much importance is given to each of the three purposes of education as an institution? What shifts do you think might be needed?
2. The development of autonomy is not just a matter of giving students choices. How well are the three conditions required for the development of autonomy met in your context?
3. In your system, is educational leadership seen as distinctive from other forms of leadership? What makes it more or less distinctive? Do you agree with the argument for distinctiveness put forward in this chapter?

Linking the Purposes to the Science of Learning and Teaching[1]

2

Ideally, we would derive the right work of educational leadership from research that describes clear causal links between leadership practices, teaching practices, and students' deep learning. As I explained at the end of the previous chapter, while we have some evidence about this causal chain, it is limited by the use of standardised tests that do not assess the student competencies involved in deep learning, and it is such learning that is central to achievement of the distinctive purposes of educational institutions. In the absence of evidence about the impact of leadership on teaching for deep learning and on the success of such teaching, I adopt an alternative backwards mapping strategy, which starts from educational purpose, then asks how students learn to achieve those purposes, how teachers foster such learning, and how leaders can foster such teaching.

This backwards mapping strategy, in which I derive implications for leadership from the science of learning and teaching, is very different from much of the discourse on educational leadership and management. That discussion is often only loosely connected to the core business of teaching and learning (Bush et al., 2019; Elmore, 2004; Robinson, 2006). As Spillane (2013) claims:

> [W]ith some exceptions, many analyses dwell on leading the schoolhouse rather than the core work of the schoolhouse. As a result, descriptions, and prescriptions for leading are only weakly related to the actual work of teaching and leading its improvement. (p. 60)

[1] Portions of Chapters 1 and 2 are a slightly revised version of Robinson, V. (2022). What is distinctive about educational leadership? In R. Tierney, F. Rizvi, E. Kadriye, & G. H. Smith (Eds.), *International encyclopedia of education* (4th ed.). Elsevier.

If leaders are committed to the purposes, understand how those purposes are enshrined in competencies, and understand what they should be doing to support teachers in developing those competencies, then they know . . . what constitutes the right work.

So, even though my backwards mapping strategy is a somewhat indirect way of deriving the "right work" of educational leadership, it reinforces one of the major themes of this book—that pursuit of the distinctive purposes of education should be strongly informed by the science of how students learn and of how teachers foster that learning. If leaders are committed to the purposes, understand how those purposes are enshrined in competencies, and understand what they should be doing to support teachers in developing those competencies, then they know, at least in broad outline, what constitutes the right work.

My initial step in this backwards mapping strategy is to distil some key conclusions from recent cognitive and educational psychology research about how students learn to understand, problem-solve, and transfer their learning. I then discuss some of the implications of these conclusions for teaching, including a brief discussion of social psychological research on the noncognitive aspects of student learning with an emphasis on student choice and autonomy.

How Students Learn

There is now considerable consensus about how students learn (Bransford et al., 2000; Darling-Hammond et al., 2019; Deans for Impact, 2015). Whether or not deeper learning occurs depends in part on the type of academic task in which students are engaged, because different tasks evoke and develop different cognitive operations (Doyle, 1983).

Doyle distinguishes four types of academic tasks:

1. **Memory tasks** in which students recognise or reproduce content they have previously encountered
2. **Procedural tasks** that require correct application of a procedure, formula, or algorithm
3. **Comprehension or understanding tasks** in which students recognise new versions of previously encountered information, apply knowledge to new problems, or draw inferences from or transform existing information
4. **Opinion tasks** that require students to express a preference or position

My focus will be on comprehension tasks, because growth in student comprehension and problem-solving, particularly for students who are struggling, is what is required to achieve deeper learning.

Comprehension and problem-solving tasks require students to actively construct a cognitive representation of the relevant concepts, events, or situations. As students gain experience in a subject domain, they develop more and better-organised representations (schemata) of task-relevant material. Since schemata are stored in long-term memory, they free up limited short-term memory for the processing of new information.

Domain-specific knowledge plays a central role in students' ability to comprehend, explain, and remember. It consists

> not only of a well-formed semantic network of valid information in an academic discipline but also of strategies for using this information to represent (comprehend) problems, search for and select algorithms, use resources from the task environment and evaluate the adequacy of answers. (Graesser et al., 2018, p. 168)

In short, competence in a domain requires a deep foundation of factual knowledge that is organised into a network of schemata that aligns with the structure of the discipline or subject. There should be no opposition, therefore, between the learning of facts and deep learning. The challenge for learners and their teachers is to avoid memorising disconnected facts and focus instead on their structure and interrelationships. This requires deepening learners' knowledge of the subject matter while developing their grasp of its conceptual structure (Bransford et al., 2000).

The development of expertise in a subject domain requires accurate encoding of subject matter (Doyle, 1983). Students can develop schemata that encode faulty algorithms and concepts (Nuthall, 2007). When students have little relevant prior knowledge or misunderstand what they have previously encountered, they will be unable to engage with tasks that presume accurate prior knowledge. For these students, comprehension tasks create considerable cognitive overload as they struggle to bring meaning to apparently disconnected bits of information.

Deep learning includes development of the metacognitive skills required to regulate one's own learning.

Deep learning includes development of the metacognitive skills required to regulate one's own learning. This involves setting goals, planning ahead, activating relevant prior knowledge, and keeping success criteria in mind and using them to monitor and adjust progress towards the goal (Bransford et al., 2000). Because not all learners independently develop the internal talk that self-regulation requires, modern curricula require teachers to scaffold metacognitive strategies by explicit teaching and practice so that, over time, students will prompt themselves and monitor their own comprehension and problem-solving.

In addition to the cognitive challenges of deep learning, contextual factors are critical. Academic work is conducted in classrooms in which teachers teach not single students but one or more groups of increasingly diverse students. Furthermore, students complete academic tasks in contexts where they are either recipients of or witnesses to the frequent evaluations of their teacher. For older students, these judgments contribute to a high-stakes accountability system of credits or points that determines report cards, academic pathways, and ultimately the students' qualifications.

These features of classrooms can create teacher-student interactions that profoundly alter students' opportunities to learn the cognitive processes required for deeper learning (Doyle, 1983). Low-achieving students are likely to feel vulnerable in a highly evaluative climate and respond by withdrawal so as to minimise the risk of public exposure and embarrassment (Peeters et al., 2020). Alternatively, they may attempt to increase their chances of success by using a variety of strategies, such as copying, or requesting detailed guides and model answers, that are designed to reduce the cognitive demands of the task. Teachers who give overly detailed instructions, prompts, and advice can unwittingly turn a comprehension task into a procedural one in which students happily follow their teacher's detailed guidance without increasing their expertise in the subject domain (Doyle, 1986).

In summary, academic work, particularly that required to achieve deep learning, is complex. As Graesser et al. (2018, p. 170), write:

> Studies of the cognitive processes underlying academic work have revealed the enormously complex character of the operations and decisions that academic competence entails, a complexity that is often overlooked when the goals of schools are discussed.

Leaders should understand and accept this complexity so they can support their teachers in providing opportunities for deep learning. I discuss how this can be done effectively in Chapter 3.

Student Motivation and Autonomy

Students learn better when they are aware of their own learning and have the opportunity to take charge, in small and large ways, of elements of their lessons (National Academies of Sciences, Engineering, and Medicine, 2018). These findings are explained by self-determination theory, which "posits that behavior is strongly influenced by three universal, innate, psychological needs—autonomy (the urge to control one's own life), competence (the urge to experience mastery), and psychological relatedness (the urge to interact with, be connected to, and care for others)" (National Academies of Sciences, Engineering, and Medicine, 2018, p. 115).

When these needs are met in school, students are more likely to be motivated by their interest in and enjoyment of the task. If enjoyment and interest are not strong, students will persist nevertheless if they perceive success on the task as linked to achievement of a valued goal. Students' interest in the task, control over their learning, and belief that they can succeed mean they want to engage in the activity for its own sake—they are intrinsically motivated. When these conditions are not present, students' engagement and persistence will depend on their compliance with external rewards and sanctions—they are extrinsically motivated. There is a considerable body of evidence suggesting that external rewards can reduce intrinsic motivation, because they focus the student on the rewards rather than on their own learning processes and may undermine the learner's sense of being in control of their own learning (Deci et al., 2001). Accordingly, to help students learn better and deeper, we want to primarily nurture intrinsic motivation.

In my Chapter 1 discussion of the purposes of education, I suggested that it was the responsibility of educational leaders to ensure the integration of the three purposes—preparation, socialisation, and autonomy. Self-determination theory provides a research-based framework for such integration because it explains how and why students who are in control of their own learning are likely to be more intrinsically motivated and successful than those who have little control over and understanding of what they are learning, why, and of how they can succeed (Patall et al., 2010).

For example, students who are given a choice of homework tasks that are designed with their interests, competence, and goals in mind are more likely to complete their homework, report being more intrinsically motivated to do so, and perform better on a related test than students given no such choice. In addition, students who perceive their teachers as supportive of their autonomy are more intrinsically motivated to persist at difficult tasks than students who perceive their teachers as more controlling.

Students who perceive their teachers as supportive of their autonomy are more intrinsically motivated to persist at difficult tasks than students who perceive their teachers as more controlling.

Implications for Classroom Teaching

There are several excellent texts available that explain the implications for classroom teaching of how students learn (Bransford et al., 2000; Darling-Hammond et al., 2019; Deans for Impact, 2015).

TEACHING FOR DEEPER LEARNING REQUIRES

1. Aligning tasks to the intended deep learning outcomes
2. Inquiring into students' prior knowledge
3. Managing groups of diverse learners
4. Integrating the teaching of metacognitive skills into subject matter teaching

Here I concentrate on four implications that have particular relevance to teaching for deeper learning before focusing more specifically on enhancing student motivation and autonomy.

First, since what students learn is a function of the type of task they engage in, it is critical that teachers are skilled in the selection, design, and assessment of tasks that are tightly aligned to the cognitive processes they intend students to develop (Tekkumru Kisa & Stein, 2015). If the intended learning outcome is comprehension, then all task components, including explanations and assessments, should foster that outcome.

For example, if a math teacher wants students to understand why an algebra formula works, then setting students 20 practice examples in which they apply the formula will foster procedural accuracy rather than comprehension. Comprehension is more likely to be fostered by assessing whether students can decompose the formula, apply its various steps to concrete materials, and provide a written or oral explanation of why it works.

Second, since deep learning requires the cumulative integration of prior knowledge with new information and concepts, effective teaching requires inquiry into students' prior knowledge. The purpose of such inquiry is not just to interest students in a topic but to assess whether students have the prior knowledge assumed by the selected task and whether that prior knowledge includes misunderstandings that need to be challenged.

Third, teachers need well-developed skills in managing groups of diverse learners while they grapple with intellectually challenging tasks. As already discussed, since comprehension or understanding tasks creates more cognitive load than procedural tasks, students may resist such tasks or seek so much teacher guidance that they become, in effect, procedural tasks. Over time, this teacher-student dynamic may lead teachers to rely too much on memory and procedural tasks for which they are more likely to gain and retain students' cooperation (Doyle, 1983; Fulmer & Turner, 2014).

For example, in a study of elementary teachers' responses to professional development in implementing challenging instruction, the most common reasons teachers gave for their difficulties were the motivation and resistance of their students (Fulmer & Turner, 2014). Some teachers were able to overcome students' resistance by communicating confidence in students' abilities to do the tasks, explaining why they were going to focus on students' reasoning rather than the correctness of their answers, and giving more autonomy to students by ensuring that each member of their group understood the task and could explain their reasoning (Fulmer & Turner, 2014).

Fourth, teaching of the metacognitive skills required for the development of critical thinking, independence, adaptability, and other competencies should be integrated into the subject matter students are learning rather than presented as separate content-free processes (Bransford et al., 2000). The reason for this advice is that different metacognitive strategies are used in different subjects.

Teaching of the metacognitive skills required for the development of critical thinking, independence, adaptability, and other competencies should be integrated into the subject matter students are learning rather than presented as separate content-free processes.

For example, the types of questions students ask about a word problem in math ("What pattern or principle might be relevant here?") are quite different from those they should ask in their analysis of a historical document ("Who was the intended audience?" "Why was this written in this way?"). Teachers should also be mindful that explicit teaching of metacognitive skills, even when embedded in content, adds cognitive load (Van Gog et al., 2011).

In summary, teaching for deep learning involves careful inquiry into students' relevant prior knowledge and the provision of multiple opportunities for students to develop rich and well-organised domain-specific knowledge. There should be an integration of, rather than opposition between, the learning of facts and higher-order thinking, for the "ability to plan a task, to notice patterns, to generate reasonable arguments and explanations, and to draw analogies to other problems are all more closely intertwined with factual knowledge than was once believed" (Bransford et al., 2000, p. 16).

Self-determination theory suggests specific ways that leaders and teachers can foster student autonomy, intrinsic motivation, and learning. Fundamental to all such strategies is the need for adults to be curious about and inquire into the perspectives of students so that they learn how to create a bridge between their curriculum and the values, interests, and goals of their students. Such inquiry involves careful listening, including to students' reasons for their dislike of particular tasks and teacher actions. Without such information, it is very difficult for teachers to provide choices that meet students' need for autonomy, competence, and relatedness. In short,

> having choice or the act of selecting alone is not enough to support motivation. Rather, choices need to be relevant to students' interests and goals, provide a moderate number of options of an intermediate level of complexity, and be congruent with other family and cultural values in order to effectively support motivation. (Patall et al., 2010, p. 898)

In addition to providing meaningful choices, teachers support the development of autonomy by linking tasks to students' values, interests, and goals. Once again, maintaining a student-centred perspective is critical in making these links. For example, intrinsic motivation is much more likely to be increased when students themselves, rather than their teachers, explain why particular tasks and activities are relevant to their lives (Yeager & Walton, 2011). Just as respectful teacher inquiry into student thinking is critical to uncovering cognitive understanding and misunderstandings, so it is key to uncovering aspects of their socioemotional learning—to discovering whether they are intrinsically motivated, whether they are truly engaged or "doing school" and why.

So far, I have argued that the science of learning and teaching tells us quite a lot about how to achieve the distinctive purposes of educational institutions. In Part B, I take the argument further by discussing the implications of that science for doing the right work of educational leadership.

SUMMARY

Pursuit of the distinctive purposes of education should be strongly informed by the science of how students learn and of how teachers foster that learning. If leaders are committed to the purposes, understand how those purposes are enshrined in competencies, and understand how teachers should develop those competencies, then they know, at least in broad outline, what constitutes the right work of educational leadership.

The competencies that are enshrined in modern curricula require deep learning—that is, the ability to learn and transfer learning to real-world problems. Such learning is fostered by multiple opportunities to complete problem-solving and comprehension tasks. It requires students to develop well-organised bodies of knowledge that align with the structure of the discipline rather than to learn isolated facts. Deep learning also includes the development of the metacognitive skills that enable students to regulate their own learning.

Self-determination theory suggests that students learn better when three basic psychological needs are met. Their need for control is met when they have the opportunity to exercise autonomy, in small and large ways, of elements of their lessons. Their need for competence is met when they can see that they have succeeded in their learning, and their need for relatedness is met when they work collaboratively. Students who are in control of their own learning are likely to be more intrinsically motivated and successful than those who have little control over and understanding of what they are learning, why, and of how they can succeed.

Teaching for deep learning involves careful inquiry into students' relevant prior knowledge and provision of multiple opportunities for students to develop rich and well-organised domain-specific knowledge. There should be a predominance of comprehension and problem-solving rather than procedural tasks and an integration of, rather than opposition between, the learning of facts and higher-order thinking.

In addition to providing meaningful choices, teachers support the development of autonomy by linking tasks to students' values, interests, and goals. Just as respectful teacher inquiry into student thinking is critical to uncovering cognitive understanding and misunderstandings, so it is key to uncovering aspects of their socioemotional learning—to discovering whether they are intrinsically motivated, whether they are truly engaged or "doing school" and why.

REFLECTION AND ACTION

1. How familiar are you and your colleagues with the science of learning and teaching as summarised in this chapter? Is it assumed in your context that you have sufficient knowledge in these areas and that your professional learning should thus be focused on leadership itself?
2. How would you tell if the teachers in your area of responsibility were planning, teaching, and assessing in ways that promoted deep learning?

3. Teachers may be unwilling to assign cognitively demanding tasks because they fear losing control of the class. How would you help such teachers?
4. Deep learning requires integration of rather than opposition between the learning of facts and higher-order thinking. To what extent is the importance of this integration recognised and applied in your context?

PART B

Doing the Right Leadership Work

3 Implications of the Science of Learning and Teaching for Leadership

This morning I received three unwelcome emails from a state department of education in Australia, requiring me to complete, within six weeks, three mandated courses: human rights and responsibilities, addressing workplace bullying, and equal opportunities. I received these emails, along with all school leaders, because I work for the department on leadership development contracts. I have no doubt that such mandated courses are important, but what puzzles me is why there are no such mandated courses on the core business of teaching and learning. Is it assumed that all leaders have already gained the knowledge of deep learning that was summarised in Chapter 2?

In my experience, this is unlikely, because the science of teaching for deep learning is relatively new, and it is only in the last decade or so that curricula have emphasised the competencies—such as creativity, collaboration, critical thinking, and problem-solving—that require deep learning. My goal in this chapter is to use the science of learning and teaching (Chapter 2) to sketch out what I consider to be the right work of educational leadership—that is, the work that the science suggests is needed to achieve the purposes of educational institutions: ensuring the development of self-directed and well-prepared students.

Of course, deriving the right work from this science is no straightforward matter, and there are huge gaps in our knowledge about how leaders can achieve educational purposes by ensuring high-quality opportunities for deep learning. In this chapter, however, I show that there are some clear implications of the science for educational leaders—implications that leave plenty of room for tailoring the right work to context-specific requirements. Precisely how those contextual adjustments are made is the subject of Chapter 4.

I have organised the implications under five dimensions of leadership practice: goal setting, strategic resourcing, ensuring quality teaching, leading professional development, and ensuring a safe and orderly environment. I have used these headers because the frameworks that guide leadership development policy in many jurisdictions employ these or similar dimensions. They do so because there is a body of research, including several meta-analyses, about the average effects of these dimensions on student outcomes (Marzano et al., 2005; Robinson et al., 2008). It must be remembered, though, that the student outcome measures employed in this research are usually standardised tests of literacy and math, and these outcomes are considerably narrower than those required as evidence of deep learning.

Dimension 1: Setting Goals and Expectations for Deep Learning

If the distinctive purposes of education are to be anything more than philosophical or policy abstractions, leaders will need to incorporate them into relevant vision, mission, and goal statements. Those statements make a difference, however, only if school-level goals are vertically integrated into the goals of subject departments, year-level teams, individual teachers, and students themselves. Achieving such integration requires a principled understanding of the institutional purposes discussed in Chapter 1 and of their relationship to curriculum competencies and deep learning. Skill is needed in engaging the relevant communities so that district personnel, teachers, and parents are committed to educating students in ways that develop their autonomy, honour their place in and contributions to particular communities, and prepare them for the educational and occupational pathways to which they and their families aspire.

In the world of education, where an argument can be made for the importance of an infinite number of activities, goal setting serves the crucial function of communicating what is more important at this time, in this context, than all the other important things. While national and local curricula signal broad goals, it is the job of school leaders to tailor abstract goals to the specific needs of local communities.

The Three Conditions of Effective Goal Setting

Doing goal setting well requires meeting the three conditions that goal theory describes as critical to its effectiveness:

1. **Clarity**
2. **Commitment**
3. **Capability**

Goals need to be **clear**, *and* those who are to achieve the goals must be **committed** to them *and* have, or acquire, the **capability** needed to achieve them (Latham & Locke, 2006).

Goal clarity requires leaders to clearly articulate and exemplify what they mean by their proposed goals. For example, what do they mean by "deeper learning," and what does their analysis of student data and teaching practice show about which students are and are not succeeding in such learning? A leader's argument to focus on deeper learning is made much more concrete and compelling if accompanied by data showing, for example, that reading accuracy results are significantly higher than those for reading comprehension, that students' factual knowledge in science is much better than their ability to provide scientific explanations, or that numeracy results are much better than those for solving word problems in math. Such data exemplify what is meant by deep learning and how it differs from more routine learning.

People commit to goals if they see a strong enough link between the goal and what they already value. Leaders need to communicate their own goal aspirations in ways that discover and connect with the values and aspirations of those whose efforts are required to achieve a proposed goal. This is a relational process requiring careful listening to those teachers who believe, for example, that deeper learning, while fine in theory, is not suitable for their students or, alternatively, that it is not worth setting as a goal because they are already doing it.

Teachers may value deeper learning in principle but still not be committed to it because their experience convinces them that success with their students is unlikely. This raises the issue of capability, which is the third requirement for effective goal setting. It is critical for leaders to recognise that by setting ambitious goals, they are likely to create a gap between their teachers' current and required levels of capability. They should then initiate respectful and nonblaming discussion of the capability issues so that teachers trust they will get the help they need (Robinson, 2018).

When the three conditions—clarity, commitment, and capability—are met, goal setting works by creating a discrepancy between current reality and the desired future. The discrepancy motivates persistent goal-relevant behaviour and focuses attention and effort on the work needed to achieve the goals. Numerous experimental studies have shown that performance is significantly higher when the three conditions are met than in comparable "do your best" conditions (Latham & Locke, 2007).

While leaders' goal setting activities are conducted mostly with colleagues, the theory of goal setting applies equally to the way teachers work with students. If school or team goals include building capability in aspects of deeper learning, it is important that leaders understand and track the implications of such goals for what should be happening in classrooms and with students.

For example, if teachers seek and reward correct answers, they unwittingly encourage students to see their role as getting the right answer rather than as building their own competency through sustained effort motivated by goals that are clear to them, that they are committed to, and for which they believe they have, or can develop, the capability required to succeed.

The three conditions specified by goal theory are generic in that they are applicable to the leadership of any type of organisation. However, as I have illustrated, their successful application in education requires leaders who can integrate their knowledge of goal theory with distinctive educational knowledge and skills. For example, leaders need to be able to articulate and defend their choice of goal (e.g., deeper learning), evaluate the match between the pedagogy required for such learning and that currently used by their teachers, and provide a compelling account of how any capability gap will be closed. The knowledge and skills involved are distinctive to the work of educational leadership.

Performance Goals Versus Learning Goals

An important distinction is made in goal theory between performance goals and learning goals (Latham & Locke, 2007). When teachers' and leaders' current capability is not sufficient for achievement of a deeper learning performance goal (e.g., student achievement in math problem solving will improve by 25% in a given year), leaders should set prior learning goals (e.g., all teachers at a particular grade level meet criteria for effective teaching of the vocabulary and strategies needed to succeed in solving math word problems).

In the context of educational leadership, learning goals are about what leaders and teachers need to learn in order to achieve performance goals that specify desired levels of student learning. By setting learning goals, leaders create an expectation of, and accountability for, teacher and leader acquisition of the knowledge and skills required to achieve the performance goal (Seijts & Latham, 2012).

If leaders set performance goals when teachers' capability is insufficient, they are likely to create stress, lower commitment, and invite goal displacement. Pressure to achieve performance goals that are beyond teachers' current capability, combined with high-stakes accountability, invites gaming and other forms of unethical behaviour (Welsh et al., 2019). Exactly the same principle applies to students' goals. If they lack some of the prerequisite skills and knowledge required for deep learning, then it is more appropriate to set learning goals that target those prerequisites rather than performance goals, such as gaining particular scores in assessments of comprehension or problem-solving.

When relevant teacher capability is low and there is high uncertainty about how a performance goal (such as improving the writing of a target group) can be achieved, leaders should set and reset a sequence of learning goals for the adults and set only quantified and time-bound performance goals and targets for what teachers should achieve with students once considerable progress has been made on the learning goals. For novel and ambitious goals, revision of targets, along with robust inquiry into the reasons for any shortfalls, should be anticipated, because it is impossible to set realistic targets without considerable knowledge and experience of what is involved in reaching them.

Dimension 2: Resourcing Strategically for Deep Learning

Once leaders have a clear and widely shared vision of what student success looks like, they need to reorganise resources of time, money, and materials to achieve that vision. Strategic leaders allocate scarce resources such as money, time on the timetable, teaching materials, and instructional expertise in ways that give priority to key goals. Staff can see alignment between where money is spent, what initiatives are being adopted, and school goals.

Leveraging Teacher Expertise

Strategic leadership pays considerable attention to recruiting, developing, and retaining teacher expertise that is matched to the learning needs of students. That time is warranted by the clear evidence that the quality of teaching is the most important in-school contributor to student outcomes (Rivkin et al., 2005).

The effect of teaching quality is cumulative, such that students who experience low-quality teaching for three years in a row are unlikely to catch up (Lee, 2018; Nye et al., 2004). Managing staff includes employing fair, transparent, and efficient procedures for exiting persistently low-performing teachers. There is a significant association between principals who are perceived by their staff to perform these tasks effectively and school performance (Grissom & Loeb, 2011).

Leveraging Student Time

Enabling all students to succeed in deep learning requires leaders to be very strategic in their management of the key resource of student time. My focus on this resource is not intended to belittle the importance of the more typically discussed management of human, material, and financial resources (Mestry, 2019). Rather, it is intended to emphasise that students need multiple and varied opportunities to learn challenging material, and for those students whose homes do not provide the cultural and educational capital required to engage with such material, school provides their only opportunity to do so.

The goal of deep learning is unlikely to be met if students and teachers are rushed through an overcrowded curriculum. Intensive exposure to a few big ideas is preferable, because students need multiple and varied exposure to concepts in order to develop schemata that encode underlying principles and interrelationships. Learning for understanding takes more time than rote learning or the application of procedures.

The goal of deep learning is unlikely to be met if students and teachers are rushed through an overcrowded curriculum.

Leaders need to address the dilemma teachers often experience between fostering the in-depth learning they espouse and covering the curriculum, for it is this dilemma that often stops them from narrowing and deepening their curriculum focus (OECD, 2019a). Many schools are now reorganising timetables to provide longer blocks of time for in-depth study of a few rich topics. Many also increase students' autonomy and motivation by providing them with meaningful choices about which topics they study.

One way to understand the use of students' time is via the concept of students' opportunity to learn. "The concept of opportunity to learn (OTL) rests on the logical proposition that students' ability to learn a subject is dependent on whether and for how long they are exposed to it in school" (Schmidt et al., 2015, p. 371). Students' opportunities to learn are eroded when time is lost through suspension of regular classes, pull-out programmes, extracurricular activities conducted in class time, disciplinary removals from class, and other disruptions (Miles & Frank, 2008). Opportunities to learn are also reduced when teachers lack confidence in teaching the scheduled lesson or do not teach the planned curriculum because they believe their students are not ready for such learning.

Leveraging Tracking and Grouping

The most important contributor to variation in OTL is the practices leaders use to group students into programmes (tracking) and into ability groups within programmes and classrooms. The 2012 PISA study of 15-year-old students in 62 countries asked students themselves about their exposure to selected topics in mathematics and analysed the links between their reported exposure to those topics, their math literacy scores, and their *socioeconomic* background (Schmidt et al., 2015). The decision to measure OTL by asking students what they had been exposed to in their math classes, rather than by asking teachers what they had taught or by examining curriculum documents, reflects a more student-centred approach and one that is easily replicated by school leaders who are curious about how their students experience the curriculum.

First, the study found wide variation within schools in students' opportunity to learn particular math content, and this variation had a strong direct relationship with math achievement. Second, students from more affluent backgrounds received far more opportunities to learn the math content on which all students were assessed than students from less wealthy backgrounds. Third, a substantial share of the relationship between socioeconomic status and math literacy achievement was explained by variation in OTL.

There is a body of research reporting similar findings for math (Schmidt et al., 2015), science (Herman, 2014), and English language arts (Wilson et al., 2016). It suggests that it is not only out-of-school factors that contribute to the well-established relationship between student home background and school achievement. How students are organised into qualification and curricular pathways are powerful in-school contributors to that relationship, and these in-school factors can be leveraged by school leaders so that all students have opportunities to learn the rich curriculum content that gives them access to advanced qualifications and capabilities.

The concept of OTL used in the PISA study was based on students' reports of their exposure to selected math content. There are broader concepts of OTL that include indicators of the quality as well as the quantity of students' exposure to curriculum content. I take up how leaders can monitor and improve the quality of OTL in the next section on the practices involved in leading teaching and learning.

Dimension 3: Ensuring Quality Teaching for Deep Learning

Improving the overall quality of teaching for deeper learning, including reducing undesirable variability in such teaching, requires leaders at all levels in a school to be skilful, consistent, and persistent in monitoring and improving curriculum and pedagogy. Improvement should be based on a shared understanding of what teaching for deep learning looks like in a given curriculum area and of how current curricula and pedagogy—as planned, delivered, and experienced by students—measure up to that standard. A key question for leaders is, "Does the curriculum, as experienced by students, provide multiple opportunities for them to develop well-organised bodies of knowledge rather than discrete facts and isolated skills?"

In helping leaders answer this question, I return to the concept of quality teaching I employed in my earlier book on student-centred leadership (Robinson, 2011) and update the ideas to reflect the evidence reviewed in Chapter 2 about how to teach for deeper learning.

In that book, I defined quality teaching as "maximizing the time that students spend engaged with and being successful in the learning of important outcomes" (Robinson, 2011, p. 92). It is important to note that this definition, which is based on the work of David Berliner (1987, 1990), provides a student-centred notion of OTL, for it is the experience of students, not the plans and intention of teachers or curriculum developers, that defines the quantity and quality of opportunities to learn.

Evaluating the Quality of Teaching

Leaders can evaluate the quality of teaching by asking the four sets of questions implied by this definition. The questions focus on (1) intended learning outcomes, (2) alignment, (3) student engagement, and (4) student success. They are summarised in Figure 3.1. In addition to the questions themselves, I provide a rationale for each set so leaders can explain why they are asking them and how they link to teaching for deep learning.

Focus 1: Intended Learning Outcomes

Assuming leaders have set deep learning goals under Dimension 1, they can monitor their salience in teaching and learning by checking the **learning outcomes** set by teachers for particular units of work and the extent to which students are aware of and able to use those goals to regulate their own learning. Leaders could check by reviewing teachers' planning, by asking teachers the questions in quadrant 1 of Figure 3.1,

Figure 3.1 Leaders' Inquiry About the Quality of Teaching

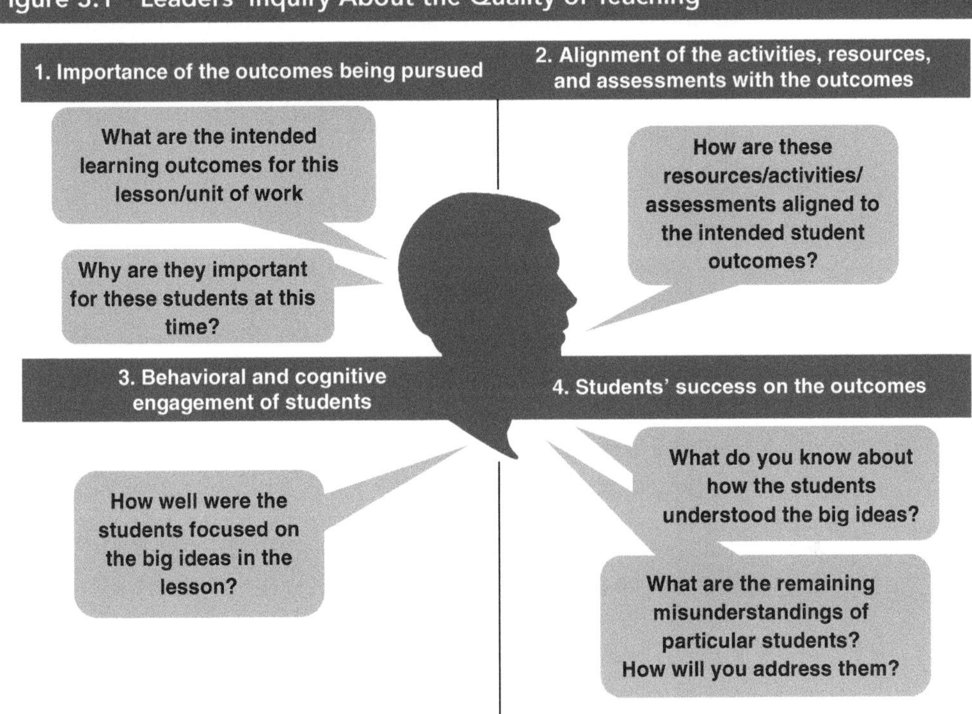

Source: Adapted from Robinson (2011).

and by asking students such questions as "Can you tell me what you are trying to learn in this lesson?"

Focus 2: Alignment

The second set of questions concerns the **alignment** of tasks, resources, and pedagogical strategies with the intended deeper learning outcomes. A good starting point for evaluating alignment is an analysis of the types of academic tasks teachers are setting. This will indicate whether teachers are setting memory, procedural, or more challenging comprehension tasks. A follow-up question could be "How do you feel about setting more intellectually challenging tasks?"

Since it is the assessments that students experience as the real tasks, alignment of intended and assessed learning outcomes is vital (City et al., 2009; Doyle, 1983). Light sampling of planned and completed assessment tasks provides an evidence base that teachers and their curriculum leaders can use to discuss the cognitive processes being assessed, their alignment with deeper learning goals, and the reasons for any misalignment.

The third aspect of alignment is the match between how the lesson or unit of work was taught and the type of teaching required to foster understanding and critical thinking. Leaders need sufficient knowledge of the pedagogy of deep learning (Chapter 2) to know what to look for when observing teaching. Table 3.1 illustrates some of the indicators that could enable leaders to distinguish higher and lower opportunities for deep learning in high school English classes.

The eight indicators are derived from observations of English lessons taught to senior students in 34 New Zealand high schools (Wilson et al., 2016). Students in schools serving higher-socioeconomic-status communities had significantly more high-quality opportunities to learn the literacy skills required to succeed in two externally examined national assessments than students in high schools serving lower-socioeconomic-status communities.

The national assessment, which was based on texts featuring complex language and ideas, required students to construct extended written responses that interpreted significant aspects of the text in original and creative ways. In the high schools serving wealthier communities, there was tight alignment between the required learning

Table 3.1 Indicators of Higher- and Lower-Quality Teaching for Deep Learning in High School English Classes

	HIGHER QUALITY	LOWER QUALITY
	FEATURES OF TEXTS	
1.	Longer	Shorter
2.	Published originals	Created by teacher (notes or worksheets)
3.	Written for adults	Written for youth
4.	Challenging	Simplified
	FEATURES OF TEACHING	
1.	Extended discussions	Fewer extended discussions
2.	More 1:1 conferences	Fewer 1:1 conferences
3.	Explicit teaching of literacy, including vocabulary, text structure, and language features	Less explicit teaching of literacy and more attention to item learning and morphology
4.	Less time on classroom management	More time on classroom management

Source: Adapted from Wilson, Madjar, and McNaughton (2016).

outcomes, the likely national assessment tasks, and the texts, assessments, and pedagogy employed in English classes. In contrast, the preparation received by students in high schools serving less wealthy communities provided students with significantly fewer opportunities to read complex texts, to learn the vocabulary, structure, and language features of such texts, and to get 1:1 feedback and coaching from their teacher.

In short, in these English classes, the quality of teaching, understood as provision of opportunities to master the deep learning required to gain the national qualification, depended on the socioeconomic status of their school community.

Leaders can modify and follow up the broad question in quadrant 2 of Figure 3.1 depending on whether they are checking the alignment of lesson planning, assessment, or pedagogy with deep learning outcomes.

Focus 3: Student Engagement

The third quadrant of Figure 3.1 refers to student **engagement** with the lesson, with engagement including behavioural and cognitive engagement. Leaders can monitor engagement by asking teachers such questions as "How well were the students focused on the big ideas in the lesson?"

Leaders can also check students' experience of the lesson by asking questions that assess their ability to regulate their own learning. Such questions as "How would you know if you are being successful" and "How are you monitoring your progress" provide some insight.

Focus 4: Student Success

The fourth quadrant is focused on student success. Success applies to any valued student outcome, including academic, social, cultural, and well-being outcomes. Providing high-quality opportunities for students to be engaged with and successful in their learning promotes their learning and their well-being, because repeated failure at schoolwork produces anxiety and threatens self-esteem (National Academies of Sciences, Engineering, and Medicine, 2018).

Well-being usually follows naturally from success at schoolwork that students value—it brings a sense of pride and self-efficacy. Of course, if "drill and kill" pedagogies are in place, a focus on academics will be in tension with well-being, but the remedy is to change the pedagogy, not to leave it in place and focus on student well-being without attending to what is happening in the classroom.

Principals and senior leaders are responsible for monitoring schoolwide student outcomes and heads of departments and team leaders for monitoring those outcomes for their groups of students. In addition to regular reviews of aggregated data, leaders can monitor success through on-the-spot inquiry into teachers' knowledge of their students' understandings and misunderstandings of the lesson. They can ask such questions as:

- What do you know about how the students understood the big ideas in the lesson?
- What evidence do you have about how they achieved the intended learning outcomes?
- What are the students' remaining misunderstandings?

In asking these questions, leaders encourage their teachers to constantly check the impact of their teaching through on-the-spot inquiry into the thinking of their students rather than through whether students can supply the right answers. Similar questions can be asked of students themselves.

The four sets of questions can be used informally as part of collaborative discussions about teaching or in more formal teacher evaluation contexts. Since they assess teaching quality by probing the experience of students rather than by prejudging the desirability of particular teaching styles, they allow considerable teacher discretion about how to teach for deeper learning in their particular context.

If leaders wish to foster deeper learning, they should evaluate whether their schools' instructional framework, and the practices that flow from it, provide adequate guidance and support for deeper learning. The tools and routines specified in their school's instructional framework, teacher induction handbook, teacher evaluation and classroom observation procedures, assessment policies, and protocols for team meetings need to be tightly aligned with the science of how to teach for deeper learning.

Dimension 4: Leading Teacher Professional Learning for Deep Learning

Leading professional learning provides powerful opportunities to influence the quality of teaching and learning. When done well, professional learning and development raises teachers' sense of efficacy, improves their practice, and most important of all, increases the capability of their students (Robinson, 2011). Done badly, it contributes to teacher burnout and cynicism about having to endure yet another round of professional development and reform initiatives.

Fortunately, a great deal is now known about the types of professional learning that are more and less likely to improve teaching practice and student outcomes (Desimone & Garet, 2015; Minor et al., 2016). Traditional approaches, in which knowledge is transmitted from an expert leader to participants, may lead to high levels of satisfaction, more knowledgeable teachers, and small shifts in teacher practices, but there is little evidence that such transmission approaches result in improved outcomes for the students of the participating teachers (Timperley, 2008). The reason is that traditional input-driven professional learning is not designed to help teachers unlearn the beliefs and practices that are in tension with those they are supposed to be adopting. Just like student learning, teacher professional learning involves an interaction between new knowledge and skills and what one already knows and can do. When there is tension between the old and the new, professional learning needs to include explicit strategies for managing the tension.

Theories of Action for Current and Proposed Teaching Practices

I described the processes and conversations involved in discovering and resolving these tensions in my 2018 book on school improvement (Robinson, 2018). Key to success is understanding and applying the concept of theories of action to the design and delivery of any professional learning that is likely to challenge teachers' current beliefs and practices. A theory of action links what teachers do (their actions) to the intended and unintended consequences of those actions and to the beliefs and motives that explain their actions (Argyris & Schon, 1974).

> If leaders understand teachers' theories of action, they understand not only what they do but why they do it and therefore why they might be reluctant to do it differently.

In short, if leaders understand teachers' theories of action, they understand not only what they do but why they do it and therefore why they might be reluctant to do it differently. When leaders of professional learning bypass the theories of action that explain teachers' current practice, they leave it over to teachers to manage any tension between their current theories of action and those required by the professional learning.

If teachers perceive little tension between the two theories, they are likely to adapt to the new material by integrating those strategies that are compatible with what they already believe and can do (Cohen & Mehta, 2017). If they perceive considerable tension, they are likely to reject the new material unless forced to do otherwise, in which case compliance will be the result.

When there is tension between the current and proposed teaching practices, a more effective strategy for leaders of professional learning is to engage rather than bypass teachers' current theories of action (Robinson, 2018). To engage is to systematically and collaboratively inquire into the theories of action that explain teachers' **current** practice and evaluate the relative merit of the current and proposed theories of action. Central to this evaluation is examination of the consequences of teachers' current practice, particularly its consequences for students.

If the consequences fall short of what teachers themselves would wish for, even though they are sceptical of making their wishes a reality, their aspirations for something better may create sufficient motivation to experiment with a new theory. Teachers' success in unlearning and relearning in order to craft a more effective theory of action will depend on many factors, including whether the professional learning is delivered as a bypass or engage approach.

Bypass Approach Versus Engage Approach in Professional Learning

To illustrate the difference between the bypass and engage approaches, I now analyse a programme of professional learning that was designed to improve the capability of 34 elementary teachers in providing the challenging instruction required for deeper learning (Fulmer & Turner, 2014). My purpose in analysing this example is to discuss what happens when a bypass approach is taken to the design of professional learning, and to point out how leaders can be more effective by switching to an engagement approach in which the tension between current and proposed theories is explicitly addressed and resolved.

Table 3.2 compares the teachers' current theory of action with that required by the professional learning on challenging instruction. Since the professional learning bypassed teachers' current theory of action, I inferred their current theory of action from the authors' analysis of the comments made by teachers as they attempted to implement challenging instruction and from their small sample of classroom observations.

The table shows the considerable tension between the two theories of action—tension that was captured in the authors' comments about the pressures teachers experienced, including their "overwhelming focus on students' resistance and disengagement" (Fulmer & Turner, 2014, p. 321).

Table 3.2 A Comparison of Teachers' Current Theory of Action With That Required by Their Professional Learning (based on Fulmer & Turner, 2014)

	TEACHERS' CURRENT THEORIES OF ACTION	THEORY OF ACTION REQUIRED BY THE PROFESSIONAL LEARNING
Beliefs	Students: • will resist challenging instruction • will not make the effort • do not have the required ability Challenging instruction: • will take too much time • is incompatible with covering the curriculum • is incompatible with preparing students for standardised tests	Students: • will be more motivated and engaged by challenging instruction • will experience more cognitive autonomy Challenging instruction: • requires challenge that students perceive as attainable
Actions	Instructional practices: • demonstrate procedures and set practice examples • ask questions that focus on accuracy of students' answers • seldom probe students' thinking, including the reasons for their answers	Instructional practices: • set rich tasks that invite multiple interpretations and strategies • ask high-level questions • enable extended student-student and teacher-student discussions • request student explanations and reasons • communicate cognitive purpose Socioemotional supports: • convey confidence in students • give greater choice • model and scaffold students' thinking
Consequences	High student capability in procedural thinking Low student capability in conceptual thinking Low student engagement, cognitive autonomy, and self-directed learning	High student capability in • conceptual thinking • providing extended responses • self-directed learning

Despite the tension, the professional development bypassed teachers' current theories by moving straight to teaching the new theory through workshops that included explanations of challenging instruction, readings, discussion, and collaborative planning of lessons using challenging instruction. As is typical of the bypass approach, a few teachers were able to resolve the tension for themselves—possibly because their current practice already incorporated aspects of challenging instruction. But many were not willing or able to do so.

The bypass design of most professional learning helps to explain the variable outcomes it typically produces (Cohen & Mehta, 2017). Teachers who are already "on board" improve their practice; those who see tensions with their current practice do not. If leaders ensure that professional learning is designed to engage rather than bypass teachers' theories of action, less money will be wasted, and it will make a more positive impact on the practices of the participating teachers and their students.

Effective professional learning engages teachers' current theories of action by collaboratively revealing and resolving the tensions between the current and proposed theories.

In the example just discussed, this would involve designing the professional learning as an interaction between the current and proposed theories of action, beginning with collaboratively revealing the current theories, comparing them with those proposed, mapping their tensions, and experimenting with how to resolve them in ways that produce more challenging instruction and better social and academic outcomes for students (Robinson, 2018).

In summary, when there is tension between current and proposed theories of action, effective professional learning engages teachers' current theories of action by collaboratively revealing and resolving the tensions between the current and proposed theories. Tensions must be resolved in ways that produce discernible improvement in the relevant student outcomes.

Further Qualities of Effective Professional Learning

While most research on effective professional learning has overlooked the importance of engaging teachers' theories of action, it has identified other important characteristics of effective professional learning—that is, learning that makes a positive difference to the students of the participating teachers. Five additional characteristics of effective professional learning are as follows:

1. It responds to evidence of a specific student and teacher learning need
2. It offers rich evidence-based content that integrates theory and practice

3. It uses external expertise
4. It provides multiple sustained opportunities to learn
5. It is personalised and responsive (Minor et al., 2016; Muijs et al., 2014)

In the remainder of this section, I give a brief overview of each of these characteristics, noting in particular how they can be misunderstood or neglected.

1. **Is based on need.** Effective professional learning is based in evidence of student learning needs. Once those needs are determined and priority student learning goals are established (Dimension 1), further inquiry is needed into possible links between current school and teacher practices and the relevant student outcomes. Such inquiry reveals the school-based causes of those outcomes and hence the leadership and teaching practices that should be reviewed and revised as part of the professional learning.

   While leaders are increasingly basing professional learning priorities on evidence of student need, it is rare that the teacher and leader practices that have contributed to those learning needs are identified, either before or during the professional learning. One implication of this omission is that teachers attend professional learning without a clear and personalised understanding of what they need to learn and unlearn to achieve improved outcomes for their students.

2. **Integrates theory and practice.** Effective professional learning offers rich evidence-based content that integrates theory and practice. Education is dogged by fads and fashions, and it is no easy matter to select interventions that are based on sound theories and have been rigorously evaluated (Datnow, 2000). Leaders can increase the chance of getting rich and worthwhile content by asking potential providers for any evaluations of their programmes, or by doing their own research on websites that provide robust syntheses of the evidence about the effectiveness of different programmes.

   Effective professional learning integrates theoretical principles and practical applications. Professional development comprising practical tips does not work, because it leaves teachers without the knowledge of underlying principles that enables them to create the conditions in their own classrooms that are the key to improved student learning (Hammerness et al., 2005).

On the other hand, theoretical content that is not linked to practical applications and rich illustration is also ineffective. When teachers complain about their professional learning being too theoretical, they are not asking for less theory, but for less theory that is disconnected from the classroom problems they are trying to solve. Effective professional development communicates clear theoretical principles and provides ample opportunity for participants to explore how they can be applied in their own contexts.

3. **Uses external expertise.** Another quality of effective professional learning is the use of external expertise. By external, I mean that the leadership of the group, whether a teacher, school leader, coach, facilitator, or researcher, has demonstrated a greater capacity to solve or prevent the relevant teaching problems than the remaining group members. Expecting teachers who share similar difficulties to solve their problems without the help of such external expertise is unrealistic.

   When the professional learning takes place in an ongoing school or network-based team, the external expert also needs the ability to foster effective ongoing collaboration between participants. Highly skilled facilitation is needed in which the leader can "challenge assumptions and present teachers with new possibilities; challenge the social norms by which collegial groups operate wherever these norms constrain professional learning; and keep the focus on students and their learning" (Allen et al., 2015; Timperley, 2008, p. 20).

4. **Provides multiple opportunities to learn.** Effective professional learning offers multiple and sustained opportunities to learn and unlearn. The opportunities should include support for participants to embed their new learning into their own contexts and time for multiple rounds of practice and feedback. To meet these requirements, leaders should ensure that their professional learning programmes are narrowly focused and intensive rather than a mile wide and an inch deep.

   In my experience, leaders overload the professional learning programme because they greatly underestimate the scope of the learning agenda associated with any particular initiative. Imagine the depth and breadth of teacher learning required to make the shift to the stronger teaching for deep learning strategies portrayed in Table 3.1. The learning agenda comprises not only new content knowledge but also new literacy teaching strategies, new texts, and new assessments. In addition, as I discussed in Chapter 2, these new teaching approaches will not take hold unless teachers are able to manage mixed-ability groups and engage students in tasks that present far more cognitive challenge than those they are used to (Doyle, 2006).

5. **Is personalised and responsive.** Lastly, effective professional learning is personalised and responsive. A personalised approach is particularly important when teachers bring widely varying background knowledge and skill to the professional learning. For example, teachers with a strong science background will learn very differently in a course on teaching science for deeper learning than teachers with weak science content knowledge (Minor et al., 2016). Just as for students, what teachers learn depends on what they already know, and an input-driven approach to professional learning accords too little attention to prior knowledge and how it interacts with the new content.

   The engage approach to professional learning is responsive to what teachers already know and can do, because it investigates their current theory of action in tandem with teaching the new one and continues to do so throughout the professional learning. (For more detail on how to do this, see Robinson, 2018.) Responsiveness is also apparent when the leaders of the learning invite and listen to doubts and disagreements, for such doubts provide windows into the tensions teachers perceive between their current theories of action and those being proposed.

Since the science of adult learning is no different from that of children's learning, it should come as no surprise that there are considerable parallels between the qualities required for effective teacher and effective student learning (Bransford et al., 2000, 2005). Just like students, teachers need multiple, sustained opportunities to learn and unlearn, including time to try things out in their own classrooms, inquire into the effects, modify their approach, and repeat this cycle until improvement is evident. In short, the development of more expert teachers of deeper learning requires teachers themselves to have high-quality opportunities for deeper learning.

Just like students, teachers need multiple, sustained opportunities to learn and unlearn, including time to try things out in their own classrooms, inquire into the effects, modify their approach, and repeat this cycle until improvement is evident.

Dimension 5: Ensuring a Safe and Orderly Environment for Deep Learning

This dimension of leadership practice encompasses what leaders must do to create a physical and social environment that makes it possible for teachers to teach well and for students to thrive, enjoy their schooling, and succeed in their learning. Dimension 5 leadership is foundational, for if teachers and students do not feel safe, if discipline codes are perceived as unfair or are inconsistently enforced, if school management routines do not run smoothly and there is low trust in the willingness or ability of leadership to fix them, then little progress is likely to be made in the other dimensions, such as ensuring the quality of teaching. As I say to newly appointed school leaders, if you are in a school where it is a challenge to get students and teachers to class on time, then you should start with Dimension 5 leadership.

The overarching purpose of this leadership dimension is to promote the willing engagement of students in their learning. That is why I will not be saying much about rewards and punishments and student discipline as traditionally understood. Achieving "willing engagement" is particularly challenging when the goal is deep learning rather than procedural or factual learning, for increased task difficulty and cognitive challenge can make sustained engagement more difficult for some students (Chapter 2). Some guidance can be gleaned, however, from an understanding of what engagement is and how it is fostered.

Student Engagement and Its Determinants[1]

Students' engagement has three aspects: behavioural, emotional, and cognitive (Wang & Holcombe, 2010). Attendance at school, being "on-task" in class, completion of homework, and involvement in learning are indicators of behavioural engagement. Depending on which aspect of behavioural engagement is of interest, it can be measured by attendance rates, rates of homework completion, observations of students' on-task behaviour, disciplinary infractions, or student surveys that ask students about their degree of involvement in their own learning.

Students who are emotionally engaged identify with their school and like at least some of their teachers, classes, and extracurricular activities. Emotional engagement with school is typically assessed with survey items such as "In general, I like school a lot; I feel like I belong to the school I go to now" and the reverse-scored item "I learn more useful

[1] This section is a revised and updated version of parts of Chapter 7 of Robinson, V. (2011). *Student-centered leadership*. Jossey-Bass.

things from my friends and relatives than I learn in school" (Wang & Holcombe, 2010, p. 643).

I discussed cognitive engagement earlier in this chapter in the section on ensuring quality teaching (Dimension 3). To reiterate, students who are thinking about the concepts and skills they are supposed to be learning are cognitively engaged. This type of thinking includes self-regulatory strategies, such as thinking about what is supposed to be learned, planning how to complete learning tasks, and checking one's own work. Cognitive engagement can be assessed on the spot by asking students what they are attempting to learn and how they will know if they are successful, or, more formally, by surveying students about how often they use such self-regulatory strategies as planning and checking their work.

Achieving these three engagement outcomes ensures a safe and orderly environment because students are intrinsically motivated and focused on their learning (Wang & Holcombe, 2010). A singular focus on behavioural engagement, when students are not motivated to learn what is being offered, is punishing for both staff and students. Although students come to school with dispositions that shape their likelihood of engagement, there is an increasing body of evidence that students' perceptions of their schooling are an additional powerful determinant of how they engage with school. That is why school leaders are increasingly gathering evidence from students about how they experience their schooling—everything from feelings of physical and psychological safety to their experience of specific units of work (State of Victoria, Department of Education and Training, 2019).

Collecting good information on how students experience their schooling is important, since their engagement is closely related to their perception of the school and classroom environment. If they perceive that environment as meeting their fundamental psychological needs, they will be far more likely to be engaged and, since engagement predicts achievement, to be successful in their learning. It is important, therefore, that leaders are aware of these needs and of how to develop classroom and school routines that satisfy them (Ryan & Deci, 2000).

The first need, a sense of personal **competence**, refers to students' feelings that they know how to succeed at important tasks and feel confident in doing so. Many of the conditions required to foster students' sense of competence, and therefore their engagement, were considered in the earlier discussion of quality teaching as providing opportunities to learn (page xx). Essentially, learning opportunities that promote success involve well-structured activities that connect with students' prior experience and interests. Teachers also promote success by preventing repeated failure through early detection and correction of students' misunderstandings (page 22). Repeated exposure to academic tasks at which students fail can lead to feelings of incompetence, from which students attempt to escape by disengagement.

As we saw in Chapter 1, one of the purposes of educational institutions is to develop students as autonomous, self-regulated, independent learners. But autonomy is not only an institutional purpose—it is also a fundamental psychological need, and meeting that need increases engagement. **Autonomy** is promoted by school and class experiences in which students influence what and how they learn. This may involve making choices, or when choices are restricted, by accepting the reasons teachers give about why learning something is important (Absolum, 2006). Ideally, it is students rather than their teachers who can articulate why intended learning outcomes are important. A sense of autonomy is also fostered by teaching that enables students to regulate their own learning through knowledge of success criteria and of the progress they are making towards them.

Relatedness is about affiliation and trust. When students sense that adults at school know and care about them, they feel more connected to the school, and their emotional engagement provides a platform from which teachers can more readily foster their cognitive engagement with tough intellectual work. Students' need for relatedness is met by teachers who are perceived as supportive, responsive, and caring. Students feel they can depend on such teachers for help with personal and social problems.

School and Class Routines That Promote Safety and Order

There are two main challenges in ensuring a safe and orderly environment. The first is ensuring consistently implemented routines, and the second is ensuring that those routines are fit for the purpose of increasing student engagement. When leaders understand the determinants of student engagement as discussed above, they can implement routines that are more likely to be effective.

Routines are important because they greatly reduce the burden of figuring out how to solve hundreds of recurring problems, such as how to assign students and teachers to particular classrooms, how to respond to parent complaints, how to ensure student safety at school crossings and on the school bus, and how to cover classes when teachers are away. Without routines, educators would be overburdened by the myriad interpersonal negotiations and choices required to figure out what to do (Becker & Lazaric, 2009). A well-managed school is a school with routines that are fit for purpose, understood, valued, and consistently implemented.

Consistent implementation is important, for without it, collective effort is undermined. It is crucial that leaders have the courage and skill required to hold to account those teachers who appear not to implement agreed routines. By "hold to account," I mean simply to ask such teachers to give an account of their behaviour, and to listen to their response. (More detail on how to do this is provided in Chapter 11.) Their account may prove that the apparent violation was justifiable because the agreed routine is not applicable in that particular circumstance, or that its application has or will bring unanticipated negative consequences. If the violation was justifiable and suggests a wider problem with the routine, then its public review and revision is important so that future noncompliance is reduced by stronger commitment to an improved routine.

The work of engaging students requires the coordinated action of their teachers and the cooperation of students and their peers. The higher the quality of leaders' management practices, the lower the number of reported serious behavioural incidents, which are one indicator of the behavioural engagement of students (Favero et al., 2016). Furthermore, the quality of management predicts growth in student achievement (Grissom & Loeb, 2011), possibly because schools with clear and consistent routines protect time for learning by reducing misbehaviour and absence and ensuring a prompt start to lessons.

The second challenge in creating a safe and orderly environment is ensuring that routines are fit for the purpose of increasing engagement by meeting the three psychological needs discussed above—competence, autonomy, and relatedness. Since there are strong interactions between these three needs, it is important to develop routines that as far as possible address all three at once rather than split them off into routines that promote one or the other. For example, much student misbehaviour in class is due to their sense of failure and shame at not being able to learn, which in turn frustrates their teacher, who has done all he can to assist and begins to give up on those students. This negative dynamic leads students to feel that their teacher doesn't like them and reduces their sense of belonging in that class. In short, students' feelings of incompetence feed into their sense of alienation, and they may reassert some control by acting out in class or absenting themselves altogether. A holistic integrated view is needed of how competence, relatedness, and autonomy work together.

A well-managed school is a school with routines that are fit for purpose, understood, valued, and consistently implemented.

Too often routines are developed that attend to one of these psychological needs without appropriate consideration of how the routines affect the others. For example, as mentioned above (Dimension 3), during the COVID-19 lockdown, many school leaders in my country of New Zealand were advised by officials to give priority to students' well-being and less priority to academic tasks. As a result, many teachers spent considerable time talking with children and their parents about their well-being and far less time tutoring those students who were already struggling with aspects of their work. Such advice overlooks the strong correlation between academic competence and well-being (National Academies of Sciences, Engineering, and Medicine, 2018). As one of my Danish school leader colleagues commented, even young children know that their job at school is to learn to read, and their well-being is diminished if they believe they are not doing so. COVID-19 remote learning routines should be designed to meet academic and well-being needs in an integrated manner.

At senior high school level, leaders are rightly concerned to increase student autonomy over what they wear to school, what they study, and where they do it. But autonomy must be given in ways that increase or at least do not jeopardise student competence and their need to relate to their teachers. When there is evidence that senior students are well behind in their learning, that they have limited ability to regulate their own learning, and that their home environments are not conducive to study, it makes little sense to give them the "freedom" to study at home for four hours a week or to send them home to do independent revision for their final exams. A more appropriate solution is to set up a study room that students are expected to attend and where teachers are expected to tutor students on individualised coconstructed study plans. Such routines are more likely to meet student needs for competence, autonomy, and relatedness than sending them home for four hours a week, or for the two weeks prior to their exams.

Cognitive engagement and the competence that it builds require classroom or study hall routines that ensure high-quality opportunities to learn and succeed (Dimension 3). Students are reluctant to attend lessons in which they are repeatedly faced with work at which they believe they will fail. Too much emphasis on competition and getting the right answer leaves students feeling vulnerable and unsafe. But neither should teachers lower expectations and provide tasks that fall well short of those required for deep learning. Rather, it is a matter of building competence while building the trusting relationships that enable teachers to inquire into and address the misunderstandings and knowledge gaps that have prevented progress.

Here is how the new principal of a failing provincial New Zealand high school describes some of the instructional leadership routines she developed to support and challenge teachers in lifting their expectations of students and more consistently providing high-quality opportunities to learn.

INSTRUCTIONAL LEADERSHIP ROUTINES TO IMPROVE OPPORTUNITIES TO LEARN

1. The leadership team checked all junior student work in the four core subjects of English, social studies, math, and science on a regular basis. They checked:
   a. the quality of the work set,
   b. the quality and quantity of students' completion of the work, and
   c. the quality and quantity of the teachers' written feedback to students.
2. At the senior school level, the leadership team increased the monitoring of students' attainment of credits towards their national qualifications.
3. Students were made aware that their work was so important that it was being reviewed by the school's leaders, who also made visits to classes to comment on their findings and expectations for students' work.
4. Quality management systems were implemented to give written feedback to teachers and their heads of department on the quality of work observed.
5. Requests for improvement were rigorously followed up with the department concerned, and these accountability measures were linked to staff appraisal and departmental review processes.
6. Teachers were supported in meeting the expectations of the leadership team through schoolwide professional development sessions that addressed the importance of teacher expectations and the use of student data in planning and teaching.
7. School targets were set that reflected the desired quality of work, and the principal reported on progress against these each month to the school's governing body to which she was accountable.

These seven leadership routines increased the quality of students' opportunities to learn and as a result significantly improved their attendance and academic success (Grainger & Byres, 2010).

When leaders understand more about how students' willing engagement in their own learning requires meeting their needs for competence, autonomy, and relatedness, they are better able to develop school and classroom routines that will increase engagement, assuming they are consistently implemented. The centrality of meeting students' psychological needs provides a powerful reason for developing leaders' skills in formal and informal ways of collecting and using information about students' experience at school. Since the three needs are closely interrelated, leaders should seek to meet them in a holistic way rather than seeking to satisfy them through three siloed and separate sets of routines.

SUMMARY

The right work of educational leadership is that which the science of learning and teaching suggests is needed to achieve the purposes of educational institutions—ensuring the development of self-directed and well-prepared students. My account of this work is organised under five dimensions of leadership practice that are included in the frameworks that guide leadership development and policy in many jurisdictions. The description of each dimension emphasises the work required to ensure that students have high-quality opportunities for deep learning.

In the first dimension, goal setting, leaders who are committed to deep learning can articulate what they mean by it, provide arguments for its importance, and set data-based goals to close the gap between the current and desired deep learning capabilities of identified student groups. They are knowledgeable about the required pedagogy, and when teacher capability needs improvement, they collaboratively set learning goals for the adults alongside student outcome goals.

If leaders have set goals to improve deeper learning, then scarce resources such as time, money, materials, and expertise need to be aligned to this goal. Leaders who are strong on this second dimension, strategic resourcing, pay considerable attention to recruiting, developing, and retaining teaching expertise that is matched to the learning needs of students. They treat students' time as the most precious resource of all, because they are aware of the time required to develop deep learning competencies, particularly for those students who have low confidence in their ability to master such learning.

When deep learning is the goal, the leadership practices associated with the third dimension, ensuring quality teaching for deep learning, are different from those associated with factual or procedural learning. Standards of quality teaching, and the observation, feedback, and evaluation protocols that apply them, are tailored to monitor and support teaching for deeper learning.

In monitoring teaching for deeper learning, leaders will identify areas where they and their teachers need more professional learning. Much is now known about what leaders can do in this fourth dimension to ensure that the professional learning changes teachers' practice in ways that make an impact on their students. Their leadership of professional learning is more effective if they ensure that it is based on evidence of the learning needs of students and their teachers; explicitly addresses any tensions between the theories of action that underpin teachers' current practices and the theories of action proposed by the facilitator; offers rich, evidence-based content that integrates theory and practice; is led by people with more expertise than the participants; and is personalised and responsive.

The overarching purpose of Dimension 5 leadership, which I call ensuring a safe and orderly environment, is to promote the willing engagement of students in deep learning. Promoting such engagement requires meeting their psychological needs for competence, relatedness, and autonomy through school management and teaching routines that are consistently implemented and fit for purpose. Since the work of engaging students requires the coordinated action of many teachers, consistent implementation is critical, for without it collective effort is undermined.

REFLECTION AND ACTION

1. Reflect on the argument that the right work of educational leadership is that which is needed to achieve the purposes of educational institutions—ensuring the development of self-directed and well-prepared students. How sound is this argument?
2. How much of your work as a leader is consistent with the right work of educational leadership as defined by the five dimensions of leadership practice?
3. Which of the dimensions do you and your team find most difficult to accomplish? Are those difficulties the focus of your leadership development?

4 Taking Context Seriously

I recently reviewed the anonymous and largely positive feedback dozens of school leaders from Victoria, Australia, gave to an independent evaluator about the state-financed professional development programmes they had participated in. Their most frequent suggestion for improvement was for greater contextualisation of workshop presentations and activities. Leaders of remote rural schools wanted more focus on the particular challenges presented by their remote location; leaders from schools serving very diverse communities or large numbers of English language learners wanted more focus on the special characteristics of their populations. In short, they wanted more attention given to their particular leadership context and more help applying the course content to that context.

Leadership providers and policy makers recognise that they are largely talking in generalities, that no two schools are the same, and that it is the job of leaders to be sensitive to the requirements of their particular context and adapt their behaviour accordingly. But what exactly is context, and what capabilities do leaders require to read or adapt to their context?

In this section, I begin by discussing traditional conceptions of context and why I consider them to be unsatisfactory. I then outline my preferred conception of context and its important implications for how leaders should notice and adapt to relevant aspects of their context.

Traditional Concepts of Context

In education, context is usually understood in categorical terms, such as school type (primary or secondary; single-sex or coeducational), school size; socioeconomic status of the school community; ethnic or language composition of the student population; and so forth. Such categories provide omnibus contexts (Shamir, 2013), suggesting that the characteristics shared by schools in the same category differentially shape the work of educational leaders in each category.

The assumption is that if leaders are knowledgeable about a relevant omnibus context, then they will be more effective in adapting their leadership to that context. Furthermore, the distinctiveness of omnibus contexts may be used as an argument for separate professional development provision for leaders of schools in different contexts.

While knowledge of the omnibus context may suggest some of the conditions that are relevant to a particular leadership challenge, there are likely to be many additional conditions, unique to a particular school and to a particular challenge, that leaders need to consider. For example, the new principal of a small rural school who encounters mistrust of him as an "outsider" works in a very different context from the principal in an otherwise similar school who does not encounter such hostility. This means that categorical similarity, such as "small rural school," provides an inadequate account of context, because there remains large variation in the contextual factors that shape the leadership of such schools.

A further difficulty with a categorical approach to context is that it can lead to stereotyping rather than careful investigation of whether a generalised claim about the category is applicable in a particular school. While there may be good system-level evidence, for example, that schools serving seasonal workers' families will suffer high levels of transience, it does not follow that the children of such workers enrolled in a particular school will be transient, or that features of the school itself, rather than family characteristics, are not contributing to that transience.

In the noneducational leadership literature, context has been defined as "the circumstance, situations, and events surrounding the phenomenon under study and affecting its occurrence, form, internal dynamics, and meaning" (Shamir, 2013, p. 344). This definition is helpful in that it moves away from categorical notions of context and suggests that context should be understood as all the factors that shape a particular phenomenon, such as absence, transience, or low achievement. We are still left with the question, however, of how leaders can discern and respond to the relevant contextual features, and I address that question next.

Proposed Concept of Context

I propose that context should be understood as all those conditions that need to be considered when attempting to understand and resolve a particular problem. The focal problem (e.g., unacceptably low achievement in writing at Grades 4 and 5) puts boundaries on what is relevant and requires detailed inquiry into the conditions that may explain the focal problem and that may need to be modified in order to resolve it.

Context should be understood as all those conditions that need to be considered when attempting to understand and resolve a particular problem.

The set of conditions that constitute the context include objective and subjective factors. For example, the context of the problem of low achievement in writing at Years 4 and 5 in a particular school might include such objective factors as the prior capability of the students in writing, the requirement to teach a mandated writing programme, the availability of external expertise in the teaching of writing, and the pedagogical content knowledge of the students' teachers. Subjective factors might include such socially constructed conditions as students' attitude toward writing, teachers' confidence in teaching it, and teachers' belief that their students cannot make accelerated progress.

This set of objective and subjective conditions constitutes the context in which the problem exists. Solving this problem requires modification of the context so that the goal of accelerated progress in writing is achieved.

Context is thus dynamic (it changes over time as objective or subjective conditions change) and particular to any given problem situation. This is not to say that generalisations cannot be made about omnibus contexts (Oc, 2018). Networks of rural principals get together precisely because *some* features of their contexts are common across their schools and those features (such as few formal leadership positions) shape part of the context of the discrete problems they have to solve.

But generalised advice will always provide insufficient guidance to leaders, because the conditions common to schools in an omnibus context (e.g., few formal leadership positions in small rural schools) do not specify the additional unique conditions that they must discern and respond to in order to solve any discrete problem. In short, the discrete context is nested within the omnibus context (Oc, 2018), and both contribute conditions that need to be taken into account.

This concept of context suggests that, rather than focusing on different capabilities for different contexts, leaders need a broad understanding of relevant omnibus contexts and, in addition, the ability to discern and modify the conditions that are unique to their discrete problem. Understanding of relevant omnibus contexts sensitises leaders to conditions, such as limited access to specialist teachers, that are likely to be relevant to many of the problems they are attempting to solve. But such generalities need to be tested rather than assumed to be applicable to the unique problem the leader is trying to solve. Yes, recruitment of specialist teachers is often difficult in small rural schools, but are there unique features of this school that are also contributing to the difficulty?

If context, as I have argued, is all those conditions that need to be considered when attempting to understand and resolve a particular problem, what exactly is involved in detecting and modifying those conditions? In the remainder of this chapter, I answer this question by explaining what a problem is, how to identify its relevant contextual features, and how those features can be modified and integrated to resolve the problem.

Doing the Right Work by Solving Problems in Context

The work of educational leaders is centrally concerned with solving the numerous organisational, staffing, and instructional problems that stand in the way of achieving educational purposes. Such problems can range from the relatively simple, such as how to schedule the school buses, to the highly complex, such as how to establish effective professional learning communities.

There may be some readers who are sceptical of the centrality I claim for problem-solving. After all, leaders are often doing routine but important management tasks that do not involve the careful deliberations we associate with problem-solving. Such scepticism can be addressed by thinking of a leader's work as comprising three parts—managing business as usual, dealing with crises and surprises, and leading improvement.

We probably recognise how problem-solving is involved in the third improvement component, but it is also relevant to dealing with crises and managing business as usual. In contrast to leading improvement, leading in a crisis requires rapid and decisive formulation of solution strategies. Leading business as usual requires the smooth operation of the hundreds of routines that enable a school to function effectively. These management routines are the product of prior problem-solving efforts. Such management work is not recognised as problem-solving because, as these carefully worked out solutions become routine, they are carried out automatically and become disconnected from the deliberative problem-solving processes that gave rise to them (Kahneman, 2011).

An advantage of solving recurring problems, such as how to schedule the buses or organise duty rosters, through such automatic processes is that they free up the cognitive resources needed to solve new problems or re-solve old ones. A disadvantage is that once problem solutions are routinised, they become so taken for granted that leaders can lose critical acumen and not recognise when changed circumstances require them to be re-solved.

Simon (1993) summarises the switch between automatic and deliberative problem-solving as follows:

> Of course, thinking is more analytic at some times and more intuitive at other times. In particular, the thinking of experts dealing with ordinary situations is highly intuitive. It becomes analytic only when the going gets tough, when novelty enters into it, when new problems have to be solved. (1993, p. 405)

An implication of the above is that leadership work involves ensuring the smooth operation of the routines generated by past problem-solving efforts, improving those routines through renewed problem-solving when they are no longer good enough, and developing solutions for completely new problems. If we are to understand what is involved in this work, we need a rich account of the nature of a problem and problem-solving. My focus is on leadership problem-solving rather than decision-making because the former encompasses all the cognitive processes involved in formulating and then solving the problem, while the latter focuses more narrowly on choosing between different solution strategies (Lipshitz et al., 2001).

What Are Problems and How Are They Solved?

At its simplest level, a problem is a gap between the current and desired situation. The problem might be identified by the gap between achievement targets and actual results, or by professional judgments that student well-being, school climate, or teacher morale is below desired levels.

While the gap definition of a problem is easily understood, it does not tell us enough to know how to solve it. More helpful for that purpose is the account of problems and problem-solving provided by philosopher of science Thomas Nickles. He describes a problem as a demand that a certain goal be achieved plus constraints on how it is achieved—that is, conditions of adequacy on the problem solution (Nickles, 1981).

Two features of this definition are very important. First, without the demand, there is no problem. Some years ago, I participated in a research-led intervention to improve the achievement of senior students so they were more likely to enrol and succeed in tertiary study. In one of the six participating high schools, teachers had given up on setting homework, even for students preparing to sit exams for national qualifications.

While the researchers perceived a gap between the current and desired homework practice, there was no demand, on the part of school leaders, that this gap be closed. In other words, this school did not have a homework problem. It took a new principal to create that demand by putting the homework issue on the improvement agenda.

The second important feature of Nickles's definition of a problem is the concept of constraints. Constraints help us to solve a problem because they specify conditions that, as far as possible, solutions should satisfy. Since Nickles's concept of a constraint is typically misunderstood as something that stops you from doing what you want to do, from now on I use the term *solution requirement* instead of *constraint*.

Without solution requirements . . . it is impossible to solve a problem, because there are an infinite number of possible solutions.

Without solution requirements—that is, conditions that, as far as possible, any solution must satisfy—it is impossible to solve a problem, because there are an infinite number of possible solutions. Imagine a leader who is asked to write a new curriculum for Grades 9 and 10. She goes ahead, assuming that literacy and numeracy are given more time on the timetable than the other learning areas, only to be told later that all learning areas are to be given equal weight. She was trying to solve the problem of writing the new curriculum with an incomplete understanding of its context—of the conditions that needed to be met by the new curriculum. This example shows why it is important to agree on what counts as a good solution—on solution requirements—*before* discussing or deciding the actual solution.

By specifying and agreeing on solution requirements, it becomes progressively clearer which solution possibilities are ruled in and which are ruled out, and thus easier to solve the problem. If people can agree on the set of requirements before suggesting solution strategies, then everyone can understand the complexity of the whole problem and take responsibility for solving it by crafting a solution that best satisfies all the agreed requirements.

In education, problems are rarely simple, and neither are their solutions. Most problems in schools are complex. Complex problems have many constituent parts that interact in ways that are hard to predict. That is why they need to be solved in a holistic fashion, by agreeing on an initial *set* of solution requirements rather than taking a piecemeal approach. Complex problems are also characterised by considerable initial uncertainty—uncertainty about what information is relevant and about what counts as a good solution (Robinson, 1993).

A complex problem is solved by working through the five stages of deliberative problem-solving summarised in Table 4.1. While the stages are described as a sequence, the process is far from linear, with iterations within and between the stages highly likely.

Since educational problems are rarely solved by one person acting alone, I describe the problem-solving process as collaborative complex problem-solving (CCPS). That is why the description of each stage in Table 4.1 includes many references to such interpersonal processes as gaining agreement, inquiring, and listening. These interpersonal processes are extensively described and illustrated in Chapters 10–12.

Table 4.1 The Five Stages of Collaborative Complex Problem-Solving (CCPS)

STAGE	PURPOSE	EXPLANATION
1. Agree on the problem to be solved	The purpose of this stage is to test whether there is sufficient agreement that there is a problem.	Completion of this stage does not require agreement about the nature or causes of the problem—that is for Stage 2. It only requires agreement that there is an important gap between the actual and desired situation and that an attempt to close the gap should be made.
2. Inquire into causes	The purpose of this stage is to generate and test causal hypotheses through a planned inquiry process before suggesting or selecting solution strategies.	For some complex problems, this stage might involve data-based inquiry into possible causes through extensive analysis of existing or new sources of relevant data. For other problems, such as a parental complaint about a teacher, causal inquiry could be completed through careful listening and cross-checking of the accounts of the parent, teacher, and student.
3. Formulate solution requirements	The purpose of this stage is to establish a set of requirements that will be used to evaluate the merit of suggested solutions by ruling in those that best satisfy the requirements taken as a whole and ruling out those that do not sufficiently meet them.	The set of solution requirements includes the goal to be met plus all those additional requirements that must be taken into account in solving the whole problem. Once key school-based causes of a problem are understood (e.g., overuse of simplified worksheets causing weak results in math problem-solving), solution requirements that address those causes (e.g., more use of rich texts in math lessons) should be included in the set. In addition, relevant practical requirements should be included, such as deadlines, resource limits, and relevant policies and regulations. The collaborative formulation of solution requirements encourages everyone to take responsibility for exploring the tensions between them and reformulating them in ways that suggest how they can best be satisfied. When the set of requirements is specified in sufficient detail, the required solutions become obvious.

(Continued)

Table 4.1 (Continued)

STAGE	PURPOSE	EXPLANATION
4. Implement and monitor solution strategies	The purpose of this stage is to monitor whether the agreed actions are being done on time and to the agreed standard, and to keep adjusting and learning until implementation standards are met.	Solutions are implemented through a progressively revised action plan. Feedback is gained about the quality and consistency of implementation. New causal factors and associated solution requirements are likely to emerge throughout the implementation phase.
5. Evaluate impact	The purpose of this stage is to determine whether what was implemented has made sufficient impact on the problem (closed the gap).	Evaluation provides feedback on the impact of the plan on goal achievement, which is usually focused on some type of student outcome. Examples of student outcome indicators include student attendance data, standardised assessments, and responses to student voice surveys and interview questions. Problem-solving should continue until the goal is achieved or until there is good reason to reduce the demand that the problem be solved.

I will now elaborate and illustrate this somewhat abstract account of the process of solving problems through two examples that, although based on real events, are somewhat disguised in the interest of clarity and anonymity. The first example addresses a social problem and the second an academic one.

Prank Day Gone Wrong

Many senior students put enormous effort into how they celebrate the end of their schooling. In New Zealand, these celebrations have attracted some notoriety, especially students' behaviour at school balls and at the increasingly risky end-of-year Prank Day, during which school leavers try to outdo their predecessors in the creativity and outrageousness of their pranks. Principals worry about their responsibility to keep their students safe during these events and about the risk to their own and their school's reputation when things go wrong and hit the headlines.

At one high school, which to date had managed to avoid such headlines, the principal was deeply upset at the risk posed to staff and students by the recent Prank Day. Despite meeting with student leaders earlier in the year, providing some funds to support their planning, and providing permission for what she believed were reasonable activities, the day turned out very differently. Among other risky activities, students' pranks included dropping water and paper cups onto stairways to induce slipping and letting off firecrackers inside the building.

At the subsequent assembly for school leavers and their families, the principal, with the support of senior colleagues and some board members, abandoned her planned speech celebrating the achievements of the leavers. Instead, she expressed her disappointment and anger at the violation of school values, the risk to others' safety, and the work the students had created for others in cleaning up the mess.

The reaction was swift. It was now the turn of parents and students to express their anger through Facebook postings, a blizzard of text messages and phone calls, and an unannounced visit to the principal's home by a couple of board members. In their view, the principal had ruined the students' celebration of the end of their schooling, and she was no longer welcome at the traditional dinner for school leavers. An apology was due.

The first stage in collaborative complex problem-solving (CCPS) (Table 4.1) was easily met. While people differed sharply in whom they considered to be at fault, it was clear that parents, students, and staff saw the situation as falling far short of their expectations. The challenge now was to learn from the past and ensure that the fiasco was not repeated the following year. Some CCPS was required!

The second stage was to learn from the past by inquiring into the causes of the recent Prank Day fiasco. An urgent review by the board, student representatives, and the senior leadership team suggested a number of probable causes. First, the planning had been rushed, leaving too little time for the student organizing committee to make the requested changes in its plans.

Second, while there had been some communication between the student organizing committee and senior leaders, the groups had not sat down to discuss and agree on the requirements for a successful Prank Day, and this had left everyone with different views about what was and was not acceptable. To be fair, senior leaders had restricted their involvement because they had genuinely wanted to provide students with as much freedom as possible in their organisation of Prank Day.

A third and related cause was that senior leaders had assumed that the school's frequently articulated values would provide a sufficiently clear set of constraints on what was acceptable but had not explicitly checked with students about how they understood the implications of those values for Prank Day. In summary, those involved had not discussed and agreed about what would count as a more or less acceptable Prank Day before the students put their plan into practice. The review suggested that future Prank Days needed, at the least, to be planned well in advance, and be constrained by the school's values.

The third stage in solving the problem of planning an enjoyable Prank Day was to formulate a set of solution requirements that ensured an enjoyable day for everyone (the goal), addressed the causes of this year's fiasco, and met the legitimate interests of all the stakeholder groups. The causal analysis suggested that planning should start much earlier in the year, that students and senior leaders should agree on broad parameters for acceptable and unacceptable activities and on shared understandings of the implications of the schools' values for the conduct of Prank Day.

In addition to these three solution requirements, the students made clear that they wanted to continue to have considerable autonomy over the planning and execution of a celebration that was creative, fun, and unique to their cohort. The principal and senior staff also wanted a day that was celebratory and that accorded students appropriate autonomy and leadership opportunities, provided that their actions did not violate important school values of respect for the school community and school property and did not pose risks to the safety and security of themselves or others.

This initial set of solution requirements included ethical requirements derived from the school's values (self-respect, respect for others, autonomy, and leadership opportunities), requirements based on regulations (reduction of risks to health and safety, adherence to legal obligations), and requirements based on the wishes of students (celebratory, unique, creative). There were also practical requirements, which included not exceeding the allocated expenditure and completing the planning in the time available, given the other duties and obligations of staff and students.

When solution requirements such as "respect for self and others" and "autonomy" are described at a high level of abstraction, it is hard to check whether staff and students have a shared understanding of their implications for the selection of permissible activities. Nor is it possible to resolve the inevitable tensions that arise between them. For example, students might argue that if some girls choose to run topless through the neighbouring boys' school, this exercise of their autonomy is compatible with respect for themselves and their peers because everyone, except a few prudes, will enjoy the prank, and the activity is freely chosen. Staff and the principal might argue that the activity violates the respect for women and girls that has been a major theme of a yearlong focus on respect for and empowerment of women and girls.

The challenge for those who lead such CCPS is not to find a compromise or trade-off between abstract requirements but to lead a series of meetings of the planning committee in which participants recognise the close interconnections between them and what they mean in the context under discussion. The goal is not to have a philosophical discussion about, for example, the meaning of respect, though that might provide useful background knowledge, but to modify each requirement in ways that preserve the principles at stake, are responsive to the context, and open up possibilities for their integration (Richardson, 1990).

The discussion of respect, for example, is made concrete and contextually relevant by posing the questions "Respect for whom?" and "How is it shown?" Respect for the janitor might be shown by having the planning committee undertake to respect school property and clean up any Prank Day mess themselves rather than leave it to the janitor, as happened the previous year. The requirement for respect has been transformed from adherence to a vague school value to a concrete understanding of what it means on Prank Day for the treatment of school property and the janitor.

The reformulation and integration of solution requirements require those involved to embrace the whole set of requirements rather than just those that are particularly important to them. They must acknowledge the tensions and seek to reduce them by recognising how certain specifications of a requirement open up rather than shut down possibilities for their integration. For example, undertaking to respect the janitor and school property in the ways described may open up more possibilities for creative activities that are likely to leave rubbish in the playground.

The reformulation and integration of solution requirements require those involved to embrace the whole set of requirements rather than just those that are particularly important to them.

Dewey described this process of deliberation as one in which "competing tendencies" are transformed:

> The aim in deliberation should be to devise an action in which all [competing tendencies] are fulfilled, not indeed in their original form but in a "sublimated" fashion, that is, in a way that modifies the original direction of each by reducing it to a component along with others in an action of transformed quality. (Dewey, 1922, p. 194)

Following Dewey's advice means moving from abstract statements about respect and risk to concrete specifications of what these might mean in relation to Prank Day. In this context, respect means such things as not creating hours of extra work for the school janitor, not frightening the intended victims of the pranks, and honouring school values about caring for members of the school community.

When parties reach sufficient interim agreement about these possible meanings, they can move to Stage 4 of the CCPS process; that is, to crafting, implementing, and monitoring solution strategies that, as far as possible, integrate all the critically examined requirements in the solution.

In this example, forging a successful problem-solving process is likely to require more than a couple of meetings towards the end of the year. Far preferable is a yearlong collaborative problem-solving process in which representatives from all affected parties come together to agree on the problem to be solved, including what has gone wrong in the past; agree on the relevant solution requirements; and then accord student leaders as much autonomy as possible in proposing activities that sufficiently satisfy the agreed requirements.

I say "sufficiently satisfy" because in complex problem-solving, some degree of tension between important requirements is inevitable. The goal is not to eliminate the tension between, for example, student autonomy and risk avoidance. Rather, the goal is to reduce the tensions between them in ways that open up rather than shut down the possibilities for their integration.

When integrating competing requirements, it is unhelpful when problem solvers give so much weight to one requirement that it is impossible to give appropriate weight to the others. More helpful are contributions that suggest how autonomy, for example, if understood as elaborated by Winch (Chapter 1), can be integrated with the requirement for respect, and how respect, in turn, implies avoiding exposing others to undue risk and stress. As Dewey explained, it is deliberation about the possible interrelationships between the requirements that opens up the possibilities for their integration.

The fifth stage of CCPS provides the acid test, for it evaluates whether the problem has been solved. It asks whether the solution strategies have had the desired impact, which in this case would mean they have resulted in a Prank Day that everyone considers to have met the agreed solution requirements. There is little point in measuring or even expecting impact if solution strategies have not been conscientiously implemented. But it is equally important to recognise that, despite thorough implementation, the impact on the focus problem may be limited (Hamilton et al., 2022). Such evidence should prompt rigorous inquiry into what happened and why in a new cycle of CCPS.

Closing the Gap in Math Problem-Solving

Problems like Prank Day are just one of the many types of problems that leaders need to solve in establishing a school culture that fosters the growth of autonomous persons—one of the three purposes of education discussed in Chapter 1. I now show how my account of problem-solving also applies to problems that arise in pursuit of the second preparation purpose.

In this example, Joshua, the head of math at Riverview High School, attempts to reduce the persistent disparity between the results of the high- and low-achieving Grade 9 and 10 students. Conscious of the increasing importance of deep learning, Joshua puts discussion of these disparities on the agenda for the next departmental meeting.

The story is presented in five sections—one for each of the stages of CCPS (Table 4.1 through Table 4.6). The left-hand column in each section tells Joshua's story and includes numbered references to the standards for CCPS listed in the right-hand column of each section. The standards communicate what constitutes good practice in solving problems involving students' academic or social outcomes. Since there is a strong collaborative dimension in CCPS, the indicators integrate interpersonal and problem-solving standards. (These standards are covered extensively in Chapters 7–10.)

Table 4.2 Stage 1: Agree on the Problem to Be Solved

JOSHUA'S STORY	STANDARDS OF GOOD PRACTICE IN CCPS
In preparing for the meeting, Joshua recognises his own disappointment at the results of the lowest-performing students, for the school has a strong commitment to more equitable outcomes and it seems that the previous year's professional development has not had the intended impact. He wonders if his teachers will be similarly disappointed and if they will be reluctant to persevere for another year. After sharing the Year 11 math problem-solving results prior to the team meeting, Joshua begins the meeting by explaining his disappointment at the results [1.1], particularly since the recent professional development in math seems not to have had the desired impact [1.2]. He explains how he believes he has a responsibility to	When leaders believe particular student outcomes are problematic, they 1.1 clearly and respectfully describe the outcomes they consider problematic (which students, which outcomes). 1.2 are honest and nonblaming about the seriousness of the problem as they see it. 1.3 give specific reasons and/or evidence to explain why they

(Continued)

Table 4.2 (Continued)

JOSHUA'S STORY	STANDARDS OF GOOD PRACTICE IN CCPS
try to reach the benchmarks set in the school's annual improvement plan so the students are not further disadvantaged in their choice of course and careers in future [1.3] and he hopes that his math colleagues will join him in that effort. He believes that a more systematic inquiry process, rather than immediately looking for another solution (new math resources, programme, or professional development), would increase the chances of making more progress. Before doing anything, though, he wants frank feedback from everyone on how they feel about persevering and learning how to achieve the goal of greatly improved math problem-solving for this low-performing group [1.4]. The team decides that a systematic inquiry process is needed before trying anything new [1.6] and that priority should be given to Year 10 and 11 classes [1.5].	think the student outcomes are problematic. 1.4 ask for frank feedback to determine whether or not others agree the outcomes are problematic. 1.5 establish sufficient agreement with those involved about the scope and urgency of the student outcome problem. 1.6 establish sufficient agreement with those involved about whether to begin a collaborative problem-solving process.

Many leaders make the mistake of moving to subsequent stages of problem-solving before establishing the demand that the problem be solved. It is the duty of leaders to create that demand on behalf of the students they serve, as Joshua did, and to openly inquire into whether others agree that the gap should be closed. If others do not agree, leaders should listen to the reasons for their reluctance, because by doing so, they will learn what conditions will enable teachers to join a collaborative improvement effort.

Table 4.3 **Stage 2: Inquire Into Causes**

JOSHUA'S STORY	STANDARDS OF GOOD PRACTICE IN CCPS
Having gained sufficient agreement to make a start, Joshua and the team plan how they will inquire into possible causes of the weaknesses in math problem-solving. First, they list the possibilities, with most teachers suggesting poor math literacy skills, classroom behaviour problems, and student absences from class [2.1, 2.2]. Joshua listens carefully, summarises the team's beliefs [2.3], and then explains that, while he does not	When there is an agreed demand that a student outcome problem be solved, leaders 2.1 disclose their own beliefs about possible causes of the problem *or*

disagree with those possibilities, it is possible that there may not be sufficient explicit teaching of comprehension strategies for students to decode word problems in math [2.1, 2.4]. This prompts a lively discussion about whether it is the math teacher's role to teach subject-specific literacy and whether there is sufficient time to do that and cover the math curriculum. The team then develops and implements an inquiry process in which they test their hypotheses about: • math literacy by assessing selected students' ability to explain key terms in math problems. • absence by using absence data for selected students and talking with students who are often absent from math class to identify the reasons for their absence. • the impact of how they teach by collaborating with a secondary math facilitator so they know what they should be looking for when they observe a small sample of math lessons. • the impact of their current math teaching by talking with selected students in the observed classes to understand more about how they are experiencing the lessons. [2.5, 2.6] Some weeks later, Joshua leads the team in a discussion about what they have learned about the causes of the math problem-solving results [2.7]. The absence data showed no real difference in attendance between the lower- and higher-achieving math students, although many in the former group talked of their dislike of math because they could not understand the work and it made them feel dumb. The class observations and associated conversations with students showed that the students got very few opportunities to learn how to understand and solve math word problems because teachers used worksheets rather than problem-solving tasks, did not teach how to decode word problems, and assessed with quizzes rather than word problems [2.7]. In discussing the data on their math teaching, some teachers disclose their reasons for relying on quizzes and worksheets. In their experience, students find complex texts too difficult, and when this happens, they misbehave and disengage. Furthermore, some teachers indicate that despite previous professional development, they are still really unsure how they can teach mathematical problem-solving to the group of lower-achieving students [2.8]. The team's inquiry process has revealed not only possible links between teaching and math results but also the beliefs that sustain teachers' current practices.	2.2 invite others' beliefs about the possible causes. 2.3 listen carefully to others' beliefs about the causes, especially at points of disagreement. 2.4 engage in collaborative discussion and preliminary evaluation of the suggested causes. 2.5 agree on an inquiry process to use relevant evidence to test the remaining most likely classroom- and school-based causes. 2.6 implement the inquiry process. 2.7 organise and lead team discussion of what the evidence suggests about the validity of each hypothesis. 2.8 repeat the above steps until a sufficiently agreed evidence-based analysis of the likely multiple causes is reached.

Research on the problem-solving processes used by educational leaders suggests that they rarely engage in explicit causal inquiry (Robinson et al., 2020). One reason is the absence of causal inquiry in the models that many educational leaders are obliged to use in their formal planning processes. Many such models move swiftly from the identification of a problem, often located in evidence of student outcomes, to the nomination of goals, targets, and action strategies.

Another reason is middle leaders' discomfort in talking about the ways teaching and teacher-student relationships may be linked to students' results (Patuawa et al., 2021). Joshua is an exception, for his honest and nonblaming stance has created sufficient trust for teachers to reveal why they teach in ways that provide few opportunities for deeper learning. His sensitive causal inquiry means he is engaging rather than bypassing the theories of action that explain teachers' current practice, and those theories provide many clues about the school-based causes of the students' results.

The omission of causal inquiry prevents learning from the past. Leaders may accept that past improvement efforts have not succeeded, but unless they engage in rigorous causal inquiry, they will not learn the reasons for past failure and what specifically needs to be done differently next time.

The emphasis on school-based causes is not meant to imply that social background does not play a causal role in students' underachievement. Rather than deny the relevance of such causes, leaders should explain, as Joshua did, that they want to focus on school-based causes because they are the ones leaders and teachers can leverage.

Table 4.4 Stage 3: Formulate Solution Requirements

JOSHUA'S STORY	STANDARDS OF GOOD PRACTICE IN CCPS
Joshua listens carefully to the discussion and summarises by listing the possible requirements that any solution strategies should satisfy [3.1]. A suitable solution must: • enable students to succeed in the work so improvement goals are reached [3.2]. • build teacher capability in planning and teaching lessons that enable students of diverse abilities to decode math word problems and explain their reasoning processes [3.3].	When there are agreed likely school-based causes of the student outcome problem, leaders 3.1 invite nominations of solution requirements—that is, criteria that will be used to evaluate suggested solutions.

• build teacher capability in assessing mathematical reasoning and problem-solving [3.3]. • engage students in the work even though it is difficult [3.3]. • ensure that the curriculum is covered [3.3]. • be manageable within the departmental budget and time allowances [3.4]. As is typical of complex problems, the team senses considerable tension between some of the requirements. Joshua believes that while teachers' desire to "cover the curriculum in preparation for the exams" is in principle desirable, a focus on "getting through the textbook" will allow too little time for in-depth teaching of the big ideas that students need to understand if they are to succeed in math problem-solving. After considerable debate, the meaning of this requirement is modified so that curriculum coverage means students deeply understand critical concepts rather than the teacher gets through each chapter of the textbook [3.5]. After this meeting, the teachers understand for the first time why their prior professional learning has not been effective. It has not been sufficiently focused on the knowledge and skills they need to plan, teach, and assess the domain-specific vocabulary and on the strategies needed to decode math problems. Nor has it addressed their concerns about students' engagement with and behaviour in such lessons [3.5]. They need a multipronged strategy that directly addresses the six requirements listed above [3.6]. The math facilitator who has helped them with the lesson observations will be invited to address the planning, teaching, and assessment requirements, and they will discuss with her whether additional expertise is needed to build capability in small-group teaching and classroom management [3.7].	3.2 ensure that the student outcome goal is listed as one key requirement. 3.3 ensure that requirements that directly address the causes are nominated (e.g., if a cause of the math outcomes is that students have not been taught discipline-specific vocabulary, one requirement must be that any new approach has to include a focus on how to teach this). 3.4 include any resource constraints on the solution (e.g., time, money, access to relevant expertise). 3.5 revise and invite reflection on the adequacy of the whole set of requirements and of how tensions between them could be reduced. 3.6 propose and invite solution strategies that best satisfy the *set* of requirements. 3.7 evaluate how proposed strategies satisfy the set of requirements.

In this third stage of CCPS, the process of identifying and reducing inevitable tensions between solution requirements is illustrated. Rather than trade-offs or compromises, the process involves seeking principled and context-specific understandings of what the requirements mean in a given context and of how those requirements can be best met alongside all the others in the set. This is what Joshua does as he leads the discussion and transformation of teachers' requirement for "curriculum coverage."

Table 4.5 Stage 4: Implement and Monitor Solution Strategies

JOSHUA'S STORY	STANDARDS OF GOOD PRACTICE IN CCPS
To save time, Joshua prepares an action plan for revision and discussion at the next meeting. He includes specific actions and timelines and decides to fill in who does what by asking for volunteers once people have accepted the plan [4.1]. At the team meeting, the action steps are revised and agreed. Joshua then explains why he thinks it is critical to monitor the implementation of the key steps, emphasising that his motivation for doing so is not to check up on individual teachers but to learn if the plan is working or needs revision. The team agrees that he will ask the math facilitator to develop indicators that she will use to give feedback to classroom teachers [4.2]. The team debates whether teachers will bring their feedback back to the team so they can learn from each other and the facilitator. Joshua advocates such sharing because he wants the team to take collective responsibility for the improvement effort. Concerns about sharing data are discussed, and protocols and schedules for meetings on how to reduce vulnerability without sacrificing opportunities to learn from evidence and each other are agreed [4.3, 4.4].	When there are agreed solution strategies, leaders 4.1 develop action plans for their implementation (what, who, when, etc.). 4.2 use solution strategies to formulate implementation indicators (e.g., teachers' use of new math pedagogy). 4.3 plan how implementation data will be collected and used. 4.4 integrate data-based monitoring and iterative adjustment into meeting routines.

Planning for evaluation needs to start early so that people are clear and confident about what will count as evidence that the problem has been solved. If, for example, the existing math assessments in Joshua's department are better aligned to numeracy than to math problem-solving, revision of math assessment tools may be needed. When assessments are aligned to valued learning outcomes, teachers can be confident in teaching to the test because the test is worth teaching to.

Since there may be a considerable lag between implementation and improved student outcomes, it is critical that there be early and frequent collection and use of implementation indicators so variations in practice and unforeseen complexities can be spotted.

Careful and timely monitoring of implementation and outcome indicators frequently reveals more information about what is required to close the gap. Sometimes action plans are radically modified because the environment has changed and new conditions must be taken into account. Complex educational problems are never finally solved. As circumstances change and leaders learn more about the consequences of

Table 4.6 Stage 5: Evaluate Impact

JOSHUA'S STORY	STANDARDS OF GOOD PRACTICE IN CCPS
In conjunction with the math facilitator, teachers trial newly developed common assessments that are aligned to district standards for math problem solving at Years 9 and 10 [5.1]. They also plan a series of short surveys of students' attitudes to math [5.1]. The new assessments are built into the assessment and meeting schedule so everyone knows when they will be administered and when the data will be discussed. [5.2, 5.3].	Leaders establish indicators for evaluating impact on student outcomes. They 5.1 plan how progress towards student outcome goals will be evaluated. 5.2 integrate collection of math data into assessment routines. 5.3 draw and discuss data-based conclusions about the extent of improvement, for which students, in which classes, and possible reasons why.

their solution, there may be a renewed demand to solve the problem by integrating a modified set of requirements. Leadership comes to the fore again when the routines that constitute the solution are interrupted so that a new round of CCPS can begin.

SUMMARY

If leaders are to be responsive to their context, they need to understand what context is and how to take it into account. Although traditional categorical notions of context (e.g., small versus large school, urban versus rural school) are suggestive of factors that schools of a given category may have in common, there is far more to context than is suggested by membership in a given category. A more practical definition is that context comprises all the factors that shape a particular problem and that leaders therefore need to consider when attempting to understand and resolve it.

Being responsive to context requires capability in discerning and modifying the factors that shape a problem so it can be resolved. Since few educational problems can be resolved without collaborative effort, I call this process of understanding and modifying problem contexts collaborative complex problem-solving (CCPS). It comprises five iterative stages.

In the first stage of CCPS, leaders test whether there is sufficient agreement that there is a problem to be solved. They use evidence and argument to describe the gap they perceive between the current and desired situations and why they think the gap should be closed.

The purpose of the second stage is to generate and test causal hypotheses through a planned inquiry process before suggesting or selecting solution strategies. For some complex problems, this stage might involve data-based inquiry into possible causes through extensive analysis of existing or new sources of relevant data.

The purpose of the third stage is to establish a set of solution requirements in order to evaluate the merit of suggested solutions by ruling in those that best satisfy the requirements taken as a whole and ruling out those that do not sufficiently meet them. The collaborative formulation of solution requirements encourages everyone to take responsibility for exploring the tensions between them and reformulating them in ways that suggest how they can be best satisfied. When the set of requirements is specified in sufficient detail, the required solutions become obvious.

In the fourth stage, solutions are implemented through a progressively revised action plan. Feedback is gained about the quality and consistency of implementation of the solution strategies. New causal factors and associated solution requirements are likely to emerge throughout the implementation phase.

In the fifth stage, the impact of the solution strategies on student outcomes is evaluated. Problem-solving should continue until the goal is achieved or until there is good reason to reduce the demand to solve the problem.

Since, for educational leaders, solving the teaching and organisational problems that prevent deep learning constitutes the right work, the leadership, problem-solving, and interpersonal virtues that enable successful CCPS are the subject of the remainder of this book.

REFLECTION AND ACTION

1. Individually or with your team, reflect on the approach you have taken in a recent improvement project. How systematic were you in working through the five problem-solving stages in Table 4.1? Typically, leaders skip Stages 2 and 3 and move straight to solution strategies (Stage 4). Did you skip these stages? If so, what were the consequences in terms of the success of your improvement project?
2. Work with your team to prepare an introductory presentation on the model of collaborative complex problem-solving described in this chapter. Illustrate your presentation with an original example.

PART C

Doing the Right Work the Right Way

5 Virtues for Doing the Right Work the Right Way

A leader can be highly capable and use that capability for either good or bad ends. For example, virtuous leaders employ their capability in goal setting to good ends by setting goals that are critical to achieving educational purposes and do so with full knowledge of the challenges they pose. They are open with others about why they believe the goal to be important and about the learning that they and others may need to do to achieve the goal. Contrast such leadership with that of leaders who are equally knowledgeable and skilled in goal setting but choose to use their capabilities to set goals that have already been achieved or pose little risk of failure. In these cases, goal setting is being used not for educational purposes but to reduce the reputational risk posed by a mandated goal setting and accountability process.

In short, high capability in goal setting does not preclude using it in ways that are misleading or inequitable. Nor does it preclude using it in ways that are interpersonally reprehensible, as seen, for example, in the leader who unilaterally sets goals for others as a way of pressuring them to improve.

My challenge in this book was to go beyond the concept of a capability to specify the qualities of leaders that ensure that their capabilities are used for worthy purposes and in worthy ways. In short, my first reason for turning to virtue theory was that it went beyond the neutral descriptive language of a capability to provide a way to think about leaders' motives and the ends being pursued.

My second reason for employing virtue theory reflects the autonomous nature of the teaching profession. Educators aspire to be professional in the sense of operating largely free from close bureaucratic surveillance. The more autonomous the professionals, the less anyone knows about the details of their practice. Even when their practice is observable, increased specialization makes it hard for colleagues or supervisors to evaluate the quality of others' practice, assuming they are willing to do so.

The combination of professional autonomy, specialist knowledge, and reluctance to intervene means that the day-to-day responsibility for maintaining standards of practice largely shifts from external supervisors to the self-regulation of the individual professional. Under these circumstances, and given educators' enormous power, "the professional better be virtuous" (W. F. May, 1994, p. 77). They better have character traits that provide internalised standards of good conduct, and virtues provide such standards. As May (1994) explains, "one test of character and virtue is whether a person is virtuous when no one else is watching and a society that rests on expertise needs more people who can pass that test" (p. 77).

By employing the clearly normative language of virtues rather than the more neutral language of capabilities, I am being explicit about what I consider to be the admirable qualities of character that are particularly relevant to the work of educational leaders. Of course, there will be debate and controversy about every aspect of a normative framework—about the educational purposes, about the nature of the work needed to achieve the purposes, and about which virtues are critical to pursuing that work in the right way.

Consideration of leadership virtues takes us beyond knowledge and skills to, in addition, the motivations, thoughts, and emotions of leaders. It enables us to consider not only what our leaders need to know and do but also what type of person they should be.

Providing an empirical grounding, as I have done in Chapters 2 and 3, for claims about what constitutes the right work is an essential step in specifying role-relevant virtues, but empirical research cannot be the whole answer. As will become clear in the remainder of this chapter, consideration of leadership virtues takes us beyond knowledge and skills, to the motivations, thoughts, and emotions of leaders in addition to the knowledge and skills. It enables us to consider not only what our leaders need to know and do but also what type of person they should be. In other words, I propose that virtues provide the standard against which we judge the extent to which the right work is done the right way.

Although the philosophical literature on virtue theory and virtue ethics is extensive, it is not well known in education, with the exception of the work of some educational philosophers who have written about its centrality to teaching (Rice & Burbules, 2010; Sockett, 2012). In positive psychology, there is a strong tradition of empirical study of different virtues, best represented by the *Character Strengths and Virtues* handbook published by the American Psychological Association

(Peterson & Seligman, 2004). While virtues find a place in the general leadership literature (Ciulla, 2004, 2012), to my knowledge virtue theory has seldom been applied to educational leadership, hence the brief introduction to virtues in the next section.

Virtues Explained

In her book on virtue ethics, Swanton (2005) defines a virtue as "a good quality of character, or more specifically a disposition to respond [to a situation] in an excellent or good enough way" (p. 19).

Like many modern virtue theorists, Swanton has embraced Aristotle's view that virtues are entailed in practically everything that bears on human happiness and well-being and therefore should not be confined to matters of morality or religion (Rice & Burbules, 2010; Swanton, 2005). The Aristotelian account of virtue is inclusive of many different types of virtue, including intellectual virtues such as creativity and open-mindedness and interpersonal virtues such as tolerance, honesty, and patience. In Aristotelian virtue theory, there are no rules, definitive lists of virtues, or universally applicable virtuous behaviours. Instead, there is an account of virtues in general and encouragement of flexibility and context-sensitive application. For Aristotle, it is not enough to know about virtues—it is the way we act on our knowledge, or as Swanton puts it, our disposition to respond to particular situations in virtuous ways, that is of central importance.

In this chapter, I provide a general account of virtues as applied to leadership character and identify three clusters of virtues that have particular relevance to the role of educational leaders. In the subsequent chapters I show, with numerous examples, how these clusters enable leaders to do the right work the right way.

Virtuous Thinking and Acting

Virtues are deep-seated personal qualities that are central to the way of being of the virtuous leader (Annas, 2011). A leader demonstrates the virtue of respect, for example, not by acting in a respectful way only with powerful parents and administrators but in all her interactions, including with her students. Furthermore, the virtue of respect is evident not just in face-to-face interactions. The respectful leader *characteristically reasons, acts and reacts in respectful ways* (Annas, 2011).

Virtue theory directs us, therefore, to evaluate the overall excellence of leaders' thinking as well as their actions. We do not judge an act as virtuous because the right words happen to be spoken. The leader may be imitating others or dissembling or have bad underlying motives. A virtuous act springs from good motives, is consciously crafted, and is derived from a reliably virtuous disposition (Swanton, 2005).

The virtuous leader chooses to be virtuous on every occasion even though, being human, they will fall short on many occasions. Their choice to be virtuous is not compelled by external rules, regulations, incentives, or sanctions, but voluntarily exercised. "Actions undertaken solely for external reasons cannot be considered virtuous, precisely because they are coaxed or coerced, carroted or sticked" (Peterson & Seligman, 2004, p. 19).

Virtues and Values

Virtues are very different from values. Virtues are desirable character traits evident in the thinking and action of persons. Philosophers disagree about whether values are qualities that are believed to be worthy (Ciulla, 2004) or qualities that are objectively worthy, whether or not they are believed to be so (Swanton, 2005). When people or institutions espouse values in this subjective sense, they are declaring some of the standards they intend to live by. The difference between what is valued, in this subjective sense, and virtues is starkly portrayed by the story of Enron—the Wall Street energy, commodity, and financial services company whose bankruptcy revealed a financial scandal that led to the downfall of other accounting and finance firms and brought financial ruin to many of its clients. The corporate values that took pride of place in the company's annual reports were communication, respect, integrity, and excellence. As subsequent events revealed, these values were hollow, for they provided no constraints whatsoever on the behaviour of its executives and employees (Lencioni, 2002).

Leaders may espouse being respectful and even think they are, but they may not have the attitudes, motivations, or skills required to act respectfully with those who disagree or with those who frustrate them. To develop the virtue of respect, they need to adopt the right attitudes towards others and learn the relevant interpersonal skills, especially in those contexts in which they find it difficult to be respectful.

Virtues and Vices

Virtues are often understood as corrective, that is, as counteracting some flaw in the human condition, some temptation that must be resisted or some motivation that must be redirected into something good (Foot, 2002). That is why virtue theory pays close attention to the vices that are counteracted by particular virtues. For instance, taken to extremes, the virtue of courage becomes the vice of foolhardiness, the virtue of being honest becomes the vice of rudeness, and the virtue of determination turns into stubbornness.

Educational leaders need the virtue of perseverance to counteract the natural tendency to give up when progress on improving the attendance of particular students proves resistant to multiple interventions. They need the virtue of open-mindedness to counter the human tendency to ignore or resist objections to their ideas. There is so much that is difficult about educational leadership, so many pressures to endure and so many vices to which one might succumb in responding to them, that the moral compass provided by strong virtues, or at least by the striving for them, is essential.

Some readers might be concerned that my focus on the internal drivers of virtues and vices locates them in individual leaders exclusively rather than including the institutional and community contexts in which they work. Let me be clear—individual virtues are not the sole answer to the challenge of developing excellent educational leaders. There is no doubt that the cultures of too many political and educational organizations discourage rather than enable virtuous leadership by giving too much weight to the "optics," populist opinions, the risk of personal grievance, or political correctness.

Accordingly, while virtuous leaders are aware of and on guard against the various external factors that undermine virtuous behaviour (Swanton, 2005), the considerable personal and political risks of swimming against such virtue-inhibiting tides must be taken seriously. If they are not, then virtue theory is at risk of being idealist, of not recognising the power of context-specific external factors to overwhelm the exercise of an otherwise virtuous character.

While the creation of more virtuous institutional cultures is not the focus of this book, suffice it to say that such a task requires leaders who have a deep practical understanding of relevant virtues, a strong personal motivation to be virtuous, and at least moderate skill in doing so. Without such knowledge and commitments, those leading any institutional reform are unlikely to know what a virtuous institution looks like, let alone how to design the structures and processes that would strengthen and enable virtuous behaviour in the "real world."

Acquiring Virtues

There would be little point in using virtue theory in an applied field like educational leadership if virtues, like personality traits, were fixed rather than learned. Fortunately, unlike personality traits, virtues are acquired through conscious and unconscious lifelong learning (Sockett, 2009, 2012). Although an educational leader may have been described in childhood as having a timid personality, this personality trait does not preclude their learning to be more courageous as an adult. They may never be consistently courageous enough to be described as having the virtue of courage, but perfection is not required (Swanton, 2005). Of greater practical importance is the strength of their motivation to overcome their timid personality and learn how to be more courageous in pursuit of the responsibilities of their role as an educational leader.

As Annas writes, virtues are "not a state you achieve and then sit back, with nothing further to do" (2011, Chapter 3 PDF). Although virtues are developed over a lifetime of character formation, they can be deliberately fostered through interventions that deepen role-related understandings of virtues and that provide context-embedded opportunities for practice, coaching, and feedback (Peterson & Seligman, 2004). That is why I will incorporate discussion and illustrations of how leaders can learn to be more virtuous throughout the subsequent chapters.

Virtues as Inclusive of Motives, Knowledge, and Skills

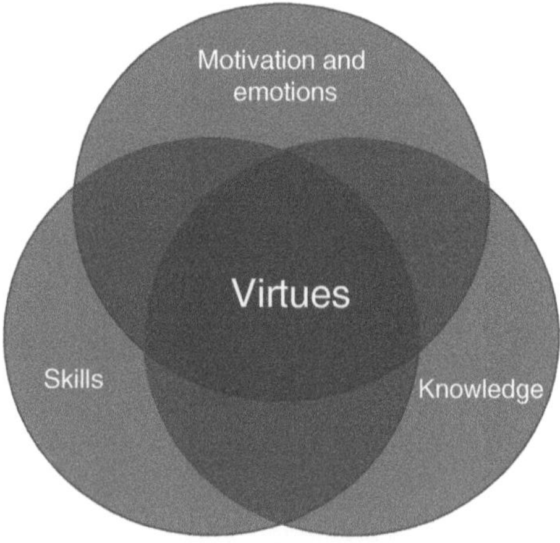

Virtues comprise desirable motivations, knowledge, and skills. Leaders cannot be virtuous in their professional role without sufficient relevant knowledge; they cannot be virtuous without the right motives, and those motives need to shape the way they deploy their skills. Although this is not the place for a philosophical treatise, it is worth establishing a working definition of these three aspects of virtue, for how leaders understand these terms makes a difference to how they practise leadership.

Leaders cannot be virtuous in their professional role without sufficient relevant knowledge; they cannot be virtuous without the right motives, and those motives need to shape the way they deploy their skills.

Motives and Emotions

Modern motivation theory conceptualizes motives as powerful conscious or unconscious personal goals that shape attention, perception, and response tendencies (Bargh et al., 2010). Leaders who are motivated to be more virtuous set and pursue overarching personal goals about the type of leader they would like to be and link their "be" goals to lower-order "do" goals. For example, an assistant principal might set a personal goal of being a more inclusive leader ("be" goal) and plan to do so by widening the representation of a committee they chair and systematically seeking feedback from those who rarely speak up in their meetings ("do" goals) (Bargh et al., 2010). Virtuous leaders think about and can articulate the type of leader they want to be, including the ethical principles to which they are committed. Because they include those commitments in every relevant set of solution requirements, they become increasingly skilled at reaching virtuous, or what Swanton (2005) calls "overall excellent," problem solutions.

The virtuousness of leaders' motives can change the impact of their behaviour. For example, the teacher observation and feedback routines that are associated with instructional leadership can be detrimental to teachers and their students when the leaders who conduct these activities are motivated by the desire to be seen in classrooms or to check up on their teachers rather than by the more virtuous motive of supporting their improvement (Grissom et al., 2013). The leadership lesson is that it is not good enough to do the observations and give the feedback—they have to be done for the right reasons.

Here is a second example of the profound difference motivation makes to the virtuousness of leader behaviour. A leader can set a school goal of improving the attendance of indigenous students because they are deeply committed to the students' well-being and attendance, or they can do so because they know they will be audited on their attendance. If the former motivation prevails, the leader is more likely to strive to achieve that goal by persisting in the face of difficulty, shielding the goal from distractions, disengaging from ineffective strategies, and not overextending themselves (Bargh et al., 2010).

Emotions, which are rooted in evaluative judgments of whether something is good or bad (Keltner & Lerner, 2010), also influence the ability to be virtuous. For example, leaders who evaluate certain conversations and tasks as likely to produce fear, anxiety, or stress are more likely to procrastinate than those who do not anticipate such negative emotions. This may explain why so many educational leaders report putting off what they anticipate will be difficult conversations with colleagues, parents, and teachers (Sinnema et al., 2013).

Strong countervailing virtues such as courage and fairness to students help leaders overcome such negative emotions. The cognitive basis of emotions means that leaders need not always be hostage to their feelings, because they can learn how to reframe their thinking, and hence their emotions, so they can act more virtuously.

One of the important findings from modern motivation research is that personal goal setting and goal striving operate on both conscious and nonconscious pathways, with the latter operating outside conscious motivation and awareness. The goal of being liked, for example, can be activated by features of the environment, and once activated, this goal will guide the leader's thoughts, feelings, and behaviour without conscious awareness (Bargh et al., 2010, pp. 305–306). Such unconscious motivation helps explain why people behave in ways that run counter to their self-concept. Sometimes it is not they who are in charge but their unconsciously activated personal goal.

Even though it is possible to gain more conscious control over personal goals, it is important to recognise the considerable difficulty in doing so. With such recognition comes more tolerance and more understanding of the neuropsychological limits of our self-regulation.

Knowledge

To pursue educational purposes in virtuous ways, leaders need to have deep context-specific knowledge of educational purposes and a rich understanding of how relevant virtues rule in and rule out different ways of pursuing them. In addition, virtuous educational leaders require technical expertise and practical wisdom in its application, both of which are built up through years of practice and experience as classroom teachers and in various educational leadership roles (Swanton, 2016).

Technical expertise includes domain-specific knowledge (knowledge that is particular to education) and more generic knowledge that is relevant to any type of leadership. Domain-specific knowledge includes knowledge of how students learn and of how leaders and teachers facilitate that learning in a manner consistent with the purpose of educational institutions (Chapters 1–4). Just as students develop expertise by gaining a rich repertoire of well-organised conceptual schemata in a subject or topic area, so leaders become technical experts by developing rich domain-specific knowledge structures about learning, pedagogy, assessment, and curriculum.

The generic knowledge that is relevant to educational leadership includes such things as strategic planning, goal setting, budgeting, interpersonal relationships, communication, and problem-solving. Such generic knowledge remains a contentless abstraction, however, unless it is integrated with educational knowledge and context-specific requirements. As Stein and Nelson (2003) argue, it is educational (domain-specific) knowledge that enables effective leadership, for "without knowledge that connects subject matter, learning, and teaching to acts of leadership, leadership floats disconnected from the very processes it is designed to govern" (p. 446).

Before proceeding further with this discussion about what knowledge is required for virtuous educational leadership, two caveats are in order. The first is that there is no consensus among educational policy makers and leadership developers about the relative importance of domain-specific and generic knowledge in educational leadership preparation and development.

While my own position on the importance of domain-specific knowledge has been made clear (Chapters 1–4), politicians, policy makers, and governors with a corporate or public service background are likely to assume that experienced teachers have adequate educational knowledge and that when they step up to more senior leadership roles, it is knowledge about leadership that they need. In England, this belief has produced such experiments as the 2010 Tomorrow's Heads programme, which allowed individuals without teaching experience to train as a headteacher (the equivalent of a principal in the United States). The programme was small and short-lived, and very few of the noneducators in the programme took up headship (principal) positions (Higham et al., 2015).

The second caveat is about the breadth and depth of the knowledge leaders need to solve problems of teaching and learning. How does the need for leaders to have substantial technical knowledge square with the reality of multiple subjects in elementary schools and even more in high schools? What depth and breadth of those subjects is it realistic to expect?

Stein and Nelson (2003) argue that every school and team leader needs in-depth knowledge of at least one subject and experience in using that knowledge to make leadership decisions about such matters as the design of classroom observation tools and student assessments, the choice of texts and teaching materials, and the evaluation of classroom teaching. Leaders with in-depth knowledge of at least one subject appreciate what it means to induct students into the knowledge and modes of inquiry appropriate to a discipline and to teach for deeper learning rather than curriculum coverage. They are also more likely than those with less such knowledge to understand the depth and quality of teacher professional learning that is required to increase student engagement with and success in the subject (Steele et al., 2015; Stein & Nelson, 2003).

Having deep rather than superficial knowledge matters, particularly when it comes to implementation of improvement strategies. Too often such strategies fail to achieve the expected results because leaders have not been sufficiently conscientious about attending to the details of the improvement strategy, and without knowledge of the details and why they matter, successful implementation is unlikely. For example, in discussing how small group tutoring could be a powerful way of combating the effects of COVID-19 school closures, Bob Slavin (2020) warned about the need for attention to dozens of details:

> An effective tutoring program has to get right crucial features, such as the nature and quality of tutor training and coaching, student materials and software, instructional strategies, feedback and correction strategies when students make errors, frequency and nature of assessments, means of motivating and recognizing student progress, means of handling student absences, links between tutors and teachers and between tutors and parents, and much more. Getting any of these strategies wrong could greatly diminish the effectiveness of tutoring.

The depth of leaders' knowledge should match the requirements of the tasks for which they have responsibility. As expectations for school leaders to be instructional leaders grows, so should the responsibility of district administrators and school leaders themselves to ensure they have the knowledge needed to perform that role.

Leadership positions that are closer to classroom teaching need more fine-grained knowledge of teaching and learning than do those positions that are further removed. Nevertheless, senior leaders who are more removed from classrooms still need sufficient knowledge in their areas of responsibility to know what high standards look like, to call attention to gaps between those standards and current practice, and to know how to support their teachers in closing the gaps and to evaluate the progress being made. In short:

> Without an understanding of the knowledge necessary for teachers to teach well—content knowledge, general pedagogical knowledge, content specific pedagogical knowledge, curricular knowledge, and knowledge of learners—school leaders will be unable to perform essential school improvement functions such as monitoring instruction and supporting teacher development. (Spillane & Seashore Louis, 2002, p. 97)

The depth of leaders' knowledge should match the requirements of the task for which they have responsibility.

In many jurisdictions there is a strong expectation that middle and senior leaders act as instructional leaders by focusing on the continuous improvement of teaching and learning. For leaders with limited educational knowledge, it is difficult to meet such expectations, unless they are strongly committed to learning alongside their teachers (Louis & Robinson, 2012).

Skills

Virtuous leaders are not only knowledgeable but also skilled in using their knowledge in excellent ways. By "excellent," I mean that their response to a situation meets, as far as possible, all the relevant solution requirements (Swanton, 2005). The know-how associated with virtue is not a routine skill performed habitually and automatically. Virtuous skill is like adaptive expertise in which the leader actively assesses the situation, integrating situational requirements with their virtuous motives to form a new response.

The concept of adaptive expertise was first proposed in the 1980s by Japanese researchers who were attempting to explain variation in the performance of experts (Hatano & Oura, 2003). One group, who came to be known as routine experts, were highly skilled in applying well-practised routines to the solutions of complex problems. They were very efficient and accurate but less inclined than a second group, called adaptive experts, to recognize when old solutions were no longer applicable and to invent new ones.

The distinction between adaptive and routine experts rests largely on the greater flexibility and innovation of the adaptive expert, which is based on their deep conceptual and practical knowledge and on their ability and willingness to use it to adapt old routines and invent new ones when required.

Educational leaders need both routine and adaptive expertise. The former is essential to ensure the smooth running of the hundreds of routines required for efficient management of the school. Leaders also need adaptive expertise so they can recognise when the old routines are not working well enough, investigate the causes of the difficulties, and specify and integrate a new set of solution requirements.

Such deliberative problem-solving produces a new solution that is then evaluated, adapted, and modified until it becomes a more effective routine than the one it replaced. Literacy leaders display routine expertise when they quickly observe and evaluate the quality of a reading lesson. The danger of such routine expertise, however, is that beliefs about what is typically required in such lessons may not hold true in a particular classroom. Adaptive experts would be open to that possibility, able to check the validity of their assumptions, and, if needed, able to use their deep knowledge of literacy to design and assess new approaches to the evaluation of literacy teaching.

There are many similarities between the concept of adaptive expertise and the knowledge and skill requirements of virtues. Virtuous educational leaders are adaptive experts in the sense that they can use their knowledge and skills to invent solutions to problems they have not previously encountered or solved. What some accounts of adaptive expertise omit, however, is consideration of the worthiness of the means and ends to which the expertise is being applied.

Virtues and skills have practicality and learning in common. The naturally timid leader learns how to be more courageous in the virtuous sense by thinking deeply about the practical and virtue requirements of the situation, attempting to act courageously, and then evaluating the extent to which he integrated the requirement for courage with other relevant virtue and practical requirements. Of course, the improvement of his skills through practice and reflection requires the correct motivation—just like the skilled sports person or musician, the virtuous leader aspires to improve (Annas, 2011). With increased skill, reliance on guidance from mentors and coaches gives way to self-directed understanding and practice of what is required to be virtuous in particular contexts.

As for knowledge, domain-specific skills are more critical to the effectiveness of educational leaders than is often acknowledged. After decades of controversy, "the weight of the evidence suggests that critical thinking, problem solving, and creativity skills are largely domain specific" (Campbell, 2013, p. 412). The more generic skills of educational leadership are the social skills deployed in exercising the influence that is central to leadership, such as skills in feedback, coaching, giving direction, and encouraging participation.

Even those generic skills, however, as we shall see in the subsequent chapters, need to be informed by relevant educational knowledge. No matter how skilled leaders are in generic interpersonal skills, it is hard for them to offer useful guidance if they know very little about the educational matters that are the subject of the conversation.

No matter how skilled leaders are in generic interpersonal skills, it is hard for them to offer useful guidance if they know very little about the educational matters that are the subject of the conversation.

In short, a practical endeavour like school leadership involves a seamless and dynamic integration of the three components of virtue—motives, knowledge, and skills. This can be illustrated by the way leaders learn the virtue of trustworthiness. Theoretical knowledge about trust provides leaders with an understanding of what it is, how it is developed, and why it is desirable. They will not build trust in their leadership, however, unless they are motivated to learn and use trust-building skills in such contexts as staff meetings, dealing with parental complaints, and discussions of resource allocation.

With increased skill, leaders gain practical wisdom about what trust looks like in a variety of contexts and about how they can foster it in themselves and others. With increased knowledge and skill, their confidence and motivation strengthen. They now not only understand that careful listening is important for building trust, but they also become more motivated to listen in an open-minded manner.

As leaders listen more, including to those who disagree with them, relationships of reciprocal respect develop. Improved relationships further strengthen their motivation to be respectful and open-minded even in difficult situations. As they experience the consequences of their more virtuous interpersonal practice, a virtuous cycle develops of more skilled and knowledgeable practice producing more satisfying relationships, which in turn increase the motivation to continue learning how to build trust in ever more difficult contexts (Bryk & Schneider, 2003).

The Place of Virtues in Leadership Frameworks

The writers of the leadership frameworks that guide the selection and development of school leaders in many jurisdictions make no explicit reference to leadership virtues, preferring instead to organise their frameworks under more neutral headings such as capabilities, dispositions, psychological resources, or "requirements." This does not mean that virtues (desirable dispositions) are not included in those frameworks, for typically there is some reference in the entries under each heading to desirable qualities of leadership character.

For example, the Ontario Leadership Framework (OLF) lists optimism, self-efficacy, resilience, and proactivity as desired "psychological resources," which are defined as qualities that allow leaders to cope with complexity and contribute to "leader initiative, creativity and responsible risk-taking behavior" (Leithwood, 2012, p. 50). The leadership framework developed by the Australian Institute for Teaching and School Leadership (AITSL) gives brief mention to dispositions in their discussion of leadership requirements. Under the first requirement, Vision and Values, principals meet this requirement when they "behave with integrity underpinned with moral purpose" and "model values and ethical perspectives" (Australian Institute for Teaching and School Leadership, 2014, p. 20). Another leadership requirement "recognises the importance of emotional intelligence, empathy, resilience and personal well-being in the leadership and management of the school and its community" (Australian Institute for Teaching and School Leadership, 2014, p. 22). In the United States, the 2015 Professional Standards for Educational Leaders promulgated by the National Policy Board for Educational Administration include an expectation that leaders act ethically and in accord with professional norms, but there is little attention given to the personal dispositions required to do so (National Policy Board for Educational Administration, 2015).

When educational policy makers employ the clearly normative language of virtues rather than the more neutral language of capabilities, dispositions, psychological resources, and requirements, they signal the importance of character and invite discussion of the particular character traits required for excellent performance of the role. The goal of leadership frameworks should be to set a standard by describing the virtues (motives, knowledge, and skills) required for excellent pursuit of educational purposes and, by implication, excluding those dispositions that enable their pursuit in unworthy ways.

A Taxonomy of Virtues for Doing the Right Work the Right Way

Which virtues are of critical importance to the work of educational leadership? The selected virtues must be highly relevant to the purpose and role of educational leaders, that is, to doing the right work, and must enable leaders to do that work in the right way. I propose three broad clusters of virtue—leadership, problem-solving, and interpersonal virtues. While all three clusters are central to the work of leadership, I reserve the term *leadership virtues* for those that pertain to a leader's motivation to lead and to the sources of leadership influence they typically draw on. The second two clusters are selected for their central importance to the work of collaborative complex problem-solving (CCPS), with three categories of problem-solving virtues addressing the work of solving complex problems and the interpersonal cluster addressing the relational side of leadership work, including but not confined to CCPS.

Leadership Virtues

Educators with leadership virtues have worthy motives for seeking and holding leadership roles. Carefully articulating these motives is important because some reasons for being an educational leader are more virtuous than others. For example, a leader whose career advancement is motivated mainly by competitiveness or the desire for more money is less virtuous than one whose leadership motivation is firmly rooted in a passionate commitment to educational purposes and to helping other educators succeed in achieving them (Peterson & Seligman, 2004).

Strong convictions about the importance of educational purposes and a willingness to lead others in their pursuit are a prerequisite for virtuous educational leadership. Educators with leadership virtues are not afraid of leading; indeed, they seek it out, but they do so for the right reasons—reasons grounded in their desire to help their colleagues and thereby make a greater contribution to educational purposes. (Chapter 6 is devoted to elaboration and illustration of this cluster.)

Problem-Solving Virtues

The rationale for the second cluster, problem-solving virtues, is firmly grounded in the work involved in pursuing the purposes. I earlier argued (Chapter 4) that the work involves both the smooth operation of hundreds of management routines and the resolution of nonroutine problems, whether they be crises and surprises or long-standing problems such as how to improve persistent low student achievement. Problem-solving is implicated in all this work because the routines involved in school management are the products of past problem-solving efforts and the quality of school management will depend on the quality and consistency of those routines. Crises and surprises require problem-solving under very tight time frames, and improvement problems are solved by being very deliberate and systematic about the processes described in Chapter 4.

Since all of this work requires some type of problem-solving, then an important criterion for selecting relevant virtues is that they are required for excellence in problem-solving. Leaders demonstrate excellence in problem-solving when they craft a solution in which all the solution requirements have been sufficiently satisfied (Swanton, 2005).

Three categories of problem-solving virtues have been selected that are tightly linked to the problem-solving process presented in Chapter 4. (Each of these three categories of problem-solving virtues is elaborated in Chapters 7–9.)

Problem-Solving Virtues

- **Strategic virtues** are required to keep purpose constantly in mind and discern which of all the important problems is the most important to pursue now.
- **Analytic virtues** are required to seek and use valid information, to inquire into the causes of persistent problems, to discern the principles that are at stake in particular solution requirements, and to formulate them in ways that open up rather than close down possibilities for their integration.
- **Imaginative virtues** enable leaders to step outside the status quo, forgo polarities, and envisage how multiple virtue and nonvirtue solution requirements may be integrated.

What distinguishes the problem-solving of virtuous leaders is their deliberate and regular inclusion of relevant virtues in the set of requirements they establish for the solution of any problem. Certain courses of action that may be acceptable to less virtuous colleagues are ruled out because they sufficiently violate the leader's commitment to relevant virtues. In short, virtues set an internalised standard for how to lead.

Interpersonal Virtues

Since leadership involves the exercise of influence over others, how that influence is exercised and the quality of relationships that are forged as a result are critical. When the work requires collaborative problem-solving, as it so often does, interpersonal virtues are required to recruit others to the problem-solving process, to make the meetings and conversations productive, and to gain the trust and commitment required to motivate the collective endeavour.

Educational leaders should treat problem-solving as a collaborative process because the knowledge and perspective of any single leader are inevitably limited. When leaders collaborate, they access a diversity of views and experience, making it more likely that the validity of their own and others' assumptions is checked and valuable perspectives are integrated into a new solution.

In addition to conferring such cognitive benefits, collaborative problem-solving can enhance coordination through shared understandings, shared commitments, and collective effort. Such joint work can also bring social benefits, such as increased enjoyment of and trust in colleagues. That is why I argue that educational leaders need interpersonal and problem-solving virtues as well as skill in integrating them in myriad instances of collaborative problem-solving.

I have identified four specific interpersonal virtues—integrity, respect, courage, and empathy—that I argue in Chapter 10 have particular relevance to the work of educational leadership (see Table 5.1). There are, of course, many other relevant virtues, such as humour, optimism, patience, and tolerance. My goal, however, is not to provide an exhaustive list but to discuss the difference that these four, and by implication other role-relevant virtues, make to the work of educational leaders.

Table 5.1 A Taxonomy of Virtues for Educational Leaders

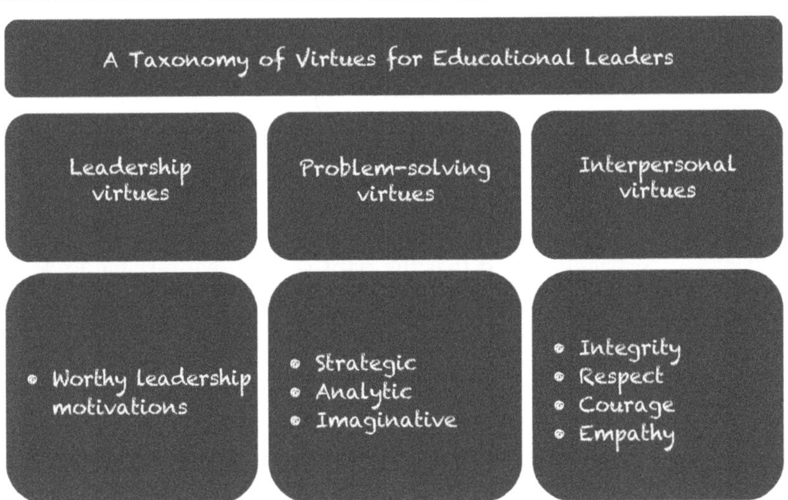

We shall see throughout Part C of this book that virtuous practice requires the seamless integration of several virtues at once, with the integration applying between and within the three clusters of leadership, problem-solving, and interpersonal virtues (Table 5.1). For example, within the interpersonal cluster, the virtue of courage must be integrated with the virtue of respect and empathy if difficult messages are to be communicated in a virtuous way. Blurting out what one thinks of another is not virtuous if what is blurted out is rude and the speaker is closed to the possibility that they are wrong. Virtues are not discrete skills to be separately mastered and evaluated (Rice & Burbules, 2010). Virtuous leadership requires crafting a response that constitutes an excellent integration of multiple relevant virtues.

The three clusters of role-based virtues constitute a taxonomy of virtues tailored to the work of educational leadership. As with all such taxonomies, there will be debate about the universality and comprehensiveness of the clusters and the location of particular virtues within each cluster. For those interested in such debates, the American Psychological Association's *Character Strengths and Virtues* handbook is a good reference point (Peterson & Seligman, 2004).

In elaborating on these clusters and illustrating their utility for educational leaders in the remainder of this book, my goal is to show how they provide a framework for evaluating the excellence of leadership work. The point of such evaluation is to arrive not at a generalised assessment of a leader's character but rather at an evaluation of the virtuousness of how leaders think and act in particular problem situations. Nevertheless, the more a leader is able to act virtuously across a range of situations, the more likely it is that they will garner a reputation as a leader of good character.

SUMMARY

Having argued that the right work of educational leaders is the dedicated pursuit of educational purposes, I use virtues and virtue theory to answer the question of how to do that work in the right way. Virtues are desirable qualities of character that provide internalised standards of good conduct that shape the motivation, emotions, reasoning, and actions of educational leaders. Leaders cannot be virtuous in their professional role without sufficient relevant knowledge, they cannot be virtuous without the right motives, and those motives need to shape the way they deploy their skills.

By being explicit about desirable qualities of character, I go beyond the neutral language of leadership capabilities to specify the qualities of leaders that ensure their capabilities are used for worthy purposes and in worthy ways. Virtuous leadership is self-regulated, consciously crafted, and derived from a reliably virtuous disposition.

Virtues are very different from values, for they are evident in practice, whereas values too often remain at the level of fine words. They are acquired through conscious and unconscious lifelong learning, much of which involves learning how to counteract the many vices that are an inevitable part of the human condition. For instance, leaders learn to counteract timidity through striving to be more courageous; they become aware of their impatience and strive to become more tolerant in the contexts that trigger their frustration; they cultivate a more thoughtful approach to overcome their tendency to show their staff that they "have the answers."

I propose three clusters of virtues that have particular relevance to the work of educational leaders. The first cluster, which I call leadership virtues, pertains to a leader's motivation to lead and to the sources of leadership influence that make it worthy.

The second two clusters (problem-solving and interpersonal) are selected for their central importance to the work of collaborative complex problem-solving (CCPS), with three categories of problem-solving virtues—strategic, analytic, and imaginative—addressing the work of solving complex problems and the interpersonal cluster addressing the relational side of leadership work, including but not confined to CCPS.

REFLECTION AND ACTION

1. Discuss with colleagues the virtues that you believe are the most important for excellence in educational leadership. In your discussion, explain what you mean by each virtue, provide an example, and give your reasons for why it is important. Compare your list with the typology of virtues provided in Table 5.1
2. How big is the gap between the leader you would like to be and the leader you currently are? Have you set "be" goals to help you close the gap?
3. How much emphasis has been given to leadership virtues or character in the leadership training and professional development you have experienced? What is your view of the adequacy of the emphasis?

Leadership Virtues 6

With so many examples of toxic, corrupt, and even pathological political and corporate leaders in the world today, it is crucial that we can distinguish between those who seek leadership power for reasons of self-aggrandisement, protection of ill-gotten gains, or to defeat rivals and those whose motives for seeking leadership power are virtuous. In education, finding and fostering teachers who want to lead for the right reasons is doubly important, because unlike in the corporate and political worlds, the consequences of leaders' actions are felt not only by other adults but by the children and young people for whom those adults are responsible.

In this chapter, I explain what I mean by a virtuous leadership motivation—a virtuous disposition to lead. I also address some of the considerable challenges involved in recruiting and nurturing leaders who want to lead for the right reasons when the pool of aspiring leaders is limited. As the following definition makes clear, it is the motivation for becoming a leader that characterises leadership as a desirable character trait. The trait comprises "an integrated constellation of cognitive and temperament attributes that foster an orientation toward influencing and helping others, directing, and motivating their actions toward collective success" (Peterson & Seligman, 2004, p. 414).

Virtuous leadership is motivated by a desire to influence others for collective rather than individual success. Teachers who are motivated to help more children than those in their own classes, who want to collaborate with colleagues to solve important problems of teaching and learning, who are not afraid to stand up and stand out in order to encourage high standards of practice—those are the motivations that, when reliably demonstrated, characterise a virtuous leadership disposition.

Sources of Leadership Influence

But there is a bit more to virtuous leadership than influencing others "towards collective success," for such influence can be exercised in either virtuous or nonvirtuous ways. The notion of success must be worthy—that is, in accord with educational purposes—and the influence must be voluntarily accepted. Leadership is a form of power because, like the exercise of force, coercion, and manipulation, it results in people doing things they would not have done otherwise (or forbearing from doing things they would have otherwise done).

The practical and moral difference between leadership and these other forms of power relationship is that in leadership, followers voluntarily accept the leader's influence (Fay, 1987). They accept voluntarily because they judge their leader as:

1. exercising their positional authority in a reasonable manner or
2. as possessing admirable personal qualities, such as trustworthiness or
3. as offering good ideas and suggestions

These three sources of influence are what distinguishes leadership power from the power involved in force, coercion, and manipulation (Fay, 1987). Specifically, the virtuous educational leader seeks to influence others for the good of students through one or more of these sources of influence.

This account of leadership is inclusive, since it does not confine leadership to those with positional authority. Those without such authority can still be leaders by drawing on relevant personal qualities and ideas. Virtuous acts of leadership are open to anyone.

In my experience, the preference of all educators, including those with positional authority, is to exercise influence through personal qualities and ideas rather than by appealing to their positional authority. Helen Timperley's research on a two-year New Zealand national literacy initiative provides a lovely example of the impact of principals who can draw on all three sources of leadership influence. From a cohort of 100 schools participating in a two-year literacy initiative, she studied the practice of the five elementary school principals whose students achieved three times the expected rate of progress over the course of the initiative (Timperley, 2011).

Teachers in one of the five schools described their principal as "a leader of teaching and learning who they could approach for help because he had knowledge and experience applicable to a variety of situations" (Timperley, 2011, p. 157). At the same time, the teachers commented on the respectful way in which their principal used his knowledge: "He has a lot of experience in other schools, and he always shares that with everybody and talks about it and he doesn't kind of put us down on a different level" (p. 160). While holding positional authority, the principal was experienced by his teachers as helping them through other forms of leadership influence—through his knowledge, experience, and personal qualities.

The distinctions between leadership, coercion, force, and manipulation apply to teacher-child as well as adult relationships. A teacher leads students when he explains the rationale for requiring them to walk in single file in the corridor and the students accept the reasonableness of the explanation ("we need to make room for the others coming in the opposite direction") or when students accept that the teacher has the authority to require them to walk in single file ("teacher said we must walk in single file").

The teacher coerces students when the source of influence is the threat of deprivation (e.g., revoking participation in a cultural or sports activity); the teacher controls students through force when removing their choice to act otherwise (e.g., by locking the classroom door before school starts to prevent entry and possible damage); the teacher manipulates students by encouraging certain behaviours and discouraging others without disclosing the strategy (e.g., boosting confidence by providing more positive feedback on students' work than is warranted and keeping the strategy secret).

So far, my account of the distinctive forms of leadership influence has assumed that leadership influence operates through virtual or physical interaction. But leadership influence is often exercised indirectly without interacting with others. Leaders can help others succeed in achieving educational purposes by empowering them—that is, by creating the psychological and material conditions that enable them to do something they did not previously have the resources or will to do (Fay, 1987). For example, leaders can empower a group of parents who are wary of getting involved in their children's schooling by encouraging them to meet, by providing the resources that enable them to feel comfortable in doing so, and then, when they are ready, by listening carefully to what they say they need to get more involved.

The notion of empowerment is also applicable to teacher-student relationships. Teachers empower their students when they foster their deep learning and self-regulation so that the students come to see themselves as more able and more likely to achieve their dreams than they would have otherwise. They are not manipulated into such self-conceptions by false reassurance and inaccurate positive feedback but are empowered by the trust their teachers have in them and their teachers' skill in developing their capabilities.

Virtuous Leadership Motivations

Virtuous leaders are motivated to help others succeed in achieving worthy purposes, and they do so, if they have a formal leadership position, through the reasonable exercise of their authority, or if they do not, through their personal qualities, ideas, and example, or by empowering others.

With this account of leadership in mind, we can return to the idea of leadership as a desirable character trait. Virtuous leaders are motivated to help others succeed in achieving worthy purposes, and they do so, if they have a formal leadership position, through the reasonable exercise of their authority, or if they do not, through their personal qualities, ideas, and example, or by empowering others. The latter sources of influence are of course also open to and often preferred by those with formal authority. Having been successful in their own classrooms, those with virtuous motivations seek leadership positions so they can help other teachers be more successful and through them help more students.

Those who want to lead for the right reasons endorse such statements as "I am often able to help others to do a task better; I am often able to organise others so they can work together more effectively; people generally look to me to help solve complex problems; people generally look to me to help resolve conflicts and keep a group together; I am often the spokesperson for my group" (Peterson & Seligman, 2004, pp. 414–415). People who strongly endorse these statements are confident in their exercise of leadership whether or not they currently hold or aspire to a formal leadership position.

A classic study of leadership motivation sheds more light on the nature and consequences of a virtuous disposition to lead. The authors studied the relationship between the motivation profiles of US business managers and the morale of their employees (McLelland & Burnham, 1976). Employee morale, which included measures of employees' sense of responsibility, organisational clarity, and team spirit, was used as an indicator of their manager's effectiveness. The managers' motivation profiles included the need to influence people for the benefit of the institution as a whole rather than for the manager's own personal aggrandisement. Since this concept of influence is very similar to the concept of leadership I am using (Fay, 1987), I see the findings of this study as informing my own discussion of virtuous leadership.

The most important factor determining high employee morale was whether their manager's need for influence was higher than their need to be liked. The employees of managers with high affiliative and low influence needs had low morale because their managers made exceptions to rules and agreements depending on who was in their office at the time.

In contrast, the employees of high-influence, low-affiliation managers had higher morale because their managers were motivated by collective achievement of organisational purposes and were skilled in creating clear pathways and processes for achieving them. As a consequence, employees felt stronger about their ability to achieve those purposes.

Although motivated to influence, effective managers acted in democratic ways, employing a coaching rather than authoritarian style. They were more able than less effective managers to exercise self-control, resulting in less rudeness and exploitation of others than their less-effective counterparts demonstrated. In conclusion, more effective managers had a virtuous disposition to lead in the sense that they were "not motivated by a need for personal aggrandizement, or by a need to get along with subordinates, but rather by a need to influence others' behavior for the good of the whole organization" (McLelland & Burnham, 1976, p. 100).

Identifying and Nurturing a Virtuous Disposition to Lead

The motivations that make educators want to be leaders are critical, for the role accords them considerable power to shape the lives and learning of their staff and students. We need to exclude candidates who are not passionate about serving students in ways that meet educational purposes while at the same time addressing the factors that deter too many teachers from aspiring to leadership positions.

We need to attend to the motivations of aspiring leaders, because how they frame their goals is likely to predict their leadership behaviour. For example, teachers who frame their goal of becoming a team leader as a strategy for advancing their career are likely to direct their attention and effort differently from teachers who want to become team leaders so they can help their colleagues make a bigger difference to the achievement and well-being of students. The latter framing suggests a more virtuous motivation than the former because it signals a deep commitment to the purposes and responsibilities of the role of team leader.

Virtuous educational leaders are unconflicted about being student-centred, particularly when the needs of students are in tension with the preferences of adults.

Virtuous educational leaders are unconflicted about being student-centred, particularly when the needs of students are in tension with the preferences of adults (Robinson, 2011). Their low need for affiliation means they are able to challenge long-established practices—such as ability grouping, tracking, allocation of the most experienced teachers to high-ability classes, and the suspension of the regular timetable and curriculum in the last two weeks of school—if they believe such practices, even though supported by staff, exacerbate inequity in students' opportunities for deeper learning.

The leader who is motivated by the need to be liked rather than respected, or who is overly concerned about the possibility of conflict, will struggle to be student-centred in situations where they perceive a tension between the needs of students and the wishes of staff. Of course, the goal is a principled resolution of the tension, but the virtuous educational leader will always be a strong guardian of and advocate for the interests of students.

In a national study of high- and low-instructional leaders in the United States, it was a stronger educational vision and passion for social justice that motivated principals who were described by their teachers as strong instructional leaders (Louis & Robinson, 2012). In contrast, those principals who were reported by their teachers to engage in less instructional leadership were more focused on warm and caring relationships with staff and students. The point of the comparison is not that such relationships do not matter but that the stronger instructional leaders saw such relationships not as an end in themselves but as enabling collaborative pursuit of a social justice agenda by providing students high-quality opportunities to learn a rich curriculum.

In some jurisdictions it is difficult enough to recruit sufficient candidates for school leadership roles, let alone recruit those with a virtuous disposition to lead. Clearly, the larger the pool of candidates, the greater the opportunity to be appropriately selective. One of the most comprehensive attempts to increase the pool was the U.S.-based Wallace Foundation's principal pipelines initiative, which was motivated by research on the impact of principals on student achievement and on their importance in turning around underperforming schools. The initiative comprised seven districtwide strategies (Table 6.1).

In a comprehensive evaluation of the initiative in six large school districts, evaluators compared the performance of matched-pipeline and

Table 6.1 The Components of the Wallace Foundation's Districtwide Principal Pipelines Strategy

	STRATEGY
1.	Districtwide adoption of **rigorous performance standards** that specify what principals need to know and do and are used in principal preparation programmes, hiring, and evaluation
2.	A **dedicated leader tracking system (LTS)** that provides up-to-date information about applicant characteristics and school vacancies and is used for forecasting, support, and hiring purposes
3.	Delivery of **high-quality preservice programmes** through partnerships between district and external providers
4.	**Selective hiring based on high-quality data from LTS** to match candidates with vacancies
5.	**On-the-job evaluation and support** for new principals aligned to the standards
6.	A **change in the job description of principals' supervisors** to reduce compliance focus and increase support of principals' instructional leadership
7.	**Centralisation of responsibility for the pipeline** at the district level with a dedicated multidisciplinary team and budget

nonpipeline schools. Pipeline schools with newly appointed principals outperformed nonpipeline schools with newly appointed principals in a three-year follow-up of math and reading achievement in Grades K–12.

In addition, principal retention was significantly better in pipeline than in nonpipeline schools (Gates et al., 2019). The systematic and multipronged initiative not only increased the availability, quality, and retention of quality principals but enabled them to achieve significantly better student results than their counterparts in nonpipeline schools.

While the pipelines strategy has provided one solution to the problems of principal recruitment and retention, it does not directly address the issue of principal character. A strong focus on virtues could be included in the strategy by making it explicit in the rigorous performance standards developed by each participating district (Table 6.1). In a stock take of principal pipeline activities across a national sample of school districts (Gates et al., 2020), 85% of respondents reported using principal standards, but little information was provided about their content.

When asked, however, about the type of person they would encourage to be a principal, many district leaders, like the one quoted below, made reference to desirable aspects of leadership character:

> We are looking for someone who is self-aware and results-driven, service oriented to our community and is able to enact high expectations. Someone who is interpersonal, can communicate effectively, and is able to collaborate effectively. Someone with courage and a positive work ethic who is committed to equity and is able to instil trust in their division and organization. Someone who can ensure a positive climate and culture, makes great decisions, and can remain focused on stakeholders, students, and [the] community instead of what is important for them. (Gates et al., 2020, p. 20)

What comes across strongly is the importance of a service ethic, of courage, a commitment to equity and selflessness. Such traits can be assessed with performance tasks such as presentations, role plays, and scenario responses (Wildy et al., 2011). The US national stock take of pipeline practices study showed, however, that few districts used such tasks in their selection processes (Gates et al., 2020).

While teachers might set out on their leadership journey with the right motivations, those motivations will change in response to their day-to-day experiences on the job (Cameron & Lovett, 2015). If teachers work in schools and systems where such motivations as a passion for reducing inequity are treated as naive or idealistic, or where their day-to-day experience tells them that there is little hope of making the difference they aspire to, then such teachers will either give up their leadership aspirations or switch to ones that are more self-serving.

In other words, the worthiness of teachers' leadership motivations is not just a matter of individual character. It is responsive to the contexts they experience, and in many contexts, there is too little evidence that making a significant and sustained educational difference is possible. This is problematic not only from the point of view of achieving institutional purpose but from the point of view of recruiting and developing aspiring leaders who seek to advance their career for the right reasons. If the purpose is too hard to achieve in too many contexts, then less virtuous motives will inevitably come to the fore.

If the purpose is too hard to achieve in too many contexts, then less virtuous motives will inevitably come to the fore.

Recruiting and Retaining Virtuous Leaders

At this point it is worth digressing to consider why it is so hard to recruit good leaders. Does it have to be? There have been many investigations of this question, most of them focusing on the working conditions of teachers and leaders and their consequences for job satisfaction, well-being, and stress. While these factors are important, I believe there is a more fundamental reason, and that is the difficulty of the work itself, and the way that difficulty is linked to the weakness of educational technology. By "weak technology," I do not mean limited use and availability of digital strategies. I mean "the absence of tight routines, or aspects of them, that are powerfully effective and have wide applicability" (Nelson, 2008, p. 493).

Just before writing this section, I took time out to watch a TV special on the sustained decline in New Zealand's math results relative to other countries. The panel of educators, researchers, and mathematicians agreed that while the national ministry of education had rolled out several different professional learning programmes, they had not produced the desired lift in results and had probably confused teachers.

What they did not agree on was how to assess and teach math or the importance of teaching number skills, including times tables, before expecting students to tackle math problems. Like the notorious "reading wars," we have an incipient "math war" in New Zealand, with student-directed learning winning the pedagogical battle over direct instruction. In math and many other curriculum areas, in New Zealand at least, we do not have nationally accepted proven programmes and pedagogical approaches. We have proven approaches, as discussed in Chapter 2, and we have unproven national strategies, as has happened in math, but we do not have a widely shared technology of teaching that produces reliable results the same way science-based professions do.

The result is a huge burden on leaders and teachers to invent what works in their context—a burden that will be willingly and successfully carried out by the outstandingly dedicated and knowledgeable members of the profession but will never be scalable. Weak technology and the forces that sustain it are insufficiently recognised drivers of the complexity of the role and of the difficulty in recruiting and retaining the right sort of educational leaders. To address this, a good first step is to recognise and debate the role of weak technology in maintaining the persistent problems of teacher and leader stress, overload, and inequitable educational outcomes.

Reluctance to Lead

While I have spent most of this chapter discussing the need to recognise and develop leaders with the right motivations, there is the additional challenge of those who are already in leadership roles, particularly teacher leadership roles, who are reluctant to lead. They lack virtuous leadership, not because they exercise power in inappropriate ways but because they so seldom exercise it at all.

They lack virtuous leadership, not because they exercise power in inappropriate ways but because they so seldom exercise it at all.

I am thinking of those teacher and team leaders who are reluctant to influence their colleagues except in the most subtle and indirect ways. They accept the role, and the time allowance and salary increment that may come with it, but are reluctant to influence their colleagues. They are nonvirtuous leaders in the sense that they are not performing the duties associated with the role. Of course, they may have accepted the role because the principal was desperate to fill it and it was their turn, or they may have interpreted the role as entirely administrative based on their observation of how it was carried out by their predecessor.

Without appropriate induction and role models, one can hardly blame teachers who accept leadership roles without understanding or accepting that, by definition, such roles require them to influence their colleagues in the pursuit of the proper purposes of education. I explore the complex reasons why too many teachers are reluctant to exercise leadership, whether or not they have a designated leadership role, in Chapter 10.

SUMMARY

Leaders' motivations for seeking and retaining leadership roles matter. Virtuous educational leadership is motivated by a desire to influence others to achieve collective rather than individual success in the pursuit of educational goals. Teachers who are motivated to help more children than those in their own classes, who want to collaborate with colleagues to solve important problems of teaching and learning, who are not afraid to stand up and stand out in order to encourage high standards of practice—those are the teachers who are likely to reliably demonstrate a virtuous leadership disposition.

Leadership virtues are evident in the worthiness of the educational purpose being pursued and in the sources of influence that are employed in its pursuit. Virtuous leaders recognise that leadership rests on fundamentally consensual rather than coerced influence processes and therefore that the sources of their influence lie in their knowledge and ideas, their admirable personal qualities, and the reasonable exercise of any authority that their role accords them. This account of leadership is inclusive because it does not confine leadership to those with positional authority. Those without such authority can still lead by drawing on relevant personal qualities and ideas. Virtuous acts of leadership are open to anyone.

In addition to these direct sources of influence, leaders may exercise influence indirectly by empowering others—in other words, by creating the conditions that enable others to achieve what would not otherwise have been possible.

There are major challenges in recruiting and retaining a pool of leadership applicants with a virtuous disposition to lead. In education, such applicants are unconflicted about wanting to help teachers guide their students toward successful deep learning. Virtuous leadership motivations are hard to develop and sustain in systems that do not nourish such virtues. While most of the obvious causes of leadership recruitment difficulties are being addressed—as seen, for example, in the Wallace Foundation principal pipelines project—I argue that a more fundamental cause is weak technology, meaning "the absence of tight routines, or aspects of them, that are powerfully effective and have wide applicability" (Nelson, 2008, p. 493). The result is a huge burden on leaders and teachers to invent what works in their context—a burden that will be willingly and successfully carried by the outstandingly dedicated and knowledgeable members of the profession but will never be scalable. Weak technology and the forces that sustain it are insufficiently recognised drivers of the complexity of the role and of the difficulty in recruiting and retaining the right sort of educational leaders.

REFLECTION AND ACTION

1. Reflect back on leaders you have worked with. Which would you say were leading for the right reasons? How were you able to tell?
2. Now apply that same analysis to yourself. How virtuous are the motivations that inform your own leadership practice?
3. To what extent is reluctance to lead an issue in your own educational context? What do you think contributes to the reluctance, and how could those barriers be overcome?

Problem-Solving Virtues 7

Strategic

When teachers feel burdened by too many initiatives, when they are unclear about the purpose of the meeting they are sitting through, when they sense there is little agreement about what is the most important thing to be doing—they are experiencing the consequences of a lack of strategic focus. Leaders with strategic virtues prevent and correct such experiences through their ability to establish and sustain a clear, shared focus that is consciously and collaboratively pursued in every relevant meeting and conversation. In addition, their strategic virtues are finely attuned to the purpose and role of the educational leader.

In this chapter, I explain and illustrate how strategic virtues are essential to solving the problems that prevent achieving educational purposes. Strategic virtues are one of three categories of problem-solving virtues (introduced in Chapter 5). The two remaining categories—analytic and imaginative—are discussed in Chapters 8 and 9, respectively. Since the resolution of educational problems typically requires collaborative effort, there is an inevitable overlap between problem-solving virtues and interpersonal virtues (see Chapters 10–12).

The Role of Knowledge and Skill in Virtuous Strategic Leadership

Virtuous strategic leaders are not afraid to identify problems because they believe it is their responsibility to do so in the interest of better serving their students. They have the knowledge and skills required because they know what good practice looks like and believe that, given the right conditions, it can be attained by all. They are not satisfied with the status quo, because they believe that better student outcomes are possible and that "our way" is not the only or necessarily the best way.

Their knowledge and skill bring confidence that they can make progress in resolving tough problems even when others before them have failed. While they acknowledge that the origins of many of the problems they face lie outside their schools, their commitment to educational purposes and their strong sense of agency nevertheless motivate them to find the school-based levers of change that enable them to make progress.

In a fascinating account of a professional learning programme for senior leaders participating in a districtwide reform of math teaching, Stein and Nelson (2003) describe how increased knowledge and skill foster higher standards and thus dissatisfaction with the status quo. An associate superintendent brought a transformative vision to his math curriculum leadership because, for the first time, he had experienced the difference between "arithmetic practitioners" and "mathematical thinkers" and learned how to recognise curricula that promoted one or the other.

His new knowledge, combined with his open-mindedness, enabled him to detect a gap between the current situation (teaching that produced arithmetical practitioners) and what he now desired (teaching that produced mathematical thinkers) because he knew what the latter looked like. His transformative vision was not "pie in the sky" but solidly grounded in the knowledge and experience he had gained through his recent professional development in mathematics. That experience led him to question the quality of math teaching in his district, to envision an alternative approach, and to design and lead a problem-solving process that enabled his committee to make an informed decision about which curriculum to adopt.

The Role of Motivation in Virtuous Strategic Leadership

Virtuous strategic leaders are internally rather than externally motivated, even when strategic goals and targets are allocated to them by districts or state agencies. In the latter cases, virtuous leaders strive, within the degrees of freedom they have been given, to make those targets serve the educational needs of their students (Louis & Robinson, 2012). They internalise rather than oppose external accountability for improved student outcomes by integrating policy requirements into their own improvement agenda (H. Mintrop, 2012).

By treating policy as a lever for accomplishing goals to which they and their staff are already committed, leaders use external accountability for improvement as an opportunity to strengthen the collective internal accountability culture of their school (Elmore, 2004; Louis & Robinson, 2012). Striving to achieve strategic goals becomes very important, not because the school is externally accountable to a board or district, but because it is the right thing to do for identified groups of students. If the school leadership does not value the accountability indicators used by the external body, it develops additional indicators of its own so that the relationship between what it values and the measures used by the external agency can be empirically tested.

Connecting the Details With the Big Picture

Strategic thinking requires the ability to connect the details with the big picture. Henry Mintzberg, one of my favourite writers on management, puts it like this:

> It is [managers'] ability to bounce back and forth between the concrete and the conceptual—to understand the specifics and be able to generalize creatively about them—that makes for successful strategists. . . . Remaining in the stratosphere of the conceptual is no better than having one's feet firmly planted in concrete. (Mintzberg, 2009, p. 163)

If the big picture is improved teaching of writing, the leaders of this effort act strategically when they know such details as how many opportunities to write extended prose are provided to which students by which teachers, how those opportunities are planned and delivered, and how the progress of teachers and students is being monitored.

Virtuous strategic leaders are not dismissive of the details in the interest of staying at a "strategic level." Yes, they take a helicopter view and focus on the big picture, but they ensure that the helicopter lands regularly so they can check the match between, for example, their abstract big picture of "cross-curricula literacy instruction" and the on-the-ground realities of what is happening in the teaching of writing. They are motivated to monitor the details, not so they can enforce their strategic plans but so they can learn more about the implications of those plans and make any necessary adjustments.

Commitment to the strategic goal of improving writing motivates attention to such things as a teacher who, despite attending high-quality professional learning, is not teaching writing as required. Virtuous educational leaders address this problem, even if the teacher in question is due to retire in eighteen months, because they care about the learning and experiences of the hundreds of students who will be in his classes during that time.

They are truly student-centred in the sense that when there is irreconcilable tension, as there may be in this example, between the interests of students and the wishes of teachers, they give more weight to the former than the latter. The moral purpose they are committed to—the lives and learning of their students—means they do not use the teacher's impending retirement as a rationalisation for their tolerance of what they believe to be his poor teaching.

Finding the Strategic Focus

One of the dangers of ambitious leaders is that they tackle too many problems at once and overload themselves and their teachers. Leaders with strong strategic virtues are able to discern those problems that are relatively more important than others and to create the space to learn how to pursue them by scaling back or stopping lower-priority initiatives. To be strategic is to know, at any point in time, what is top priority, what is lower priority, and why.

To be strategic is to know, at any point in time, what is top priority, what is lower priority, and why.

Considerable work may be needed to gather the evidence and mount the arguments needed to settle on one or two strategic priorities. In some education systems, support is provided for this purpose by system leaders who work with principals to review a comprehensive set of evidence about the school before settling on improvement priorities. In other systems, school leaders must gather their own formal and informal evidence and use it to select the highest-priority problems.

Some of the virtues involved in finding a focus are illustrated by the mentor in the following three excerpts (Tables 7.1, 7.2, and 7.3) from her meeting with a leader who has just begun her first principalship at a small rural elementary school. In this early meeting, the principal recounts a litany of problems she has already detected and expresses her bewilderment at knowing where to start in tackling them. She recounts a long, jumbled list of difficulties, including caretakers who want to work only in daylight hours, dilapidated signage, complaints about student behaviour from the bus company, difficulty in getting relief teachers, a demoralised staff, hostility from the deputy who did not win the principalship, poor reading results, and a falling roll.

In the first excerpt, the mentor helps her to think more strategically by listening carefully to her brief description of all the problems and then summarising the list. These behaviours indicate an acceptance of the complexity of the situation and prevent a premature settling on one issue. The mentor's summary helps the principal move beyond a problem-by-problem approach to consider the set of problems she faces so she can think more strategically about their relative importance and interrelationships.

Table 7.1 Strategic Virtues: Accept the Complexity

Mentor	That sounds like a lot on your plate.
Principal	It feels a little bit muddly, actually. I don't know where to start. There are so many things, and they all seem important.
Mentor	Yeah. Well, in a way, they are all important. That's what's so difficult about this job, that they are all important. Maybe what I can help you with today is just answering that question about where to start, so that you get a sense of, even though they're all important, "This is the most important place for me to start now." Is that a good goal for today?
Principal	Yes, it is. I don't think I've told you . . . When you say, "Which is the most important?" I haven't talked about the falling roll yet.
Mentor	Oh, okay.
Principal	That's a real issue. And I don't know if the caretaker, or the cleaners who leave early, if they aren't doing a good job, so parents aren't happy about that. Is it because the teachers are stuck, or the staff don't seem very motivated? Is that the problem? Or is it our shabby sign at the gate? I just don't know where to go, really.
Mentor	All right. Well, you've given me a sense. I suspect it's just a wee snippet, but it's a sense, I think, of what you're up against at the moment. What I've heard you say is that there's just a whole range of issues, and they're very different. So I want you to work with me on sorting them.
Principal	Okay.
Mentor	I've heard about the caretaker not coming after hours. I've heard about a problem with the buses, the signage, staff who don't seem to have a lot of energy and drive, to put it frankly. And I've heard about a falling roll. What's your sense of what's the most important?

Once the principal had disclosed all her "top of mind" issues, the mentor sought her view about what was most important. In the next excerpt, having agreed with the principal's choice of the falling roll as the priority problem, the mentor inquired further into her views of its causes, because without a clearer idea of what the likely causes were, the principal would still struggle to know where to intervene.

Table 7.2 Strategic Virtues: Find the Focus

Mentor	Okay, that makes good sense to me. So let's just focus on the falling roll, which is a biggie. What I want to help you with is how to get a handle on how to think about it, terms of where to start. What's the cause of the falling roll in your view? I know you haven't been here long, but I really want to get inside your head around what you think is causing it.

(Continued)

Table 7.2 (Continued)

Principal	Well, when I said the staff are stuck, I don't know if that's where the problem is. I've had a look at the kids' books, and I don't think some of them are really working as hard as what I would have expected. I don't think that, because it's a small country school, that should be a reason why they haven't been exposed to good teachers or anything. Because I know that there's some really buzzy smaller schools. I think that there's something not right with the grades that we're getting. And I know that the school down the road, there's been a bit of a shift there, and kids who used to come to our school are now going down there. I'm not sure if it's a combination of some of these things, or if it's around . . . When I look at what some of the reading results are, I think that really, we could be doing better.
Mentor	So you've looked at the reading results already. You've got a sense that they're not good enough, in your view?
Principal	Yes.
Mentor	Okay. Well, you've given me a pretty clear sense of what some of the issues might be. You've said there's two possibilities in your view. One is that the teaching and learning is not where it needs to be, in terms of challenging the students enrolled in this school in terms of the literacy achievement that you've looked at. And the second thing you've suggested, in terms of your thoughts about the cause, is that the school down the road has lifted its game, and the community's noticed that. So that's pretty clear. What do you know about what your staff thinks is the cause of the falling roll?

The mentor's last question—"What do you know about what your staff thinks is the cause of the falling roll?"—was motivated by her belief that finding the strategic focus should be a collaborative endeavour. Leaders need to recruit others to the problem-solving process, and this requires collaborating with teachers to find and commit to a strategic focus.

In Table 7.3 we see how, in response to the mentor's question, the principal revealed her reluctance to speak with staff about the falling roll and her hypothesis about its cause. The excerpt shows the close interaction between strategic and interpersonal virtues—or lack of them. The mentor uses her knowledge and skill in CCPS to check the ability of the principal to communicate her view of the strategic priority and check her teacher's degree of agreement. She discovers that the principal's virtuous strategic leadership is hampered not only by her limited strategic thinking skills but by her limited interpersonal virtues, manifest in this example by not knowing how to conduct the nonblaming conversations and meetings required to recruit her staff to the problem-solving process.

Table 7.3 Strategic Virtues: Communicate the Focus

Mentor	What do you know about what your staff thinks is the cause of the falling roll?
Principal	I don't know. I haven't asked them. I suppose . . .
Mentor	Have you discussed the falling roll situation with them, as a staff?
Principal	No, no, not really. And I suppose I've been so sort of busy with all of these other things, and being new, that it's not until now that I'm starting to think about the falling roll as being the problem. I think also that one of my fears would be, how do I tackle the staff around the falling roll, because it may come back to reflect on them and the work that's going on. And it almost is too big, and I don't know where to start.
Mentor	Yeah. Okay. So you're saying that you haven't talked about it with the staff, partly because you just haven't really been clear enough in your own mind about that being a central issue. And you're also acknowledging that you've got some real hesitation about how to do that with them?
Principal	Yes, I do.

One of the key skills of virtuous strategic leadership is the ability to not only discern a focus but to be really specific in one's communication about what it is and the reasons for its selection. Leaders are often reluctant to be clear, as in this example, because they fear upsetting or singling out those whose practices may be implicated in the problem. The fear of singling out individual teachers or schools can lead to the introduction of unnecessary whole school or even districtwide initiatives. (For further discussion on this fear, see the section on Integrity in Chapter 10.)

Improvement initiatives should be targeted to those who are in need of them and done so in a way that is supportive and nonblaming. A blanket approach risks dilution of the effort needed to improve the work of those who are struggling and alienation of those who are already successful.

Improvement initiatives should be targeted to those who are in need of them and done so in a way that is supportive and nonblaming. A blanket approach risks dilution of the effort needed to improve the work of those who are struggling and alienation of those who are already successful.

In summary, strategic thinking is needed in finding a focus and in determining its scope. The latter decision should be guided by the evidence about where strong and weak practice is likely to be located. There is some evidence that principals who focus their instructional leadership on those teachers who most need their support have a greater impact on teaching practice than those who distribute their efforts more widely (H. May & Supovitz, 2011).

In Chapter 3, I stressed the setting of very few strategic goals, because achieving them typically requires unlearning old practices in order to learn new ones. Strategic educational leaders create room for learning by stopping or postponing work that will compete with the priorities.

In his book *Leading With Focus*, Schmoker (2016) argues that strategic educational leaders achieve better outcomes because they simplify their work by narrowing and deepening their focus on the quality of teaching and learning. His case studies of districts and schools that have narrowed the focus of leaders' work in this way provide compelling examples of what can be achieved with a relentless focus on improvement. For example, at one large low-achieving high school, the leadership team established a clear sequential curriculum with an emphasis on reading, writing, speaking, and reasoning; incorporated writing into most lessons; trained teachers in the principles of effective lessons and closely monitored their use; and trained and empowered department heads to serve as leaders of improvement. The school was held up as "a model of what can happen when leaders eschew instructional fads and instead focus on—and only on—the most critical elements of curriculum, literacy and instruction" (Schmoker, 2016, p. 64). The improvement was achieved without differentiating students into ability groups and without spending a single additional dollar.

Taking activities and initiatives off the table requires courage, because there are often groups of staff, students, and parents who are invested in them. Strategic virtues are required to think through the complexities of what should be stopped or postponed, and interpersonal virtues, including interpersonal courage, are required to gain sufficient agreement with the decisions. (See Chapter 10 for further details on interpersonal courage.) If leaders have a clear sense of educational purpose and deep knowledge of what will be required to achieve it in their context, they will be able to be transparent about the reasons for their choices and, assuming sufficient interpersonal virtues, be nondefensive in their responses to those who object.

Enacting the Strategic Focus

Educational leaders with strong strategic virtues have a passionate commitment to the lives and learning of the students for whom they are responsible. This may seem an obvious point, because there would be few leaders who do not espouse such a commitment. It is the enactment of this virtue, however, that is required for excellence—and that requires the knowledge and skill needed to find and maintain a strategic focus, to ensure that that focus cascades through all the relevant meetings and activities, and to persevere in the face of distraction and difficulty until sufficient progress has been made.

At the macro level of the system, district, and school, leaders with strategic virtues are able to discern and articulate improvement priorities and justify their preferences in terms of the purposes of schooling. Once strategic priorities are determined, they shape aligned goals, work streams, and professional learning activities. At the more micro level, the purpose of meetings and conversations is understood and agreed upon. A shared purpose determines the type of information that is likely to be relevant, who needs to be involved, and the type of decisions that need to be made.

Since strategic leadership, like all leadership, is a social process, it requires the integration of strategic and interpersonal virtues so that the work of choosing and maintaining a strategic focus becomes a collective responsibility. If leaders cannot recruit others to every stage of the problem-solving process, they will remain strategic thinkers rather than strategic leaders.

If leaders cannot recruit others to every stage of the problem-solving process, they will remain strategic thinkers rather than strategic leaders.

Strategic virtues, or what Swanton (2005) calls virtues of focus, are applicable to every problem, not just to those described as "strategic" in strategic and annual plans. When the need to be strategic is confined to the writing of such plans, the importance of every leader being strategic in their daily work is overlooked.

If, for example, improved writing results are a strategic priority, then that goal should be integrated into the solution requirements of every problem that is relevant to achievement of the goal, including how to teach and assess writing, how to develop a professional learning programme that ensures every teacher learns how to plan and deliver consistently excellent writing lessons, and how to monitor students' progress. Strategic virtues shape how leaders think about all their work because they are continually asking, "How does this meeting, activity, project, or resource add value to the most important goals we are pursuing?"

Maintaining the Strategic Focus

Even more challenging than establishing a shared focus on a strategic priority is maintaining that focus. When teachers view the problem as unsolvable, when everyone is overloaded already, and when new problems compete for leaders' attention, it is easy to drop the ball and switch to something else.

I recall asking a literacy leader in one of my workshops why her school had switched from a focus on literacy to math. Her answer was "Because we have been doing literacy for two years." When I followed up by asking about student outcomes, she said there was some improvement, but it was certainly not widespread. It was the lapse of time rather than any evidence of impact that had led to the switch.

Leaders should expect achievement of their strategic priorities to require persistent and conscientious effort, because the problems they represent are likely to have resisted previous efforts to solve them. Repeated failure increases cynicism about the possibility of improvement and reduces teachers' sense of agency and self-efficacy. That is why leaders of improvement need to persevere and maintain their strategic focus.

Perseverance is the "voluntary continuation of a goal-directed action in spite of obstacles, difficulties or discouragement" (Peterson & Seligman, 2004, p. 229). The disposition to persevere helps us overcome a natural tendency to quit when the going gets tough. It increases the chance of success and willingness to tackle what is difficult.

As with virtuous strategic leadership in general, virtuous perseverance is internally rather than externally motivated. The educational leader is determined to reach the improvement goal because they believe that is the right thing to do for their students, not because of external accountability requirements. When there are such requirements, leaders frame those requirements as aligned to and supportive of the moral purpose to which they are already internally committed (H. Mintrop, 2012).

In discussions of perseverance, virtuous perseverance must be distinguished from the related vices of stubborn or dogged persistence. While improvement efforts may fail because leaders give up on a potentially fruitful strategy too early, they may also fail because leaders persist for too long with a flawed strategy. Sometimes this happens when leaders become wedded to a particular programme, funding source, or extra staffing entitlement.

What is needed, therefore, is not persistence as such, but the ability to know when to persevere and when to quit. Such judicious perseverance is more likely when leaders are focused on achieving the improvement goal itself rather than on maintaining a particular strategy for achieving the goal.

Leaders can learn about the effectiveness of their chosen strategy by establishing implementation and outcome indicators. The former give early information about whether a strategy is being implemented correctly. For example, a literacy strategy that requires team leaders to meet regularly with their teachers to review the progress of target children should be accompanied by indicators that give leaders timely information about whether the expected data-based discussions are taking place. Such indicators will enable them to detect and inquire into any gaps between what they expect and what is actually happening.

If improvement strategies are not being conscientiously implemented, the outcome indicators (shifts in the achievement of the target children) are unlikely to improve. The persevering leader is motivated to use such indicators so they can learn as fast as possible about whether a revised or new strategy is needed (Robinson, 2018).

This reflection from an elementary school teacher on why she increased her focus on reading provides a powerful example of how a strategic plan that incorporates rigorous evaluation indicators for improvement can shape the practice of teachers:

> Well, I keep saying the word focus . . . If you don't have that focus, well then another five weeks goes by and things can crop up, like you can do some folk dancing and a marvellous unit on this and that. Now we know that every five weeks we are graphing the reading results, and so you don't let reading go, you let other things go, but you don't let that go. . . . I would like to think accountability was intrinsic, but it used to be getting through the day, keeping the room tidy, having a quiet class. At the end of the day, we would go out of the classroom not necessarily thinking "What have I done today that has helped them to learn to read?" You would go home with a warm fuzzy feeling. "Oh, that was a good day. Maybe I will do some more of that tomorrow". I think the focus has come right back to "What have I done today and who is moving and who isn't moving and why aren't they moving?" That is what you are taking home in your head. (Timperley, 2005, p. 409)

Maintaining a strategic focus requires every relevant leader and teacher to manage the constant stream of distractions that would otherwise prevent a sustained focus on the improvement priority. Whether the distractions come in the form of requests for administrative information, concerned parents, upset teachers and students, or urgent school property and management issues, strategic virtues are needed to manage distractions in ways that protect the time and effort needed to pursue the priorities.

We need more leaders like Robin, the principal of a large New Zealand high school that serves one of the most disadvantaged communities in the country. It was his determination to lead the improvement of teaching and learning that enabled him to maintain his strategic focus despite the distraction of two employment court cases about teacher competency:

> Principal: [The court cases] are a distraction and I think I just have to label it that. We've got a Trust associated with the school, and I do a presentation to them every couple of months. I just had to go back to basics with them and say, "[Teaching and learning] is what the focus is. I know you're concerned about all these other things going on, but it's about kids for me and I'm going to keep doing it." (Robinson et al., 2017, p. 32)

It was his commitment to his students that kept him focused on teaching and learning despite the stress of the two court cases.

Leaders need to decline, redirect, or terminate resources and activities under their control that distract from strategic priorities. Doing so is challenging, because time or money has often already been allocated to something else. A radical reduction in initiatives, withdrawal from interesting but nonessential projects, and the ability to say "no thanks" is often needed to create the space for an intensive focus on the strategic priority (Schmoker, 2016). Similarly, a panoply of professional learning opportunities must be replaced by a narrow and deep focus so teachers develop the adaptive expertise required to teach in ways that will ensure strategic goals are met.

Too often new principals, appointed for their innovative ideas, terminate or add initiatives before they have understood and systematically evaluated those already in place.

New leader appointments are a frequent cause of dropping rather than maintaining a strategic focus. Too often new principals, appointed for their innovative ideas, terminate or add initiatives before they have understood and systematically evaluated those already in place. By doing so, they fail to learn from history—that is, from their school's past failures and successes—and thereby risk leading another cycle of incoherent and unsuccessful improvement efforts.

Educational leaders repeatedly report their inability to pursue the most important obligation of their role, which is ensuring the quality of teaching and learning (Goldring et al., 2020; Hochbein et al., 2021). While there is no doubt that they work in environments of constant distraction, leaders' situation is sometimes made worse by the difficulties they have in learning strategic virtues.

For example, leaders with high affiliation needs may fail to protect the time they need to plan, act, and evaluate their progress in achieving strategic goals. Similarly, leaders who have an open-door policy, or who accept teachers' expectations that they will have immediate answers to their problems, contribute greatly to an environment of constant distraction.

Failure to allocate sufficient time to strategic priorities was a major contributor to the continued poor results in math at Western Heights elementary school, where I was working as a leadership facilitator. After puzzling about why so little progress was being made in achieving this strategic priority, despite considerable expenditure in teacher professional development in mathematics, I realised I had been assuming that senior leaders were actively managing the initiative.

To test this assumption, I asked the principal and her deputy to estimate the percentage of their own time they had spent actively leading the math initiative during the previous school term. I then asked each of them to make the same estimate for their colleague. When the four independent assessments were disclosed, we learned that there was very little discrepancy between the estimates they had made of their own and each other's time. Within five minutes they had agreed and accepted that they spent between 5 and 10 percent of their time leading the effort to improve math across the school and that that was considerably lower than what was required to achieve success.

In the six weeks until my next meeting with them, the principal and her deputy reviewed their diaries to find out the types of activity that were taking up their time. They then reallocated workloads and staff, wrote new job descriptions, and appointed a special-needs coordinator to relieve the deputy of the considerable work she undertook to gain services for the many high-needs children at the school. This appointment enabled the deputy to focus more on the instructional leadership that was required across multiple areas of the school to achieve schoolwide progress in math. There was now far greater alignment between the strategic priority and the allocation of leaders' time.

SUMMARY

Strategic leaders are skilled in discerning the complexity and interrelationships between apparently disparate problems and finding a strategic focus that will enable them to start on one strand of the problem while keeping the whole in mind. Virtuous strategic leaders focus on the right work by giving priority to those problems that directly impact the learning and well-being of students. They are skilled in communicating their reasons for giving some problems greater priority than others, in checking agreement with the priorities, and in creating space for pursuit of the priorities by stopping, postponing, or integrating lower-priority competing activities.

Virtuous strategic leaders show courage and judicious perseverance in maintaining their strategic focus while ensuring that progress is monitored through collaborative discussion of implementation and outcome indicators. They persevere in their efforts, motivated to reach improvement goals because they believe that is the right thing to do for their students, not because of external accountability requirements. While initial adjustments to resourcing and use of time might be painful, the radical reduction in the scope of the work and the intensity of leaders' focus mean their chances of success are greatly increased.

Strategic virtues are applicable to every problem, not just to those described as "strategic" in strategic and annual plans. When the need to be strategic is confined to the writing of such plans, the importance of every leader's being strategic in their daily work is overlooked. Strategic virtues shape how leaders think about all their work because they are continually asking, "How does this meeting, activity, project, or resource add value to the most important goals we are pursuing?"

Since strategic leadership, like all leadership, is a social process, it requires the integration of strategic and interpersonal virtues so that the work of choosing and maintaining a strategic focus becomes a collective responsibility. If leaders cannot recruit others to every stage of the problem-solving process, they will remain strategic thinkers rather than strategic leaders.

REFLECTION AND ACTION

1. Strategic virtues are essential for finding and maintaining clear improvement priorities. How clear are those priorities in your context? Are they clear in practice as well as on paper?
2. What do you notice in a school where leaders have strong strategic virtues? What difference does it make to the work of its leaders and teachers?
3. Is the virtue of perseverance strong in your own and your colleagues' pursuit of an improvement goal? What are your reasons for your view?
4. What facilitates and inhibits your own perseverance in trying to improve teaching and learning in your area of responsibility?

Problem-Solving Virtues 8

Analytic

Leaders with strong analytic virtues are motivated to test rather than assume the validity of the beliefs that guide their actions and reactions. They have a high need to inquire into the facts of the matter, to understand complex problems, and to think carefully about the reasons for their decisions. They recognise the difference between knowledge and beliefs and, therefore, that what is believed to be true may be based on mistaken or incomplete understandings. Their recognition of the fallibility of beliefs, even if strongly held, motivates them to test and check the quality of their own and others' thinking through skilful inquiry into its accuracy and reasonableness.

Analytic virtues imply a disciplined form of curiosity about what is happening, why it is happening, and what, if anything, should be done about it. The curiosity of the virtuous leader is disciplined by the requirements of her role. In the fast-paced world of leadership, a leader who is constantly seeking, for example, to check the accuracy of her teachers' self-reports about what is happening in their classrooms, or who is unable to suggest a course of action without checking out multiple possibilities, will find herself overloaded, stressed out, and stressing others. The virtuous leader senses when it is important to slow down, interrupt her typically fast interpretations, and become more curious.

Analytic virtues are evident when leaders seek to understand the causes of a problem before planning how to fix it so they can match their solution strategies to the probable causes of the problem. Their skill in causal reasoning leads them to avoid "quick fixes" when they are not convinced the "fix" is based on an accurate understanding of the problem for which it is supposed to be the solution. They are humble enough to accept that, if other leaders have tried and failed to resolve long-standing problems, some systematic analysis and learning may be required in order to succeed where others have failed (Robinson et al., 2020).

Leaders with strong analytic virtues are very aware of the ethical dimensions of their decision-making—that mistaken assumptions and taken-for-granted beliefs can produce poor-quality decisions that waste resources, do not solve the problem, and may have negative impacts on students. (For an example of the role of analytic virtues in solving a complex schoolwide problem, see Chapter 13.)

In this chapter, I return to the concept of theories of action first introduced in Chapter 3 to show the importance of analytic virtues in testing the validity of these powerful theories. Next, I describe the inner states (motives and emotions), skills, and knowledge required to exercise these virtues and avoid their associated vices. I conclude with a practical example of how strategic and analytic virtues work together in the first stage (agree on the problem to be solved) and second stage (inquire into causes) of collaborative complex problem-solving (CCPS).

Analytic Virtues and Theories of Action

When we caution leaders to test their assumptions and avoid leaping to conclusions, it is important to recognise just how hard that is. In addition to the barriers posed by the fast-paced nature of the job, the limits of our memory and information-processing capacity mean that we must impose our understandings on a situation rather than treat it afresh. With experience, leaders develop mental models, or theories of action (Chapter 3), that enable them to quickly interpret a situation and decide what to do.

When there is a lot at stake, it is critical that leaders can interrupt their fast, automatic reasoning processes and test rather than assume the validity of their theories of action.

The benefit of these tacit theories of action is that they reduce cognitive load and enable swift action. The downside of such theories is that, for leaders, just as for students, mental models may encode misunderstandings, lack rich connections, and overlook key features of the context. When there is a lot at stake, it is critical that leaders can interrupt their fast, automatic reasoning processes and test rather than assume the validity of their theories of action. They must recognise the possibility of error, slow down, and switch to a more deliberative problem-solving mode, in which the validity of preconceptions is explicitly checked.

As Daniel Kahneman (2011) so colourfully puts it, our brains are "jumping to conclusions machines." While taking cognitive shortcuts increases the speed and efficiency of decision-making, its downside is that it gets us into trouble if our assumptions are mistaken, or if we have overlooked critical features of the situation. As I have previously written, "The challenge for leaders is not to eliminate their preconceptions, for they are an inevitable feature of their memory and information processing capabilities, but to eliminate the assumption that their preconceptions are correct" (Robinson et al., 2020). Meeting this challenge requires the cultivation of analytic virtues.

The practical importance of analytic virtues and their associated vices is illustrated in a fascinating study of how nine Californian educational leaders developed the theories of action that shaped their school improvement efforts (R. Mintrop & Zumpe, 2019). During the course of two years, the authors tracked the thinking and action of these nine leaders as they completed a doctoral programme that was designed to support their school improvement work. Using repeated interviews and observations from workshops and coaching sessions, the authors described the patterns of thought and action that largely prevented these leaders, despite the efforts of their coaches, from testing the validity of the theories of action that shaped their leadership of improvement.

One of the nine leaders was Sofia, a midcareer elementary principal who was passionate about reducing the achievement gap for Black and Latino students in public schools. She believed the gap was caused by teachers not being exposed to culturally and linguistically responsive pedagogy (CLRP). Rather than testing her beliefs by coming up with alternative possibilities and then collecting relevant data so she could learn more about their validity, Sofia "tested" her framing of the problem by asking her teachers about their knowledge of and exposure to CLRP. Since her inquiry showed that they had had little such exposure, she interpreted the results as confirming the "need" to introduce this type of professional development.

Despite being urged by her lecturers and mentors to consider alternative possibilities, the authors reported that "when Sofia consults theory and research to find out more about her problem, she seeks and finds support for her view of cultural relevance as an explanation of the achievement gap" (R. Mintrop & Zumpe, 2019, p. 315). As the authors explain, "having identified literature that points to a systemic and pervasive problem of cultural relevance, . . . she believes that she has identified a phenomenon that surely exists in her school as well. The literature gives further weight to and confirmation of her conviction" (R. Mintrop & Zumpe, 2019, p. 316).

Though Sofia was possibly the most extreme, all nine leaders were unable to test the validity of the theories of action that guided their school improvement strategies. They used their skill in data-based inquiry and their reading of research to confirm rather than critically examine the accuracy of their initial framing of the problems and the actions that followed from them. Like most leaders, they were unable or unwilling to engage in double-loop learning, that is, to be open to the possibility that the beliefs and values that were central to their theories of action needed revision (Argyris, 2003).

It seems, therefore, that skill in data collection, study of research literature, and the guidance of coaches may not be sufficient to overcome the external and internal pressures that produce powerful and self-sealing theories of action. Overcoming these pressures needs, in addition, the motivation and skill that comes with strong analytic virtues.

Analytic Virtues and Truth-Seeking

At the heart of analytic virtues is a stance in which truth is treated as a regulative ideal—one that is never finally attained but worth striving for in the interest of learning and quality problem-solving (Phillips, 1987). Thus, leaders with these virtues treat their beliefs as fallible and their reasoning as potentially flawed while nevertheless striving to improve them through a process of error detection and correction (Argyris, 1976; Mazutis & Slawinski, 2008).

For many educators, the mention of truth raises thorny issues that lead them to avoid the word altogether, or to adopt a relativist stance in which they resort to such phrases as "my truth" and "your truth." Such relativism is unhelpful, for leaders are frequently in situations where they have to make judgments about whose "truth" has the most merit.

For instance, when students provide very different reports of a playground fight, or when a parent's complaint about a teacher differs markedly from the self-report of the teacher, the leader has to locate and weigh up the relevant evidence and make a judgment about the likely truth of each aspect of the various reports. A leader's claim to know what happened requires an explanation of how she arrived at her judgment, including how she evaluated the alternative accounts, what type of inquiries she made, and what types of evidence she considered. In short, while truth is never finally obtained, it certainly differs from a belief.

We come closer to the truth by examining the grounds for beliefs and making judgments about the reasonableness of the accompanying explanations and evidence. There will be many occasions on which the evidence is incomplete and the arguments turn out not to be as strong as first thought, which is precisely why we should treat our own and others' claims to know the truth not with automatic scepticism, but with an open-minded recognition of their fallibility.

Analytic virtues require a stance of truth-seeking rather than truth-claiming. The truth-seeking leader not only models such a stance but aspires to create a team or school culture in which everyone is concerned with the quality of the thinking that informs their actions. The leader's truth-seeking virtue motivates them to, for example, challenge the accuracy of rumours and gossip, question quick conclusions about how to spend money, and care deeply about the accuracy of their student data and the validity of its interpretation.

Analytic virtues require a stance of truth-seeking rather than truth-claiming. The truth-seeking leader not only models such a stance but aspires to create a team or school culture in which everyone is concerned with the quality of the thinking that informs their actions.

Truth-seeking leaders are open-minded in the sense that they are reliably willing to examine their beliefs, with the word *reliably* signalling the presence of a character trait rather than the occurrence of a few examples of open-minded behaviour. Being open-minded is "not a matter of mere perfunctory listening to contrary opinions but a genuine readiness to revise or even abandon one's views in light of new objections or counter evidence" (Spiegel, 2012, p. 8). In short, open-minded leaders ask themselves, "Ought I to hold the beliefs that I hold?" (Sockett, 2012).

Open-minded leaders avoid the vice of being uncritically open to the views of others. As Hare (2003, p. 7) explains,

> [O]pen-mindedness, as Dewey famously put it, is not empty-mindedness (Dewey, 1966, p. 175). It is a form of critical receptiveness . . . , not mere receptiveness to any idea regardless of its merits. Cranks, who find their views rejected, are quick to claim that their critics are not open-minded, but open-mindedness requires that we examine the evidence seriously, not that we accept it.

Although being open-minded in a context that often requires fast and decisive leadership can be extremely challenging, the nine leaders studied by R. Mintrop and Zumpe (2019) remind us that it is not just external factors that constrain open-mindedness, for those leaders had great difficulty testing their theories of action despite being expected to do so and having the time and support required to make it possible. In short, analytic virtues and vices are just as important as, if not more important than, any external drivers or inhibitors of open-mindedness.

Truth-seeking leaders need to be highly sensitive to cues that they should switch from their fast automatic mode of reasoning to a slower, more deliberative mode.

Like open-mindedness, closed-mindedness is also a habit of mind, and far more easily acquired than open-mindedness. The vice of being closed-minded is partly explained by the cognitive shortcuts we take to accommodate our limited information processing and memory capacity. Those shortcuts include simplifying complex situations by imposing well-learned perceptual frameworks upon them and then assuming the validity and applicability of those frameworks. Truth-seeking leaders need, therefore, to be highly sensitive to cues that they should switch from their fast automatic mode of reasoning to a slower, more deliberative mode. Such cues are found in the reactions of others and in leaders' self-regulation of their own thinking processes.

Herb Simon summarises the switch between automatic and deliberative problem-solving as follows:

> Of course, thinking is more analytic at some times and more intuitive at other times. In particular, the thinking of experts dealing with ordinary situations is highly intuitive. It becomes analytic only when the going gets tough, when novelty enters into it, when new problems have to be solved. (Simon, 1993, p. 405)

The problem with Sofia's theory of action was not that she interpreted the underachievement at her school as the result of culturally inappropriate teaching but that she was unable to make the switch from this intuitive and swift presumption to a more deliberate mode of reasoning in which she sought to test rather than confirm her belief. In this respect, her leadership was unethical because she imposed her unvalidated theory of action on her teachers and their students.

The confirmation bias shown by Sofia is a well-established cognitive phenomenon, and just one of the numerous biases that lead us to select and use information that confirms rather than disconfirms our beliefs (Dunning, 2012). Since disconfirming information provides a more powerful test of validity than information that confirms our beliefs, skill is needed in seeking and using counterexamples, alternative hypotheses, and contrary opinions to check the validity of our beliefs.

Imagine a team leader who believes that one of his teachers has just taught a poor lesson because she is still recovering from a chronic illness and is tired in the afternoons. If he is a virtuous seeker of the truth, he tests his belief about the cause of the poor lesson not by recalling confirming examples of other poorly taught afternoon lessons but by recalling any examples of well-taught afternoon lessons, for such examples would disconfirm his claim that the cause of her poor lesson was her afternoon tiredness. He could also seek disconfirming examples by thinking about the quality of the teacher's morning lessons, because if those have also been of low quality, it would suggest that his "tired in the afternoons" explanation is at best incomplete.

Motivational Aspects of Analytic Virtues

Since checking and testing the validity of one's beliefs requires substantially more mental effort than assuming their truth, leaders need to be motivated to develop the analytic virtues that cue them into this form of reasoning. Social and cognitive psychologists have identified a variety of motivations that develop analytic virtues and avoid the associated vices.

The first motivation is the need for cognition, which is defined as "an individual's tendency to engage in and enjoy thinking" (Kruglanski & Sheveland, 2012, p. 484). While situational factors influence willingness to expend effort, there are stable individual differences in the need for cognition.

Second, leaders with strong analytic virtues have high levels of accuracy motivation; that is, they are typically uncomfortable with guesswork, hearsay, and automatic acceptance of others' claims. Their desire to form accurate appraisals of situations is contrasted with the less virtuous defence motivation—the desire to defend one's existing attitudes, beliefs, and behaviours (Hart et al., 2009).

Sofia's confirmation bias was a result of her strong defence motivation—her desire to "prove" rather than test her belief that culturally inappropriate teaching was the cause of underachievement. While accuracy motivation can be activated by instructions to consider a wide range of evidence and evaluate arguments for and against a course of action and by reminders of the importance of a decision, such instructions, as we saw with Sofia, are no guarantee of a more open-minded stance.

Accuracy motivation is inhibited by severe time pressure. Virtuous educational leaders adapt to this pressure by discriminating between those decisions where there is a lot at stake and, therefore, where careful deliberation at several rounds of meetings may be needed, and those where less is at stake, so a more intuitive and less effortful approach is acceptable. The challenge for leaders is to develop their analytic virtues to the point where they can skilfully exercise them when the situation requires.

The need for cognitive closure is a third motivation that shapes how leaders think and act (Kruglanski & Sheveland, 2012). Leaders who are uncomfortable with uncertainty will terminate their inquiries and make earlier decisions than those who have less need for closure. They may be more impatient, more likely to jump to conclusions, and more rigid in their thinking than leaders for whom this need is weaker. Leaders with a high need for cognitive closure may seek definitive answers to questions that cannot and should not be definitively answered at the time.

For example, leaders with a high need for closure may want the district office to tell them exactly when remote learning under COVID-19 will end and be reluctant to accept that a definitive answer cannot be given because it depends on such unknowns as how people will behave under the latest restrictions. Leaders with stronger analytic virtues are more able to live with such uncertainty because they can regulate their need for closure.

While there are individual differences in the strength of these three motivations, they are not fixed, because skill and motivation grow in tandem. Leaders who are motivated to expend the cognitive effort needed to test and check the validity of their beliefs will, over time, become more skilled as they gain experience in testing different types of claims in different contexts (Soll et al., 2015). As their truth-seeking becomes more skilled, it will require less cognitive effort.

The Ladder of Inference: A Tool for Truth-Seeking Leaders

The ladder of inference, originally developed by Argyris (1990) and explained in the following box, is a powerful tool for helping leaders to develop their analytic virtues. It portrays how our conclusions are always fallible because they are based on a series of inferences, each of which may be faulty in some way.

THE LADDER OF INFERENCE: A TOOL FOR TRUTH-SEEKING LEADERS

- The ladder provides a visual image of how our prior beliefs and experiences may lead us to notice certain things and ignore others, and then to leap to conclusions about what it all means.
- The rungs on the ladder tell us that we are selective about what we notice (and others may notice different things); that our descriptions

are shaped by our prior understanding (so we are not neutral); that our interpretations and conclusions are also partial and not obvious.

- Truth-seeking leaders recognise that the inferences they draw at each rung of the ladder may be mistaken and are skilled at testing them by retrieving the information at the bottom of the ladder on which they are based.
- If we become more conscious of how we climb the ladder of inference, we are in a better position to evaluate the accuracy of our beliefs and the strength of the reasoning that led us to a particular conclusion.
- The ladder of inference helps us understand why others may have seen things differently from us and therefore why it is important to treat our views as fallible.

Figure 8.1 illustrates these inferential reasoning processes in the context of the evaluation of an elementary teacher's lesson. Years of experience in classrooms produce assumptions about what good teaching looks like, and these shape what is noticed, how it is described, and the conclusions that are drawn about the effectiveness of a lesson.

Figure 8.1 The Ladder of Inference

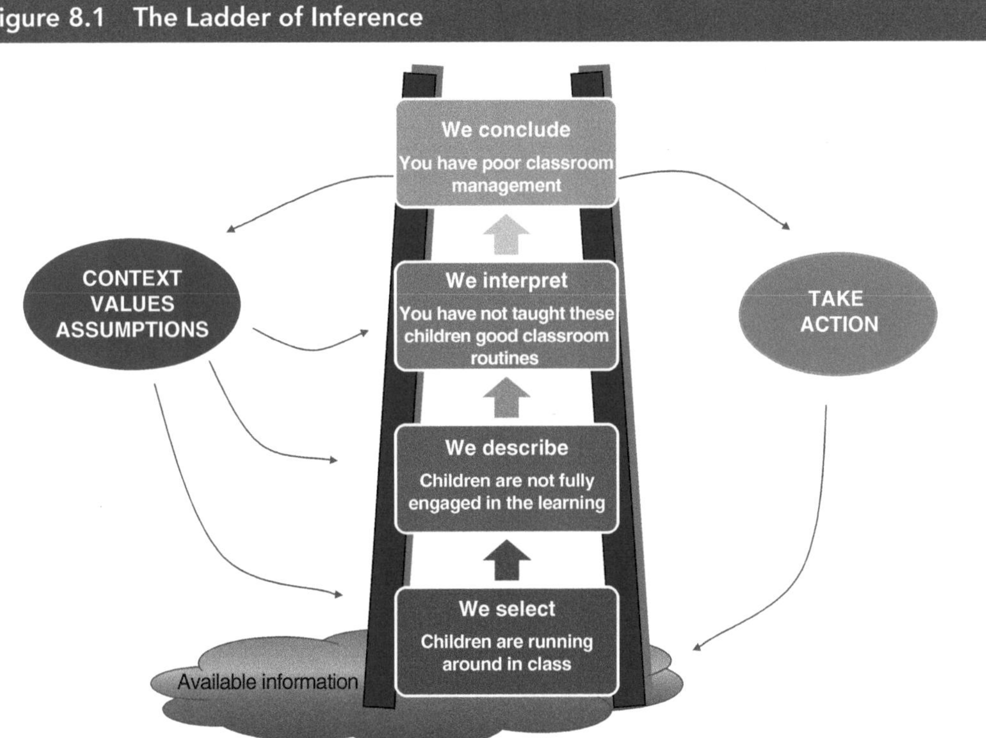

Source: Robinson, V. M. J. (2011). *Student-centered leadership*. San Francisco, CA: Jossey Bass. Adapted from Argyris and Schon (1974).

A truth-seeking leader is motivated to make the cognitive effort needed to check rather than assume the validity of her conclusion about the teacher's classroom management. Cognitive effort is needed, because testing the validity of the beliefs described in Figure 8.1 requires retrieving the information on which each belief is based, assessing its accuracy, and evaluating the quality of the reasoning that led to the final conclusion.

Figure 8.2 provides some questions that could help this leader to check the validity of her conclusion that the teacher has poor classroom management.

Figure 8.2 Questions for Checking the Validity of Inferences

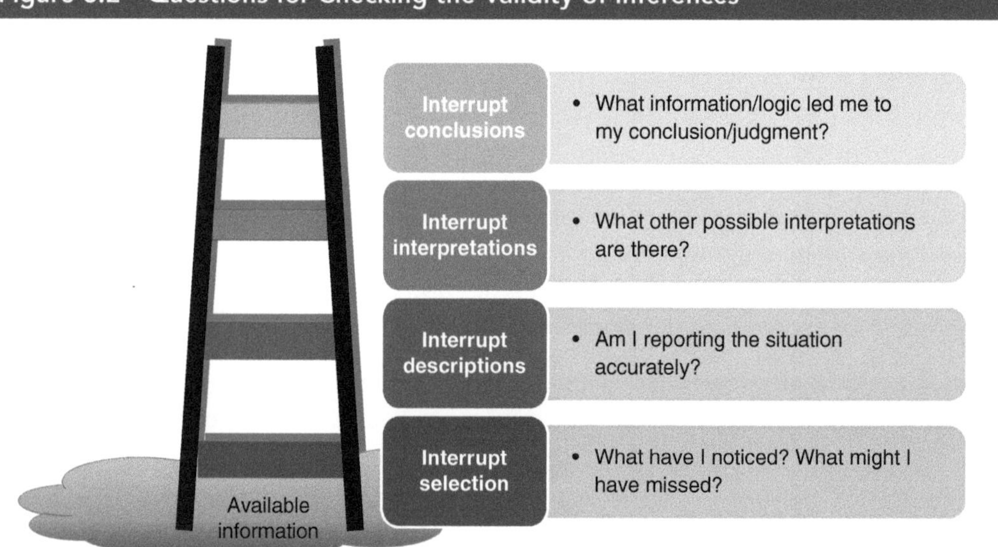

Source: Robinson, V. M. J. (2011). *Student-centered leadership*. San Francisco, CA: Jossey Bass. Adapted from Argyris and Schon (1974).

As with all virtues, there is a strong interaction between skill and motivation. The more skilled leaders are in interrupting and examining the way they move up and down the ladder, the less motivational force they will require. They will notice when they have searched for confirming rather than disconfirming examples, described what they saw in exaggerated and overgeneralised language, and failed to consider alternative interpretations. Over time, they will think more carefully and accurately and do so more routinely and automatically. As skill increases, the amount of effort needed reduces, though considerable effort may still be required to test the validity of some complex claims.

Strategic and Analytic Virtues in Action

As already explained, it is somewhat artificial to separate out the discussion of each type of virtue, because the practice of leadership requires them to be integrated in ways that are flexible and responsive to context.

In this section, I illustrate the integration of strategic and analytic virtues in the first two stages of collaboratively solving a complex problem (Table 4.1) related to student behaviour.

The context is an elementary school in which student behaviour incidents are managed by a restorative justice policy (Razer & Friedman, 2017). Under this policy, rather than excluding or punishing students, informal or more formal meetings are called at which all who are involved in or impacted by the behaviour are able to discuss what harm was caused, why the behaviour occurred, the wider emotional context, what is needed to put things right, and how such situations can be avoided in the future.

Despite the operation of a restorative justice policy in the school, the principal, Kane, notices that nearly every day, there is a line of students who have been sent out of class and are waiting for Jacqui, the deputy principal, to talk to them. Kane's purpose in having a conversation with Jacqui is to check whether there is agreement that the lineup constitutes a problem, and if so, to understand its causes, starting with the theory of action that Jacqui employs to deal with the students (Table 4.1, Stages 1 and 2). The purpose of the conversation is not to critique Jacqui's theory of action but to deeply understand some of the factors, from her point of view, that need to be taken into account in solving the problem.

In the following excerpts (Tables 8.1 and 8.2), the conversation between Kane and Jacqui is presented in the right-hand column and the thoughts that Kane had as the conversation unfolded are shown in the left-hand column. Evidence for Kane's analytic and strategic virtues is found in his thoughts and his actual speech. The thoughts are

Table 8.1 Strategic and Analytic Virtues in a Problem-Solving Conversation—Stage 1

KANE'S THOUGHTS	CONVERSATION
Collaborative Complex Problem-Solving (CCPS), Stage 1: Agree on the Problem to Be Solved	
I need to describe to Jacqui exactly what I have seen	Kane: Hi, Jacqui. I've noticed that there's another long line of students outside your office again.
Yes, Jacqui's right, and I accept some responsibility	Jacqui: Yeah, and quite frankly, it's just getting so tiresome. The behaviour of these kids is just unacceptable. Actually, I think it's probably time you stepped in.
I want a collaborative problem-solving effort	Kane: Well, thanks for being so frank about it, and yes, I am stepping in and this conversation is the start of it, and I would like to work with you on changing that. Jacqui: Great.

particularly important, because it is the combination of thoughts, feelings, and behaviour from which virtues are discernible.

In Stage 1 of CCPS, Kane's strategic virtues are apparent in the way he establishes and maintains a clear focus for the conversation. He begins by disclosing, without any judgmental overtones, that he has once again observed the line of students who have been sent out of class. His clear disclosure enables Jacqui to not only express her own concern about the student behaviour but to challenge her boss to do something about it ("It's time you stepped in"). With his nondefensive acceptance of the challenge, Jacqui and Kane conclude the first stage of collaborative problem-solving—they agree on the problem to be solved.

Table 8.2 Strategic and Analytic Virtues in a Problem-Solving Conversation—Stage 2

KANE'S THOUGHTS	CONVERSATION
Collaborative Complex Problem-Solving (CCPS), Stage 2: Inquire Into Causes	
I want to understand Jacqui's theory of action for managing behaviour. I need to start with her actions.	Kane: Okay. What I want to do first, though, is understand how you're currently handling these kids and what is producing your frustration and what you're doing with those kids and/or the teachers. So can you tell me about that? What are you doing around these kids that are lined up? Because I know it's part of your job description, the pastoral care, isn't it? Jacqui: It is, it's a huge part of my job description. Kane: Yes. Jacqui: So the teachers are sending them to me. We have a restorative philosophy through the school, as you well know, and that's hugely time-consuming as well . . . Kane: Yes. Jacqui: So a lot of the time is spent gaining some initial information from them. Sometimes the teachers don't want them back in class, and quite frankly, you know, the disruption of some of these students on the other students in the classroom is just unfair, and it's extra pressure on teachers when teachers are already pressured. So there are some times where I keep them and I set them tasks, and then when I feel that they're more settled, I integrate them back into the classroom. Kane: Right. Jacqui: I'm also running around setting up restorative meetings. I hold those meetings for the more severe cases, so it's quite a lot of work.

Gee! There is a lot here. I need to really focus . . .	Kane: I'm just going to take some notes, Jacqui, because I want to make sure that I'm really hearing you fully. Jacqui: Okay, that's fine.
I need to see if I can remember this, so summarising will help.	Kane: So, in terms of what you're currently doing, first of all, well, what teachers are doing is that they're sending you the children, the misbehaving ones. Except from . . . Jacqui: They're usually repeat offenders.
Is the problem confined to particular teachers?	Kane: Repeat offenders, right. Are these repeat offenders coming from particular classes and teachers, on the whole, or are we talking about them being widespread across the school? Jacqui: I don't know if I've actually reflected on that. Kane: Right. Jacqui: My gut feeling would be that there probably are two or three teachers . . . Kane: Right. Jacqui: . . . that those students are coming from more regularly, but, I mean, most teachers send me students to see at some time.
I didn't finish the summary.	Kane: Okay, so most teachers but possibly two or three teachers are doing those referrals to you more often. When the students are there, some of them you are setting tasks for, you are looking after [them] yourself until they settle down? Jacqui: Correct.
I have a hunch she is not working with the teachers, and I need to invite her to confirm or disconfirm.	Kane: Okay. What—and the answer to this may be "I'm not doing this," I'm genuinely enquiring, Jacqui—what are you doing with the teachers who are sending the students? Jacqui: Well, I usually just report back to them about what I've done and then, as I said, often, as a consequence of them ending up with me, a restorative chat is planned, and teachers are involved in that . . . Kane: Right.
My goodness, I need to take notice of this.	Jacqui: . . . chat. But the kids, I don't know that the restorative chats are working. I don't know they're encouraging our students to take sufficient responsibility. Kane: Okay. So you've got questions about how effective our restorative justice policy and procedures are?
I accept the challenge and now need to inquire further into Jacqui's beliefs. What is preventing her from	Jacqui: Yes, well, it certainly doesn't seem to be reducing behaviour, so I'm questioning its impact at the moment. Kane: Okay. So what's leading you to accept these students and to do what you're doing with them? And I'm asking you that,

(*Continued*)

Table 8.2 (Continued)

KANE'S THOUGHTS	CONVERSATION
working more with the teachers?	Jacqui, because you could say, "Well, I'm spending most of my time talking with the teachers and helping them and helping them understand the experiences of these students and how to manage them in their classrooms," but that's not what you're doing, so I want to understand why, why you're dealing with them so much. Jacqui: I think that once these kids come to me, I see teachers as being just overwhelmed, stressed, not knowing what else they can do. I mean, I don't think they choose to send them to me lightly. Well, I hope they wouldn't. So it's kind of they're at their wit's end, and I feel I have a responsibility as, you know, assistant principal in charge of behaviour, to allow the other students in this school to learn effectively.
Have I listened carefully enough to understand why Jacqui does it this way?	Kane: So, at the moment, you're saying that you're dealing with this in a way that's looking after stressed teachers, that the teachers are at their wit's end, and you feel a responsibility also to the other students in the class to, in fact, remove children who are really, really disruptive. Have I understood that? Jacqui: Yes, that's exactly how I'm feeling.

Kane maintains the focus throughout the excerpt by asking direct questions that serve the causal inquiry purpose of Stage 2 of CCPS. These questions are motivated by a genuine desire to learn, in very specific terms, what Jacqui is doing with the students and their teachers and why. He is systematic in his questioning by first probing for information about her actions and then for the beliefs that drive those actions.

Kane's analytic virtues are particularly evident in the way he pursues his causal inquiry. His desire to listen carefully and check the accuracy of his understanding of Jacqui's theory of action is perhaps the most obvious manifestation of his analytic virtues. But his analytic virtues are also evident in his openness to causal drivers that go well beyond Jacqui's individual theory-in-use. In a second challenge from Jacqui, he learns that the restorative policy itself, or at least the way it is being implemented in the school, might be ineffective. Once again, he reacts nondefensively and recognises that there may be more to resolving this problem than he first thought!

SUMMARY

Analytic virtues are apparent in leaders who are motivated to test rather than assume the validity of their own and others' key beliefs, who are skilled in doing so, and who can explain why such testing is important to them. Virtuous leaders are very aware of the ethical dimensions of their decision-making—that mistaken assumptions and taken-for-granted beliefs can produce poor-quality decisions that waste resources, do not solve the problem, and may have negative impacts on students.

Leaders with strong analytic virtues monitor and regulate their own behaviour so that they can gain more accurate and complete knowledge about the causes of and solutions to the problems that prevent them from achieving the educational purposes of their leadership roles. They know the difference between knowledge and beliefs and are committed to testing rather than assuming the validity of what they would otherwise accept as true. They are skilled in using the ladder of inference to test the validity of the conclusions that they or colleagues have reached about what is happening, why it is happening, and what to do about it.

Learning and exercising analytic virtues is challenging, not only because of the fast pace and complexity of leaders' work but also because the limitations of human memory and information processing mean we are all hardwired to take cognitive shortcuts, largely by imposing our preconceptions on the world. These shortcuts increase the possibility of erroneous reasoning, closed-mindedness, and various forms of confirmation bias.

Despite inevitably limited cognitive capacity, leaders have the choice of interrupting their fast and intuitive reasoning processes and being more deliberate and thoughtful about the accuracy and adequacy of their beliefs and theories of action. Leaders with strong analytic virtues are more likely than those with weaker virtues to recognise when more cognitive effort is required, to be skilled in rigorous testing and correction of inadequate assumptions and beliefs, and to be less defensive about their revision.

The effort required to reason in a more deliberate manner is motivated by enjoyment of thinking (need for cognition), high accuracy motivation, and low need for cognitive closure. The stance of leaders with strong analytic virtues is that of truth-seeking rather than truth-claiming.

REFLECTION AND ACTION

1. Analytic virtues include being open-minded, especially in the face of difference and disagreement. With a colleague, think of leaders you have known who have the virtue of open-mindedness. What do they do that leads you to call them open-minded?
2. Three psychological needs—the need for cognition, accuracy, and closure—shape a leader's analytic virtues. How strong are those needs in you? How do they shape the way you lead?
3. Apply your knowledge of strategic and analytic virtues to Tables 8.1 and 8.2 by identifying specific behaviours that you believe are indicators of Kane's strategic and analytic virtues. Discuss your views with colleagues in a team meeting or study group.

Problem-Solving Virtues 9

Imaginative

While analytic virtues are required to discern the elements of a complex problem and their interrelationships, imaginative virtues are required to reconfigure and integrate those elements in ways that suggest how the problem could be solved. In deciding what to call this category of virtues, I considered calling them synthetic virtues to emphasise the contrast with analytic ones. I also considered calling them integrative virtues, as that name conveys what I consider to be a hallmark of excellent leadership—the ability to forge principled integrations of diverse requirements. In the end, I settled on imaginative virtues because that name links the category to the virtue of creativity and to the ability to transcend conventional thinking about a situation to envisage how competing tendencies can be reconciled in ways that create a more satisfactory solution.

In his book *The Opposable Mind*, Roger Martin defines what I call imaginative virtues as "the ability to face constructively the tension of opposing ideas and, instead of choosing one at the expense of the other, generate a creative resolution of the tension in the form of a new idea that contains elements of the opposing ideas but is superior to each" (Martin, 2009, p. 15). The new idea is the creative solution that integrates apparently disparate elements by transforming them in ways that reduce the tensions between them.

Martin characterises the personal stance of integrative thinkers as

1. understanding the difference between reality and the mental models through which that reality is understood. This understanding enables them to question taken-for-granted assumptions and examine the implications of different mental models.

2. embracing differing mental models for the insights they provide into various elements of the problem, including possible solution requirements.
3. feeling comfortable with complexity and tolerant of multiple interpretations because they see them as providing opportunities to learn and test the validity of various interpretations of the problem.
4. having a strong sense of efficacy and confidence in their ability to solve, or learn how to solve, a complex problem by formulating a solution that sufficiently satisfies all the solution requirements.

The need for educational leaders to have strong imaginative virtues stems from the multiple purposes of educational institutions and the complexity of much of the work. Too often that complexity is overlooked because leaders are unwilling or unable to make the cognitive effort required to reconcile competing requirements or because they privilege one purpose over the others.

During the COVID-19 school closures, leaders and teachers in many jurisdictions were urged to prioritise their own and their students' well-being and not to stress themselves and their students about keeping up with lessons. While the intention behind such advice was laudable, it reinforced the unfortunate opposition in education between well-being and academic goals and significantly eroded the opportunities to learn for those students who needed them most. In my view, the challenge during COVID was not to look after students' mental health nor to stick rigidly to the academic schedule, but to imagine how these two requirements, plus a third requirement for equity of provision, could be satisfactorily integrated.

Leaders with imaginative virtues might have experimented, for example, with making high-quality lesson resources available to all their students and then scheduling teaching time so that those students who were stressed by repeated failure to understand and complete their lessons before the pandemic could receive high-quality specialist tutoring that enabled them to succeed, gain confidence, and finally enjoy their remote and in-school lessons. Students who were able to succeed at their largely self-managed lessons would receive fewer check-ins with their teachers unless they or their teachers believed them to be required.

Such experiments explicitly address the need to find innovative solutions that sufficiently satisfy the requirements to provide all students with opportunities to learn, to meet equity goals by tailoring those opportunities to diverse learning needs, and to address school-based causes of stress and disengagement.

No doubt there is a great deal more complexity to this example than I have covered here, but my point is that leaders with imaginative virtues will question the opposition that is set up between psychological well-being and academic goals and the thinking that encourages prioritizing one over the other (Clarke, 2020).

This example also provides a telling reminder of the role of knowledge in virtues. Leaders who are knowledgeable about the close connection between students' psychological well-being and academic success are more likely to be critical of policies and directives that set up oppositions between them (Clarke, 2020; Kaya & Erdem, 2021). They know that the cause of student unhappiness and disengagement at school is often their repeated failure to succeed in their lessons. They know that intensive high-quality tutoring will improve the achievement and the psychological well-being of such students.

Imaginative Virtues and the Integration of Solution Requirements

In Chapter 4, I quoted John Dewey's (1922) description of the deliberation required to transform competing requirements in ways that open up more possibilities for their integration. Such deliberation requires the exercise of imaginative virtues, and such virtues are particularly important in the third stage of complex problem-solving, which involves formulating and integrating solution requirements.

To make this more concrete, let's look at an illustration. Simon, a school leader with strong imaginative virtues, is leading a staff discussion of how to address the poor math achievement of many Years 3–7 students in his school. The results indicate that the students are well behind age-related benchmarks and particularly weak in math problem-solving.

Simon's recently completed graduate study in education has made him aware that the ability grouping that is used in nearly all math lessons in his school is a likely contributor to the inequitable results (Schmidt et al., 2015). The school's indigenous and minority students are nearly always placed in the lower-achieving groups and seldom move into the more advanced groups, where they would have greater opportunity to learn the forms of mathematical reasoning required to solve word problems.

At a series of staff meetings, Simon learns that teachers hold strong and opposing views about the merits of ability and mixed-ability grouping. While one or two teachers are already experimenting with mixed-ability groups in which students of different abilities collaborate on rich tasks by tackling different elements of the task and articulating how they draw their conclusions, the majority of teachers see the range of abilities in their classes as far too great to make mixed-ability grouping workable.

Furthermore, these teachers argue that if they were to shift to mixed-ability grouping, lesson planning and behaviour management would be far more challenging than it is at present. They are not sure how to plan a series of rich tasks or how to formatively assess students' strategies for tackling such tasks, nor are they confident of the ability of many of their students to cooperate with each other in productive ways. Why would the higher-ability children be patient with and listen to those who are struggling?

Simon listens carefully and realises that the debate could quickly become an unproductive battle over whether or not to introduce mixed-ability grouping. Furthermore, if schoolwide mixed-ability grouping was to be introduced right now, he argues, it would be bound to fail, because many teachers have had little opportunity to learn the types of lesson planning, teaching, and assessment practices that are required to make it work. He knows from his graduate study that successful mixed-ability grouping requires adequate teacher capabilities in the design and assessment of rich math tasks, in the mathematical understandings and misunderstanding that are likely to be evoked by the tasks, and in teaching the dispositions and skills required for productive group work.

Simon knows that without such capabilities, the strategic priority of improved mathematical reasoning and problem-solving will not be met. To achieve the performance goal of improved math, he needs to gain agreement on prior teacher learning goals (Chapter 3, Dimension 1), so that all teachers will be in a position to experiment with high-quality mixed-ability math teaching, and to then make an informed evaluation of the relative effectiveness of ability and mixed-ability grouping.

Simon's imaginative virtues are evident in his knowledge of the conditions required for effective teaching of mixed-ability math groups and in his ability to use that knowledge to transform the problem so that there is a deeper appreciation of the set of solution requirements that need to be satisfied if the goal of improved math teaching is to be met.

One of those additional requirements is to manage the disruptive behaviour of students so that their group work is productive. While some teachers see considerable tension between these two requirements and reject mixed-ability grouping on that basis, Simon can imagine ways to minimise the tension through explicit teaching of protocols for group behaviour during mathematical discussions. Similarly, he can see ways to resolve the tension some teachers see between learning number facts and focusing on mathematical reasoning.

The imaginative virtues that Simon brings to these discussions are based in knowledge and experience gained in his graduate study and in his growing willingness to embrace and work with complexity. He has learned to listen to his teachers, for their concerns suggest the solution requirements that are important to them, and the sooner they are on the table, the sooner everyone understands the complexity of the problem. Simon is not afraid of the complexity of multiple solution requirements, because his past experience of resolving such tensions gives him confidence that it can be done again.

Imaginative Virtues, Creativity, and Problem-Solving

The process of formulating and integrating constraints is a highly creative process. In the context of leadership work, creativity refers to "the production of viable or workable, new, or original solutions to complex, novel, ill-defined problems" (Mumford et al., 2014, p. 758). This definition incorporates the two defining features of creativity—it produces original or novel solutions and is adaptive in the sense that those solutions are workable.

Creativity applied to educational leadership, therefore, is not an undisciplined process of inventing or embracing the unusual, the risky, or the fanciful. It is, rather, the application of an imaginative disposition to the resolution of complex previously intractable problems through reimagining how the various solution requirements can be formulated in ways that enable their principled integration.

Absolutist thinking is the enemy of creativity in complex problem-solving.

Absolutist thinking is the enemy of creativity in complex problem-solving. Such thinking produces opposition and conflict and stymies the creativity involved in specifying constraints in ways that reveal rather than foreclose possibilities for their integration (Richardson, 1990).

Unfortunately, educational discourse is replete with unproductive oppositions and polarities, such as autonomy versus accountability, formative versus summative, and leadership versus management. Such binary thinking is of little use to educational leaders, for their practical and policy world requires grappling with the details of concrete problems, many of which require the integration of one or more of these so-called oppositions.

Leaders with strong imaginative virtues resist oppositions and trade-offs because they understand the principles that are at stake in each of the opposing forces and can imagine how the relevant and worthy aspects of each might be reconciled. The deeper their knowledge of the science of learning and teaching and of other relevant theories, the more likely they are to achieve such integration.

For example, they will be critical of oppositions between formative and summative assessment if they are familiar with the argument that formative assessment can be viewed as rehearsal summative (Scriven, 1991). Similarly, if they have experience with reading programmes that integrate whole language and phonics approaches, they will resist being forced to choose between the two.

Conventional trade-off thinking erodes aspiration and imagination, for it accepts oppositions as inevitable rather than as a likely consequence of the abstract and decontextualised manner in which the so-called oppositions are debated. If oppositions are accepted, then leaders give up on integration and pursue compromise and trade-offs instead.

Doubtless there are complex problems for which tensions between solution requirements are so strong that a compromise or trade-off between them is the only practical option. But there is considerable evidence from research on conflict resolution and problem-solving that strategies that attempt to integrate the legitimate requirements of all parties produce more effective relational and task outcomes than strategies such as forcing or compromising (De Dreu, 2010; Euwema et al., 2003).

Leaders with strong imaginative virtues are likely to be innovative, not because they are attracted to innovation per se or are caught up in the fads and fashions that bedevil education, but because their skills in the specification and integration of competing requirements produce innovative solutions. Education does not need innovations in the sense that manufacturing and technology companies need to tempt consumers with new products. It needs innovative solutions to long-standing and emerging problems, most of which will require new combinations of what is already known, but implemented with more dedication, resources, and focused attention than is typically the case.

As for other forms of creativity, leaders' knowledge is intimately connected to their imaginative deliberations (Mumford et al., 2014). For example, the leader with little knowledge of the relationship between academic success and student well-being is less likely than one with more such knowledge to recognise the relationship between the two and therefore the possibilities for their integration.

Similarly, the leader who is familiar with the debates about the validity of the distinction between leadership and management is in a far better position to confront those who insist on its separation than those who are unaware of the debate and take the validity of the distinction for granted (Mintzberg, 2009). Creativity in any field, including educational leadership, requires mastery of the relevant domain-specific knowledge and skills (Peterson & Seligman, 2004).

Strategic, Analytic, and Imaginative Virtues in Action

I now return to the story of Kane and Jacqui, whom we met in Chapter 8 as they started to tackle the problem of the long line of students who had been sent out of class by their teachers. Kane's strategic and analytic virtues had enabled him to gain agreement with Jacqui that the lineup was a problem worth tackling (Stage 1, Table 4.1) and to discover, through systematic inquiry into her theory of action, some of the causes of the problem (Stage 2, Table 4.1).

In their subsequent meeting, Jacqui and Kane formulate the requirements for a more satisfactory solution to the problem (Stage 3, Table 4.1). It is at this stage that we see Kane's imaginative virtues at play as he seeks to reduce the tension between the various solution requirements by finding a principled way of integrating them.

In the following excerpt (Table 9.1), the conversation between Kane and Jacqui is presented in the middle column, the thoughts that Kane had as the conversation unfolded are shown in the left-hand column, and a commentary on the various virtues at play, excluding interpersonal virtues, is presented in the right-hand column.

In Kane's prior discussion with Jacqui (Chapter 8), he learned that the first four solution requirements in Table 9.2 were important to Jacqui. At their second meeting, Kane was clear that he wanted teachers to manage most student behaviour in their lesson without recourse to exclusion, and Jacqui added that she wanted more joy in her job—joy that would come with spending less time on managing disruptive students.

Table 9.1 Strategic, Analytic, and Imaginative Virtues in a Problem-Solving Conversation—Stage 3

KANE'S THOUGHTS	CONVERSATION	VIRTUES DEMONSTRATED
Collaborative Complex Problem-Solving, Stage 3: Formulate Solution Requirements		
This was hard to accept, but Jacqui is right about the restorative justice. I need to also tell Jacqui what is important to me.	Kane: I'm really pleased we've started talking about, you know, the long line of students, and I think I probably share your view that the restorative justice isn't working as well as it should be in the school. I just wanted to summarise quickly what I think I've learnt about what's important to you, and then I want to add some things to it and see whether you agree with what's important to me, by giving you my view on what's happening. Jacqui: Okay.	Imaginative: Kane embraces complexity by signalling that there may be multiple solution requirements.
I need to summarise my understanding of Jacqui's theory of action. *Don't beat about the bush. Tell her what my critique is.*	Kane: Because I think I need to be up front with you about that as well. I understand that you've been really caring for the teachers and the students by taking these disruptive students, looking after them and then reintegrating them back into the classroom when they're ready, and I think that that's an important part of your pastoral role. I thought about it and thought, well, one of the unintended downsides, possibly, of that is that the teachers are not learning how to manage the students in their own classes better. And these patterns of behaviour with the students—I think you used the words they're "repeated patterns of behaviour," which suggests to me that we're not progressing with those students. Is that a fair summary of what you were telling me?	Analytic: Kane offers a critique of the strategy Jacqui is currently using and provides grounds for the critique. Imaginative: Kane suggests an additional solution requirement—teachers learn to manage students better.
Oh. Another challenge!	Jacqui: Yep, it is a fair summary. And I do understand where you're coming from when you say that we are possibly not building teacher capability, but, look, if I'm honest with you, we're building teacher capability in so many areas at the moment, there's huge emphasis in the school on the numeracy strategy and the literacy strategy, and I just feel like they're overwhelmed and overloaded, and I'm really trying to protect them from that.	

Don't get defensive. There is a lot going on.	Kane: Right, thanks for that. And I think you've raised another issue, which is "Do we have too much going on in terms of initiatives and professional development in the school at the moment?" And I'm open to the fact that the answer to that might be yes. Jacqui: I think that's a really good reflection. I think it's something we do need to think more about.	Imaginative: Kane modifies his understanding of the "reduce stress" requirement by accepting it applies to more than stress caused by disruptive students. Analytic: Kane stays open-minded in his acceptance of the critique.
I need to be clear about how I see the priorities.	Kane: So, then that comes to priorities. Which of these things do we need to be working on first? And for me, if the students aren't in the class, if the classroom routines aren't really focused on academic learning time, then numeracy initiatives, literacy initiatives, and all the rest of it, you know, we're going to have too many kids missing out on that because the fundamentals of having learning routines and a learning culture in the classroom is not in place. So that's why I'm thinking maybe we just need to shift our priorities a wee bit.	Imaginative: Kane clearly states how he sees the interrelationships between aspects of the problem. Strategic: Kane links those interrelationships to his argument for which aspect should be given first priority.
She is trying to keep learning going.	Jacqui: I can see that, and I want to reassure you that when they are with me, as I said to you, I'm often retaining them, settling them, and I do try to provide tasks that are very close to what I would expect them to be doing when they're with their teachers. Kane: Yes.	
Good! She shares my priorities.	Jacqui: But obviously it's not the same stuff. So I think that's a really fair point is that this does need to be a bigger priority than it currently is in our school.	
I need to directly check again.	Kane: Right. In my view, every teacher in the school should be able to manage classroom behaviour, set norms that support learning most of the time for most students. Of course, there are the exceptions where we need other strategies like restorative justice conferences.	Strategic: Kane articulates the gap he sees between the current and desired situation.

(*Continued*)

Table 9.1 (Continued)

KANE'S THOUGHTS	CONVERSATION	VIRTUES DEMONSTRATED
	But do you share my view that we may have to inquire into and discuss that expectation with the staff?	
As usual, this is much more complex than just dealing with the immediate issue!	Jacqui: Yeah, I think that's fair, and I think maybe a wider review of the place of restorative justice in our school, both how does it work at the classroom level, what are the expectations on teachers in terms of the restorative philosophy in their classrooms, and then how does that then look schoolwide and for the more severe behaviour incidents or those that are the "repeat offenders," for lack of a better word.	
I'm hoping we can support each other in doing this.	Kane: So there's two things I would like you and I to take to the senior leadership team when we're ready, and one is our view that we need to focus more on building the expectation and the capabilities of all our teachers so they can establish and maintain a climate for academic learning in their classrooms. And the second thing I'd like us to take is the restorative justice programme that we've got going and whether that's being effectively implemented, what its place is. I mean, in my view, conferences are not for everybody. They are for the extremes which can't be managed in classes, etc. So that's my sense of what our next steps are. Jacqui: That sounds fantastic. Kane: Okay.	Imaginative: Kane suggests a consultative process for integrating the need for fewer exclusions from class with the need for a priority focus on building teacher capability in classroom management.
Oh goodness! I'd hate to lose Jacqui! I'm glad she has been frank about her feelings.	Jacqui: Pastoral care is just supposed to be one part of what I do. If you can shift some of the pressure in that, that's going to allow me to do some of the things that I'm more passionate about, and it will bring joy back to my job.	
We have a next step.	Kane: Well, that's another fantastic benefit, Jacqui. Okay, we'll make a time to get organised so we can lead this discussion at the next senior leadership meeting. Jacqui: Sounds great.	Imaginative: Kane accepts an additional solution requirement—Jacqui finds more joy in her job.

Table 9.2 Six Solution Requirements for Solving the Problem of Student Exclusion From Class

	INITIAL SOLUTION REQUIREMENTS	COMMENTS
1.	Reduce repeated class exclusions	Jacqui and Kane agree on this goal and agree that little progress has been made in meeting it.
2.	Reduce teacher stress	Jacqui currently gives this solution requirement considerable weight.
3.	Be fair to well-behaved students by preventing disruption to lessons	This requirement is also very important to Jacqui.
4.	Maintain learning for excluded students	Jacqui has attempted to fulfil this requirement but gives it less weight than #2 and #3.
	ADDITIONAL REQUIREMENTS	
5.	Increase teacher capability in classroom management	This requirement is not currently important to Jacqui, who sees it as incompatible with reducing teacher stress.
6.	Increase job satisfaction for Jacqui	This requirement is in considerable tension with #2.

By listing all six solution requirements, we can see the complexity of the problem and why simplistic solutions such as declaring that teachers must limit their exclusions would not work. Teacher compliance with such instructions would be unlikely because a limit in exclusions does not meet their wish for reduced stress nor their desire to be fair to other students. A satisfactory solution requires imagining ways of meeting all six requirements, either as currently stated or in a modified form.

There is considerable tension between some of the listed requirements. When Kane suggests that teachers learn more effective classroom management skills, Jacqui objects that this will add further stress. Rather than set up an opposition between stress reduction and building capability, Kane imagines how both could be achieved by reprioritising and reducing the professional learning load for teachers, a strategy that will be debated further at the next meeting of the senior leadership team.

Kane recognised and reduced the tensions between the various requirements through a combination of strategic, analytic, and imaginative virtues. The latter virtues enabled him to recognise that the lineup was not inevitable but a consequence of a widely shared set of assumptions about how to deal with disruptive students. He embraced rather than resisted the growing complexity of the problem, because he knew the current routines were not working and he had the knowledge and confidence to imagine how a collaborative process of debate and learning could produce solution strategies that sufficiently satisfied all six requirements.

Analytic and strategic virtues were evident in Kane's ability to argue that improved classroom management should be a professional learning priority because it was a necessary foundation for implementation of the literacy and numeracy initiatives. Kane and Jacqui agreed that their next steps would be to take the problem, their solution requirements, and their initial suggestions for how to satisfy them to the next meeting of the whole senior leadership team.

Although Table 9.1 shows the three categories of problem-solving virtues at play (strategic, analytic, and imaginative), complex problem-solving is a collaborative endeavour, with progress being just as dependent on interpersonal virtues as on problem-solving virtues. It was Kane's nondefensive response to Jacqui's challenges, his careful listening, and his respectful critique of Jacqui's theory of action that enabled him to learn that there was much more to the problem than he had initially recognised. The critically important cluster of interpersonal virtues that make productive collaboration possible is discussed in Chapters 10–12.

Complex problem-solving is a collaborative endeavour, with progress being just as dependent on interpersonal virtues as on problem-solving virtues.

SUMMARY

While analytic virtues are required to gain an accurate understanding of the elements of a problem and their interrelationships, imaginative virtues are required to reconfigure and integrate those elements in ways that suggest how the problem could be solved. Imaginative virtues are seen in the creativity with which some educational leaders are able to reimagine apparently conflicting solution requirements so that they can be integrated in ways that advance multiple educational purposes. Such creativity rests on a foundation of deep knowledge of the relevant concepts because such knowledge enables flexible yet principled interpretations of solution requirements.

Imaginative virtues are critical to the third stage of complex collaborative problem-solving (CCPS)—the stage in which solution requirements are modified in ways that increase the possibilities for their integration. Leaders with strong imaginative virtues accept the initial uncertainty and complexity of multiple solution requirements because their past experience, their deep domain-specific knowledge, and their ability to learn give them confidence that they can craft a satisfactorily integrative solution.

Absolutist thinking is the enemy of creativity in CCPS because it produces opposition and conflict and stymies the creativity involved in specifying requirements in ways that reveal rather than foreclose possibilities for their integration. When imaginative virtues are weak, leaders accept oppositions as inevitable and turn to trade-offs and compromises. Research on negotiation and conflict resolution suggests that such solution strategies produce less effective relational and task outcomes than integrative strategies.

REFLECTION AND ACTION

1. Is staff discussion in your context hampered by opposition between educational ideas and preferences? What are the ideas that are most commonly treated as oppositions?
2. How could you use imaginative virtues to foster integration rather than opposition between those ideas and preferences?
3. Discuss the argument that leaders with strong imaginative virtues resist oppositions and trade-offs. Why might this be the case? Do you agree?

10 Interpersonal Virtues

There is no dispute about the critical importance of relationships to the effectiveness of educational leaders. After all, leadership, in contrast to force or coercion, requires the voluntary acceptance of the leader's influence, and a major determinant of such voluntary acceptance is the leader's relationships (Fay, 1987). But what sorts of relationships should educational leaders cultivate? What may be considered a good-quality relationship between friends, between doctors and their patients, between lawyers and their clients, and between business associates may not be applicable to the relationship between educational leaders and teachers.

The challenge for educational leaders is to develop the types of relationships that are required to collaboratively pursue the educational purposes and resolve the complex problems that stand in the way of achieving them. What must be avoided are good relationships with teachers that do not serve students well because the adult relationships are not sufficiently focused on achieving those purposes.

In this chapter, I argue that it is relational trust that enables leaders and teachers to collaborate and succeed in resolving problems. Using research on relational trust and its consequences, I argue that leaders need to cultivate certain interpersonal virtues in order to build the trust required for CCPS. I supplement the argument with additional material drawn from my own research programme on leaders' capability in building trust.

In Chapter 11, I turn to the central challenge of integrating problem-solving and interpersonal virtues, for it is this integration that is at the heart of doing the right work the right way. I give considerable attention in that chapter to how ubiquitous interpersonal vices prevent the desired integration and how they can be overcome.

Relational Trust: A Guide for Deriving Interpersonal Virtues

Trust is critical in contexts where the success of one person's efforts is dependent on the contribution of others. In the context of schooling, making significant shifts in student achievement and well-being requires the collective effort of many teachers, and each one's success will be partly dependent on the effort and skill of others. This interdependence creates risk and vulnerability. Teachers ask themselves, "If I go the extra mile, will others do the same?" Relational trust involves a willingness to be vulnerable because one has confidence that others will be respectful and play their part. It should not be mistaken for feelings of warmth or affection.

Research on trust in schools provides good guidance on the interpersonal virtues required to build trust. The seminal study was conducted in four hundred Chicago public schools involved in a major school reform process (Bryk & Schneider, 2002). In a four-year follow-up, researchers found a strong relationship between annual gains in student reading and math and growth in levels of trust between teachers and their leaders.

The Chicago study found that teachers' trust of their leaders was based on four factors: **integrity** (e.g., saying what one means, doing what one says, giving frank feedback); **interpersonal respect** (e.g., listening carefully to disagreements, treating others fairly, taking others' legitimate interests into account); **personal regard** (e.g., caring for others as people, not just as role incumbents) and **role competence** (e.g., ability to do one's job to a high standard, thus enabling others to do their jobs without unnecessary risk, and dealing competently with incompetence).

Since the Chicago study, other researchers, using different teacher surveys, have identified similar determinants of teachers' trust of their leaders and also confirmed its consequences for students (Goddard et al., 2009; Tschannen-Moran & Gareis, 2015). In schools where trust levels are higher, teachers take more risks, such as disclosing what they need help with, and experience a stronger sense of professional community and collective efficacy. It is that type of school culture that enables collaborative problem-solving and improved social and academic outcomes for students.

Four Interpersonal Virtues

Based on the research on relational trust and on my own research programme on leaders' interpersonal capabilities, I suggest that four interpersonal virtues are required to build the type of trust that is needed to collaboratively resolve complex improvement problems. They are

1. Integrity
2. Interpersonal respect
3. Courage
4. Empathy

As mentioned in Chapter 5, my purpose here is not to provide an exhaustive taxonomy of all relevant interpersonal virtues but to argue for a few that are critical to building the trust required to succeed in CCPS. Additionally, some key concepts from the research do not apply here because they relate not to virtues but to other aspects of relational trust. For instance, while role competence is one of four key determinants of trust (Bryk & Schneider, 2002), I have not included it in the interpersonal cluster because role competence is an outcome of many virtues, not a virtue in itself. Throughout, I tailor my discussion of the four virtues to the role of educational leaders and to their pursuit of educational purposes.

Integrity

According to the *Character Strengths and Virtues* handbook (Peterson and Seligman, 2004), we attribute the virtue of integrity to leaders who can be relied on to report honestly and tell the truth, not only about external situations but also about their own thoughts and feelings. The accuracy of their self-representations means we understand their thinking and can get to know them for who they truly are.

Leaders with integrity can be taken at their word. They follow up on public commitments, justify their actions with reference to clear principles, and eschew ad hoc and arbitrary decisions (Favero et al., 2016).

This generic account of integrity needs some refinement, however, so that it better fits the role of educational leader. While "being true to self," "practising what one preaches," and "keeping one's word" are necessary conditions for integrity, they are not sufficient, for the word of the educational leader must also be in accord with the obligations and purposes of the role.

For educational leaders, integrity requires not only congruence between words and actions but also that the words and actions be educationally worthy. In other words, they serve the interests of students. Bryk and Schneider (2002) remind us of the centrality of educational purposes when they write that "integrity demands resolutions that reaffirm the primary principles of the institution. In the context of schooling when all is said and done actions must be understood as advancing the best interests of children" (p. 26). Leaders who make unprincipled exceptions, take the easy way out of difficult situations, and most of all, put the interests of the adults above what is best for students lack integrity on those occasions.

For educational leaders, integrity requires not only congruence between words and actions but also that the words and actions be educationally worthy. In other words, they serve the interests of students.

Integrity requires transparency so others can understand the reasons why the leader takes a particular position. This can be difficult for leaders who fear that disclosure of their point of view will create upset or conflict. What such leaders often do not realise is that nondisclosure also brings risks, for in the absence of clear communication, teachers will speculate about the leader's motives, and their attributions may generate mistrust. When full disclosure is not possible, integrity is demonstrated by declaring that to be the case, along with the relevant reasons for nondisclosure, such as confidentiality agreements, privacy concerns, or ongoing investigations.

Integrity includes clearly explaining and giving appropriate weight to the bottom lines and nonnegotiables that need to be taken into account when solving a specific problem.

In the context of educational leadership, integrity is of critical importance, for without it leaders are likely to give too little importance to the duties and responsibilities of their role. Integrity includes clearly explaining and giving appropriate weight to the bottom lines and nonnegotiables that need to be taken into account when solving a specific problem. It means disclosing rather than withholding one's relevant points of view, including feelings and reactions, but doing it in a way that also accords respect to others. Integrity also means leading in accordance with one's own critically examined standards for excellent leadership rather than giving in or giving up because it is easier to do so.

Integrity is closely related to the idea of self-respect. Self-respecting leaders articulate and defend the standards of leadership to which they hold themselves to account and feel disappointed when they fall short of them (Dillon, 2021).

Integrity in Action

In Table 10.1, I illustrate leadership integrity by focusing on how a Norwegian high school principal was transparent and principled in his follow-up of his teachers' progress in implementing a new national curriculum. The purpose of the new curriculum is to teach for deep learning, with students working across various disciplines to develop the knowledge, skills, and values required to live rich and productive lives in a world in which there are major societal challenges.

Table 10.1 Declaring One's Agenda

SPEAKER	MEETING EXCERPT	ANALYSIS
Principal	Welcome to our planning group meeting. Since we are halfway into the school year, we planned to talk today about the new curriculum. Our specific theme today is the interdisciplinary themes, and I believe I asked you to come prepared to talk about what is happening in your teams. Because I would like to hear from each of you how it's going with your teachers and how they are using the themes in their teaching.	***Integrity:*** *Principal provides a clear statement about his understanding of the purpose of the meeting. He recalls the expectations he communicated about the required preparation for the meeting.*
Principal	Is that your understanding?	***Open-Mindedness and Respect:*** *Principal checks rather than assumes the validity of his recollection of prior agreements.*
Team Leaders	Yeah, yeah.	
Principal	I have, as you know, seen some classes myself. I have also been speaking to the teachers, besides you in these meetings. So, I have an assumption that it's not being fully	***Integrity:*** *Principal discloses rather than withholds the information he has gathered from his classroom visits*
	implemented throughout the school, and with all the teachers in all the subjects. So that makes me concerned about how it has changed for the pupils. So I would like to hear what you think. What I'm going to do is to ask you just to give a short status report on each of your teams. And then afterwards we're going to discuss them before we go further. Do you agree this is okay? Yeah? Would you like to start, Year 8?	*and his evaluation of that information.* ***Respect:*** *Principal signals desire to hear others' point of view and checks agreement with his suggestion about how to proceed.*
Team Leaders	[Nod their agreement]	

Source: Robinson (2020).

The new curriculum requires teachers to integrate the teaching of values, skills, and subject content through three interdisciplinary themes: health and life skills, democracy and citizenship, and sustainable development. Teaching such interdisciplinary themes requires many high school teachers to switch from teaching their subjects to collaboratively planning lessons in which subject content and basic skills are learned through in-depth study of the themes.

The principal has called the meeting with the leaders of Years 8, 9, and 10 to review their progress in developing units of work that are consistent with the broadly specified national curriculum guidelines. The analysis section is annotated to show how integrity is manifested in the principal's speech. The close interaction of multiple virtues in any leadership practice means that other interpersonal virtues, such as respect, and problem-solving virtues, such as open-mindedness, are also noted.

The principal acts with integrity by being transparent about the purpose of the meeting, the evidence he has gathered, and his somewhat critical evaluation of that evidence ("I have an assumption [the curriculum] is not being fully implemented"). His critical stance is grounded in a principled concern about how the limited progress he has observed is impacting students. He is motivated not by a desire to comply with external curriculum mandates and deadlines but by his concern about the impact of the team's progress on students.

Leaders with integrity resist pressure to act contrary to their principles and articulate how those principles are guiding their decisions. As I indicated earlier, however, not just any principles will do. Integrity requires that the principles at stake serve educational purposes.

In the next example, we again see a transparent and principled approach, but this time the context for virtuous behaviour is that of declining a request rather than setting an agenda. The principal comes under pressure to approve a physical education teacher's request for $1,500 to fund his visit to an out-of-state school and university to research the possibility of setting up a sports academy. In the following excerpt, the principal gives several reasons for turning down the teacher's request.

Table 10.2 Saying No

SPEAKER	MEETING EXCERPT	ANALYSIS
Principal	Hi, Ron, thanks very much for coming and talking to me today.	
Ron	No problem.	
Principal	I was surprised when Mary came to me on Thursday with your proposal about you having two weeks in Christchurch based on your plan. From my perspective, I'm concerned about whether there is a need for the trip to investigate the sports academy concept. I'm concerned that the academy investigation doesn't appear to have any link to our focuses and planning; I don't see any evidence of it in the Physical Education (PE) plan or the review report that went to the board last month. I would really like to know what your thought process is behind it and how you see this going. *Ron explains what he is contemplating . . .*	***Integrity:*** *Principal is explicit about the principle he is using to evaluate Ron's proposal:* • *linked to relevant strategic plans* ***Strategic virtues:*** *Principal assesses the alignment of the proposal with strategic plan and priorities.*
Principal	I think you should go ahead and inquire with the Physical Education team, do a bit more research on the concepts—for us to spend $1,500 at this stage without having the PE team on board, it's pushing things a bit much at this stage. Maybe next year this is something that the PE team will put on their annual plan.	***Integrity:*** *Principal is explicit about a second principle he is using to evaluate Ron's proposal:* • *idea has been discussed with relevant colleagues*
Ron	So if I get back to the team and we get this ball rolling, can I do it next year?	
Principal	It will depend on what you've found out along your lines of enquiry. I certainly don't want to commit to it at this stage . . .	***Integrity:*** *Principal is explicit about a third principle he is using to evaluate Ron's proposal:* • *do not preempt the results of an inquiry process*
Ron	Yeah.	
Principal	We need to be sure we really want to do this—that it fits with our aims.	

The analysis in Table 10.2 is inevitably partial, because virtues are character traits that cannot be judged on the basis of a few leadership behaviours. The behaviour of the principal was, on his own admission, somewhat novel, for he described himself as "the caring, sharing guy who likes everyone being happy!" Nevertheless, if virtues are to be more than philosophical or psychological abstractions, we need to be able to point to specific examples of virtuous behaviour, even though we cannot make generalisations from a few examples to the virtuousness of this leader's character.

Interpersonal Respect

The virtue of interpersonal respect is manifest in leaders who appreciate others on their own terms, without reference to their own interests and desires. They see them as having goals and interests of their own and as entitled to pursue them in an autonomous and self-directed manner as long as such autonomy is compatible with the pursuit of agreed educational purposes and role responsibilities. To respect all members of a school community is to treat their points of view as worthy of attention and open-minded consideration, even though those interests and points of view may differ markedly from one's own.

Respectful leaders give due consideration to the critically examined interests and contributions of all parties. The qualifier "critically examined" is important, for respect does not require acceptance of everyone's point of view. I made this point in a different way in Chapter 8 when I discussed the analytic virtue of truth-seeking and open-mindedness and distinguished the latter from uncritical acceptance. What respect does require is that everyone's interests and points of view be publicly examined for relevance to the particular problem, for the principles that are at stake, and for the educational implications of attempting to meet them. Leaders are respected when they are open to being influenced by the ideas and arguments of others.

Mutual respect may evolve into friendship, liking, and even love, but the motivation of the virtuous leader is to respect and be respected, not to be liked.

Virtuous educational leaders want to be respected rather than liked. Respect implies keeping a professional distance from colleagues—a distance that grants appropriate autonomy and independence and recognises that much of a colleague's life is not the leader's business unless it impinges on professional responsibilities. Mutual respect may evolve into friendship, liking, and even love, but the motivation of the virtuous leader is to respect and be respected, not to be liked.

The virtue of interpersonal respect is most obvious in leaders' consistent ability to pay attention and listen. Listening is a key determinant of teachers' perception of the trustworthiness of their leaders (Bryk & Schneider, 2002). It is much easier to listen to views that accord with our own than to listen to contrary views. A frequent question leaders ask me is what to do when teachers challenge them about the need for improvement. My advice to those leaders is to listen carefully to why their teachers disagree and refrain from attempting to persuade them otherwise until the teachers in question confirm that the leader has listened and understood their concerns. (I provided an example of how to listen to challenges in Table 8.1 in my previous discussion of analytic virtues.)

In a healthy school culture, there is a close association between respect and accountability. When educators make agreements, whether or not those agreements are formalised in policies and minutes of meetings, respect requires that those involved hold each other accountable for abiding by those agreements unless there is further agreement that they be waived or revised.

Take the example of a teacher who requests exemption from their team's after-school meetings because they are a single parent and need to get home to their young children. The team leader shows respect for this teacher, whether or not they agree to waive attendance at the meeting, by listening carefully to the request and disclosing their concern about the implications of granting it for building the desired professional learning community. Respect is also shown by inviting a collaborative search for an integrative solution that enables the teacher to meet their childcare needs and be part of the professional learning community. The team leader is disrespectful of the teacher if their request is prejudged as unreasonable, or if it is granted despite the leader's belief that it is unreasonable.

Educators who unilaterally ignore or violate agreements disrespect their colleagues by, in effect, signalling that their own interests are more important than those of others. Educators who perceive others to be violating agreements and choose to do nothing are also disrespectful of colleagues, as they are treating the violators as not worthy of being held to the same high standards as everyone else and undermining the interdependence and collective effort that enables everyone to do a good job.

Dealing with a perceived violation in a respectful way requires disclosure of one's belief that there has been a violation, gaining agreement on what happened, inquiring into the circumstances, and listening to the other's explanations. Such open-minded and respectful "giving account" to one another builds trust and respectful reciprocal accountability.

Respect in Action

Being respectful is particularly difficult in unfamiliar situations, for it is in those situations that the leader's assumptions about what it is to be respectful may not be shared by others. In Table 10.3, I show how a new team leader navigates a situation in which she is unsure of how to be respectful of a male teacher, Fetu, who is a Samoan elder. She needs the elder's help in understanding the cultural issues that may explain the reluctance of a young Samoan woman teacher, Lili, to speak up in the team meetings in the presence of the elder. She has already spoken with Lili, who has confirmed her reluctance and suggested that it would be best if the cultural issues were explained by Fetu. The team leader believes that it is important that every member feel comfortable about sharing their practice and learning together, and she hopes that Fetu can help her achieve this.

Table 10.3 Navigating Cultural Difference With Respect

SPEAKER	MEETING EXCERPT	ANALYSIS
Team Leader	Talofa, Fetu.	***Respect:*** *Talofa is a salutation in the Samoan language.*
Fetu	Talofa.	
Team Leader	Thank you so much for your time and for meeting with me. I think I need your help, and I'm going to try and explain why I think that and then get your reaction. We have committed to trying to get a really effective professional learning community going between us. And yet I've been concerned for the last three or four meetings, there's a dynamic developed in the group where we're actually not sharing our teaching and our stumbling blocks and our successes in the way that I think is critical to an effective professional learning community. And I'm particularly concerned about Lili. As you know, in terms of our last meeting, for example, where we were looking at the creative writing. I was amazed at how Lili's work and the results of her students were so good, and yet she wouldn't talk about her teaching. Fetu, did you notice that?	***Respect:*** *Team Leader (TL) shows respect by asking for Fetu's help.* ***Strategic Virtues:*** *TL links agenda to a prior agreed purpose.* ***Integrity:*** *TL is transparent about her reasons for meeting.*
Fetu	I certainly noticed that, and I think I can explain some possible reasons around that.	
Team Leader	Okay, that would be helpful.	***Respect:*** *TL indicates willingness to accept help.*
Fetu	Now, Lili and I are both Samoans, and in our culture, there is a value called Fa'aaloalo, which is the respect for the relationship (Va fealoa'i) between any two people. Now in this case, Lili looks up to me as the	

	more experienced teacher in this school, older, and a chief as well, so in our culture we show respect by ensuring that we take into account the beliefs and values of those who are older or more experienced than us. So that is a possible explanation for that, and Lili is doing her best as a young Samoan teacher to ensure that anything that she says either has gone through me as a more senior member of the school and also will not undermine any decision that I make.	
Team Leader	Thanks, Fetu. As a Palagi (white person), I can't speak in the same way you do, but I also want to run a meeting in which you and everybody is respected. My dilemma is that I also have an obligation to lead the process whereby we all learn to improve our teaching. And so I want to find a way, with your help, of making it possible for us to learn from Lili in this case, but also in a way that you and she are culturally comfortable. And at the moment, I'm at a loss to how to do that. Have you seen Lili's results? Have you looked at the sort of work that I was trying to share in our last meeting?	***Respect:*** *TL listens and acknowledges differences in understanding of respect and the limited nature of her own understanding.* ***Strategic and Imaginative Virtues:*** *TL returns to the purpose and the need to integrate cultural comfort and learning from each other.*
Fetu	Honestly, that last meeting, that was probably the first time I've actually seen, although I have actually heard from other members of the department how well she is doing. And that's a . . . and I feel good when I hear things like that, because you know I see myself also reflected in how well she's succeeded. And I truly see her as one of the real potential leaders of our community and school, and I feel that I have a part to play in that as a respected adult in the school community.	
Team Leader	So I wanted to ask you about whether you agree that it's important to try and create a dynamic in the meeting where Lili does feel able to talk about her teaching in a way that all of us can potentially learn from her, particularly around the creative writing results she's achieved.	***Respect:*** *TL directly checks Fetu's agreement with Lili speaking up in front of him.*
Fetu	Yeah, I'm sure that's not a problem, but I think you have to understand what those values are and how they actually play out in events like our meeting. So definitely I can . . . maybe as part of that I need to have some discussion	

(Continued)

Table 10.3 (Continued)

SPEAKER	MEETING EXCERPT	ANALYSIS
	with Lili as well to ensure that she's comfortable in sharing her best practice, because, like I said, I want what's best for her and our school, so I have no problems with that as long as it's done in a culturally appropriate way.	
Team Leader	Okay, so you suggested that you have a chat with Lili about her role in the meeting and about her speaking up? Did I hear you right, is that what you suggested?	***Respect:*** *TL listens, summarises, and checks.*
Fetu	That's what I suggested.	
Team Leader	Okay. I would be really happy with that. Thanks.	

The excerpt illustrates how being respectful in cross-cultural situations may require explicit testing of what would otherwise be taken for granted as respectful. Until the team leader noticed that Lili was not speaking up, she had assumed that all the team members, having agreed to build a professional learning community, would willingly contribute. When Fetu spoke about the Samoan concept of respect for elders, the team leader explicitly checked to see whether that concept of respect was compatible with Lili speaking up in team meetings. Fetu indicated that he believed it was and that he would speak with Lili to help her navigate between the Samoan world and her role as team member.

Courage

Educational leaders with a courageous disposition habitually overcome their fears, take risks, and make themselves vulnerable as they pursue a worthy goal (Goud, 2005). They make themselves vulnerable by doing what they think is right despite not knowing how others will react or despite believing that others will react negatively (Meyer et al., 2017).

In education, worthy goals are those that advance educational purposes in a manner that is consistent with a particular leadership role. For team leaders committed to improving the attendance and achievement of indigenous students (the worthy goal), courage may be required in reaching out to families about whom they know little (overcoming fear of being culturally inappropriate) and in challenging the negative stereotypes held by some of their teachers (risking adult relationships in the interest of students). For principals, courage may be needed in disclosing their personal disappointment in the latest assessment results (being vulnerable) and in publicly challenging what they see as a teacher culture of low expectations (risking adult relationships in the interest of students).

Educational leaders need interpersonal courage to be effective in the numerous situations that are likely to evoke feelings of fear, risk, and vulnerability. Such contexts include asking for critical feedback, giving critical feedback, dealing with problems of teacher performance or behaviour, tackling problems where they feel inadequate or underprepared, and confronting dysfunctional cultures of gossip, deficit thinking, or uncritical discussion.

Courage is needed to encourage colleagues, especially those in less powerful positions than the leader's, to give direct and honest feedback (see the box titled "A Principal's Courage in Seeking Public Feedback" for an example). When leaders take the risk of asking for and listening to such feedback, trust in their leadership increases, because they have made themselves vulnerable and reduced the risk for teachers of giving honest feedback.

Courage may be expressed in either virtuous or nonvirtuous ways (Robinson, 2020). This distinction is important, because without it we cannot distinguish between courageous acts that are foolhardy or unwise and those that are praiseworthy. For example, a leader who challenges a powerful parent who falsely accuses a child of bullying her daughter may be courageous in overcoming her fear of the parent, but such courage is not virtuous if the leader speaks to the parent in a rude and disrespectful manner. This example shows that in the practical world of school leadership, there is no such thing as courage "in the pure." The exercise of virtuous interpersonal courage requires being simultaneously respectful, honest without being rude, and open- rather than closed-minded about the facts of the matter.

The exercise of virtuous interpersonal courage requires being simultaneously respectful, honest without being rude, and open- rather than closed-minded about the facts of the matter.

In short, acts of virtuous courage draw on wider aspects of the leader's character—the more virtuous the leader in the overall sense, the higher the likelihood that their individual acts of courage will be virtuous. *This means that while we can understand and discuss interpersonal courage as a stand-alone concept, leaders cannot be courageous in the virtuous sense unless they learn how, in each context-specific situation, to integrate the requirement for courage with other relevant virtues.*

In my earlier discussion of trust, I summarised the four determinants of teachers' trust of their leader as integrity, interpersonal respect, personal regard, and role competence (Bryk & Schneider, 2002). Being competent in the role requires considerable interpersonal courage, for educational improvement is seldom obtained without challenging aspects of teachers' performance or behaviour. When leaders are lacking in courage or are courageous in nonvirtuous ways, they are likely to be judged as less than competent, because they will avoid those situations in which they are fearful of others' reactions or tackle them in ways that make matters worse.

In education it is often easier to discern incompetence than competence, because signs of incompetence are more public and less ambiguous. For example, teachers and parents are quick to make negative judgments about principal incompetence when buildings are not orderly and safe, when individuals interact in a disrespectful manner with impunity, and when accountability for implementing collective agreements is weak (Bryk & Schneider, 2002).

One of the reasons leaders fail to act in courageous ways is that they doubt their ability to do so without damaging relationships (Robinson et al., 2016). As they become more skilled in being courageous in respectful ways, they become less fearful and more confident that they can give and receive critical evaluation in ways that promote learning rather than defensiveness. Over time, their growing capability reinforces their commitment to improvement as they become more confident that they can give honest feedback in a respectful and learning-oriented rather than controlling manner (Hannah et al., 2010).

Learning to be more courageous is supported by institutional culture as well as by high-quality learning opportunities for individuals. A regulatory environment that sanctions leaders whose courageous acts are nonvirtuous because they violate natural justice, fail to comply with codified procedures, or trigger employee stress reactions sends strong messages about the risks of attempting to be courageous and getting it wrong.

If, in that same environment, there are few if any sanctions for leaders whose response is to take no action at all, then leaders will conclude that the risk of choosing to act and acting in a less-than-virtuous fashion is far greater than the risk of taking no action at all. Leaders' virtuous courage, therefore, can be increased by ensuring an encouraging regulatory environment, as well as by developing the interpersonal skills of individual leaders (Robinson, 2020).

Courage in Action

After attending an intensive course on interpersonal virtues taught by a colleague and me, a principal wrote to us about what had happened at her recent staff meeting:

A PRINCIPAL'S COURAGE IN SEEKING PUBLIC FEEDBACK

Today I asked my staff to help me understand what was going on for them in terms of feeling overwhelmed by workload issues and any other concerns. I also asked the question, "How may I have contributed to it?" I told them that I would take the information back to the executive and do something with it. I also said that I would try very hard to listen and not offer reasons for my actions, which could appear defensive and shut down their feedback, and at the end I would summarise their concerns to make sure I had understood. I advocated strongly at the start for building a culture where we discuss these things and we talk about issues and concerns with each other. I was anxious but knew I had to do it.

What I learned today was their angst was not from the stuff they had to do (i.e., programmes, etc.) but more from a lack of clarity about what was required and the volume of professional learning we were bombarding them with. They were also concerned about the inconsistency in staff's management of student behaviour and about the impact of students' diet on their behaviour.

The principal's courage is evident in the way she made herself vulnerable by not only asking for feedback but also asking how she may have contributed to her teachers' stress. Her courage was motivated by her virtuous disposition to lead—she wanted to be more effective in her role as leader of teacher professional learning. One consequence of her courage was that she received honest feedback and learned that some of her assumptions about teachers' dissatisfactions were incorrect. Another consequence was that she learned how to be courageous in ways that she had previously doubted she could accomplish.

Empathy

Leaders with the virtue of empathy have the ability to "understand and share another person's feelings and emotions—to see things from the perspective of another and understand another's point of view" (Tomlinson & Murphy, 2018, p. 20). Empathy should be distinguished from sympathy, which is "a soft tender emotion of pity and concern that is associated with imagining the plight of another person" (Peterson & Seligman, 2004, p. 330).

The empathy of educational leaders is motivated by a deep desire to understand their staff and students—not in an intrusive sense but in the sense of appreciating their role-related beliefs, attitudes, and feelings. As communities become increasingly diverse, empathy becomes more critical to creating inclusive and effective schools and classrooms. Empathy is needed in every context where leaders encounter students, families, and colleagues whose ways of speaking, behaving, and living differ from their own. Empathy and humility are particularly important in these contexts, because it is likely that what the leader takes for granted as the right way to behave may not be similarly understood by others.

Salvi, principal of a high school serving a highly disadvantaged community, was revered in the community for his ability to understand and get alongside his students. Despite coming from a very different background, he came to understand his students by listening to their stories, educating himself about the impact of poverty on families, greeting them, and spending his lunch breaks with them in the cafeteria. He displayed aspects of the different components of empathy (Zaki & Ochsner, 2016):

1. Taking others' perspectives to understand how and why they experience the situation as they do.
2. Setting aside any prejudgments about others, for such prejudgments prevent careful listening. Any subsequent critical evaluation should be done collaboratively once the other person trusts that the leader has understood what they are experiencing.
3. Recognising others' expressed and unexpressed emotions.
4. Communicating the recognised emotions in a manner that checks rather than assumes the accuracy of one's attribution.

Empathic leaders create commitment to improvement by empathising with rather than being controlled by the difficulties others anticipate and experience.

The second aspect of empathy, avoiding prejudgments, is critical to developing the trust required to improve teaching and learning. Empathic leaders create commitment to improvement by empathising with rather than being controlled by the difficulties others anticipate and experience. In the face of resistance, empathic leaders control their frustration and defensiveness in order to learn why others disagree and why their expectations have not been met. Without empathy, leaders will have difficulty inquiring into the theories of action that explain their teachers' difficulties. Rather than being curious about why teachers engage in practices they view as problematic, listening carefully, and summarising what they think they have heard, they are likely to interrupt, suggest ways of improving, or issue instructions. The result will be less trust and less understanding of the drivers of the practices they seek to improve.

To practice the third component of empathy, recognising and understanding another's emotional experiences, requires recognition and acceptance of similar emotions in oneself, along with the ability and willingness, when appropriate, to name and describe those emotions. This behaviour is also key for practising the fourth aspect of empathy: testing rather than assuming the accuracy of the emotions that are attributed to others. In short, the attribution of anger, sadness, or any other emotion involves recognising that, like all such "mind reading," the conclusions one draws about another's emotional state are fallible and their validity needs to be tested by describing and checking the accuracy of the perceived emotion. This is one of the ways that analytic virtues are relevant to the exercise of interpersonal virtues.

It is more difficult to recognise and respond empathically to negative than to positive emotions, particularly when the leader is the source of the negativity. In those situations, empathic leaders build trust by communicating the emotion they perceive, checking for accuracy, and inquiring into the reasons for the negative emotion.

As with all virtues, you can have too much of a good thing. Excessive empathy can prevent the leader from integrating it with other relevant virtues, such as conscientious conduct of duties. While it is important, for example, to empathise with the personal situation of a distressed teacher, the virtuous leader does not let such empathy override his duty to prevent the teacher's personal problems from negatively impacting the learning of his students. An educational leader's role is not that of guidance counsellor.

Excessive empathy can also lead to emotional exhaustion. Rather than seek to increase empathy per se, leaders should be supported in regulating their empathy so they can integrate it with the other virtue and nonvirtue requirements of the situation (Zaki & Ochsner, 2016).

Empathy in Action

Leaders frequently encounter tears when attempting to discuss a teacher's practice. When this happens, an empathic leader names the emotion she sees ("I can see this is really upsetting you"), pauses to check the accuracy of her attribution, and provides a choice about whether to continue the meeting rather than unilaterally deciding it should be postponed or redirected ("What would you like to do now?" "Do you want to carry on or schedule another time?").

The short example below (Table 10.4) shows how a leader can integrate the interpersonal virtue of empathy (in this case, empathy for the teacher's perceived distress) with analytic virtues (testing the validity of her perception), leadership virtues (commitment to her leadership duties), and interpersonal virtues (respecting the teacher by providing a choice about how to continue).

While empathy enables leaders to learn more about, for example, how staff are experiencing aspects of their job, they need additional virtues to follow their inquiries with respectful critique if relevant problems are to be solved. Note how the principal's empathy in the following exchange does not preclude addressing the challenge of improvement.

Table 10.4 Discussing Disappointing Results With Empathy

SPEAKER	MEETING EXCERPT	ANALYSIS
Principal	I must say, I am disappointed in these results. How do you feel about them?	***Integrity:*** *Principal discloses own feelings and asks about teacher's feelings.*
Teacher	Well, a bit disappointed, I suppose, but I'm not surprised. The students' literacy is so poor they can't do the social studies tests.	
Principal	So you are disappointed but not surprised. How do you feel about the possibility of improvement?	***Respect:*** *Listening is indicated by the summary and direct inquiry into teacher's views about improvement.*
Teacher	Oh, pretty pessimistic, I suppose. I've tried everything I know, and nothing seems to make much difference.	
Principal	Well, if you have tried all you know, I can see why you are pessimistic. I need to get you some more expert help, because we have a collective responsibility to try to lift these results. How do you feel about that?	***Empathy:*** *Principal shows acceptance and understanding of teacher's pessimism.*
Teacher	Depends what sort of help.	
Principal	Okay, so what does that depend on? What in your eyes would be the right and wrong sort of help? . . .	***Empathy:*** *Principal offers nonjudgmental acceptance of teacher's reluctance.* ***Respect:*** *Principal inquires further into teacher's views.*

SUMMARY

Interpersonal virtues are central to the development of trust. Trust is required because making significant shifts in student achievement and well-being requires the collective effort of many teachers, and this interdependence creates risk and vulnerability. Relational trust reduces vulnerability and defensiveness so that teachers and leaders can be honest with one another, learn together, admit mistakes, and locate competent advice and support.

Research on trust between leaders and teachers suggests that the interpersonal virtues of integrity and respect are required to build trust. In addition, drawing on my own research programme and experience as a leadership facilitator, I include two additional virtues of courage and empathy in the cluster of interpersonal virtues.

We attribute the virtue of integrity to leaders who can be relied on to tell the truth, not only about external situations but also about their own thoughts and feelings. For educational leaders, integrity requires not only congruence between words and actions but also that their words and actions be educationally worthy because they serve the interests of students.

The virtue of respect is manifest in leaders who treat others as having goals and interests of their own and as entitled to pursue them in an autonomous and self-directed manner as long as such autonomy is compatible with the pursuit of agreed educational purposes and role responsibilities. Virtuous educational leaders strive to be respected rather than liked, and their respect is evident in the way they pay attention and listen, especially to views that differ from their own.

Courage is evident in educational leaders who habitually overcome their fears, take risks, and make themselves vulnerable as they pursue their educational goals. Without courage, educational leaders may avoid situations that evoke fear, such as giving or receiving critical feedback, dealing with noncompliance, or confronting dysfunctional cultures of gossip, deficit thinking, or poor performance. A distinction is needed between virtuous and nonvirtuous courage, because courage can be foolhardy and disrespectful as well as praiseworthy. Virtuous interpersonal courage requires leaders not only to overcome their fear but to learn how to integrate the requirement for courage with other relevant virtues, such as respect and open-mindedness, in each context-specific situation.

Leaders with empathy understand others' emotions and see things from their point of view, even though they might disagree. In the face of resistance, empathic leaders are calm and focused on learning why others disagree or on why their expectations have not been met. Their empathy is evident in their skill in inquiring into their teachers' difficulties, acknowledging their feelings, and avoiding prejudgment of their behaviour.

The depth and scope of the empathy of virtuous educational leaders is appropriate to their role, for its focus is the appreciation and understanding of others' role-related beliefs, attitudes, and feelings. Just as empathy can be lacking, so can it be excessive. Neither is virtuous. Just as for other virtues like courage, self-regulation is needed so empathy is expressed in ways that enable its integration with other requirements of the role.

REFLECTION AND ACTION

1. In your team, individually generate a list of the interpersonal virtues that you believe are critical to building trust. Discuss your lists and then compare them with the four interpersonal virtues discussed in this chapter.
2. How do you understand the difference between being liked and being respected? How have each of these motivations shaped your own leadership?
3. Are there leadership situations in which you would like to be more courageous? What is it about those situations that has made this difficult?
4. Think of a situation in which you would like to show more empathy. Review the four components of empathy and then apply them to your interactions with this person. What happens as a result?

Integrating Leadership, Problem-Solving, and Interpersonal Virtues

11

When teaching graduate courses on educational leadership, I was struck by the frequent mismatch between the way the course content was structured and the practical requirements of educational leadership. When topics such as building trust are taught separately from topics such as teacher evaluation, a mismatch is created between the practice of leadership and its academic study. It is one thing to learn about relational trust and quite another to learn how to build trust while conducting a teacher evaluation. When both topics are taught separately, the most difficult challenge, which is learning how to integrate the two, is left to the student to figure out.

In this book, I do not leave the reader to figure out the hardest part. That is why I have stressed the theme of integration, and in this chapter and the next, I deal explicitly with the integration of the three virtue clusters.

Perhaps the most important principle of integration in leadership work is that while educational purpose provides the focus, the five stages of collaborative complex problem-solving (CCPS) provide the structure within which the purpose is pursued, and the interpersonal virtues guide the collaborative process that unfolds within the structure. Figure 11.1 portrays these relationships, with the compass guiding the ship towards the purposes, the stages of CCPS providing the ship's structure, and the virtues steering the problem-solving processes.

The five stages of CCPS provide the structure within which the purpose is pursued, and the interpersonal virtues guide the collaborative process that unfolds within the structure.

Integration is required between and within the virtue clusters. Leadership virtues provide the sense of duty and responsibility that motivates leaders to create the conditions required to achieve educational goals. Problem-solving virtues provide the understandings and skills required to solve the complex problems that stand in the way of achieving the

Figure 11.1 The Integration of Educational Purposes, CCPS, and Virtues

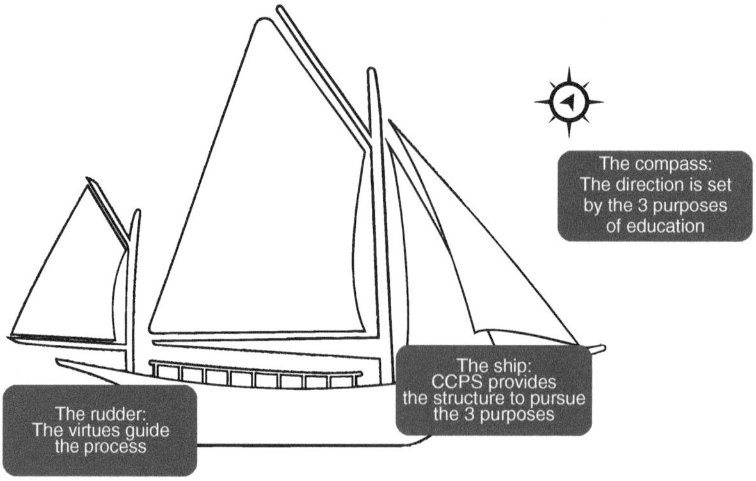

Source: Ship icon by Apvaper/iStock.com; compass icon by Stefan Ilic/iStock.com.

goals. Interpersonal virtues are essential for gaining and maintaining the collaboration required for a coordinated pursuit of the goals.

I provided numerous examples throughout Chapters 7–9 of the integration of the three categories of problem-solving virtues with various interpersonal virtues. I noted that, while strategic virtues enable leaders to discern the relative priority of numerous problems, interpersonal virtues are needed to gain sufficient agreement about the strategic focus and why it is worth pursuing. Similarly, analytic and interpersonal virtues are highly interdependent, for truth is pursued through a competition of ideas and arguments—and in hierarchical organisations in particular, interpersonal virtues are needed to access diverse points of view and to settle on understandings that are sufficiently shared to coordinate the work. Imaginative virtues enable the integration of the legitimate interests of different parties, and without interpersonal virtues, leaders may struggle to access others' interests and gain agreement on their legitimacy.

Leadership is complex because it requires simultaneous attention to the task or problem, to the relationships required to progress the task, and to the management of self—that is, to activating virtuous internal motives and emotions and inhibiting any default interpersonal vices that threaten to take hold. In other words, doing the right work the right way requires leaders to draw, in flexible and context-specific ways, on all three virtue clusters at once. At the level of the task, problem-solving virtues enable leaders to make progress on the problems. At the level of relationships, interpersonal virtues enable leaders to interact productively with others, some of whom may hold very different views from their own. Nested in all these virtues is the need to manage self so that virtuous thoughts, feelings, motives, and emotions are activated.

In the remainder of this chapter, I describe and illustrate how these three levels are woven together in contexts where leaders often experience them as pulling apart. I begin by explaining how interpersonal vices frequently prevent the integration of problem-solving and interpersonal virtues, then move to practical examples of how integration can be achieved.

The Task-Relationship Dilemma

When seeking improvement, whether it be schoolwide or focused on a team or individual, leaders commonly experience a dilemma between their desire to address the problem and their desire to maintain good relationships with the staff members concerned. I call this the task-relationship dilemma because leaders feel caught between progressing the problem-solving and maintaining their relationships. What these dilemmatic situations have in common is anticipated or actual threat or embarrassment—to the leader, others, or both (Argyris & Schon, 1974).

Perhaps the most common situation in which the dilemma is experienced is in giving or receiving critical evaluation, whether in formal contexts, such as teacher evaluation, or informal contexts of collegial discussion. In a classic study of how leaders deal with perceived teacher incompetence, Bridges (1992) found that leaders typically manage the task-relationship dilemma by avoiding the performance problem altogether or by addressing it through a range of "easing in" strategies, including making suggestions without explaining why they are needed, communicating improvement messages to the whole group instead of just to those who are the intended recipients, and minimizing the seriousness of the concern. Improvement in teaching and learning is postponed in the interest of better staff relationships.

I came across an example of this when talking with a leader who provided professional development to her whole team even though she was concerned about the practice of only one teacher. Her behaviour lacked integrity, for she was unable to be transparent about the real reasons for the professional development. Furthermore, it was disrespectful of colleagues to require them to participate in professional development in order to protect the feelings of that one teacher.

When I asked the leader why she was intervening at the team level rather than more directly with the teacher concerned, she explained,

Leader: Umm . . . it's not easy sometimes to have those conversations. You like to keep collegial feeling in the department, and we like to keep supportive of each other, but those conversations can be quite difficult.

Viviane: And what do you sense might be difficult about it?

Leader: Knocking her confidence. I think she already lacks confidence in the class, that's why we have this situation in the first place, so I think that is why—I want to build her up rather than have her think that maybe I'm criticising her.

Since this leader had set up an opposition in her mind between being supportive and being critical, and the latter was unacceptable as it "knocked confidence," she had chosen the indirect strategy of providing professional development to the whole team. She felt stuck in the task-relationship dilemma and had responded by doing what she thought would protect her relationship with the teacher.

Causes of the Task-Relationship Dilemma

The task-relationship dilemma is not inevitable; it is a function of the nonvirtuous analytic and interpersonal thinking and actions that leaders (and others) bring to such situations. There is little point in advocating the integration of interpersonal and problem-solving virtues without addressing the substantial empirical evidence that such integration is impossible unless leaders unlearn the nonvirtuous patterns of thought and action that produce the task-relationship dilemma. This unlearning process is an important part of managing the self so that interpersonal vices are counteracted by virtuous motives.

I have found the theory and practice of interpersonal and organisational learning developed by Argyris and Schon, the originators of the concepts of theory of action and single- and double-loop learning, to be the most helpful for understanding and unlearning these nonvirtuous default patterns (Argyris & Schon, 1974, 1996). They call the theory of action that produces the task-relationship dilemma Model 1, and the theory of action that prevents and transcends the dilemma Model 2.

Model 1 is our deeply ingrained default theory of action that tells us how to be effective under certain conditions. It involves unilateral control of the process and content of conversations to the extent required to win and be right, while protecting ourselves and others from negative emotion.

The shift to Model 2 requires a shift from the closed-minded desire to persuade others of the rightness of our point of view to a more open-minded stance, where the primary focus is on learning about the validity of all relevant viewpoints (Spiegel, 2012). I have picked up Argyris's emphasis on validity in my discussion on analytic virtues (Chapter 8) and his emphasis on joint rather than unilateral control in my cluster of interpersonal virtues (Chapter 10).

So how do leaders make the shift from the cluster of vices that Argyris and Schon call Model 1 to the analytic and interpersonal virtues that they call Model 2? To answer that question, I will start with two examples of Model 1—the soft-sell strategy and the hard-sell strategy—and a brief review of the negative consequences of Model 1. Then I'll explore Model 2 through a look at integrated virtues within a CCPS process.

Model 1: Flawed Approaches to the Task-Relationship Dilemma

When leaders experience the task-relationship dilemma, they typically attempt to resolve it through either a soft-sell or hard-sell strategy. Figure 11.2 illustrates how these two strategies apply to a leader who experiences a dilemma between communicating his concern about a teacher's reading programme and avoiding the defensiveness he

Figure 11.2 Soft-Sell and Hard-Sell Approaches to the Task-Relationship Dilemma

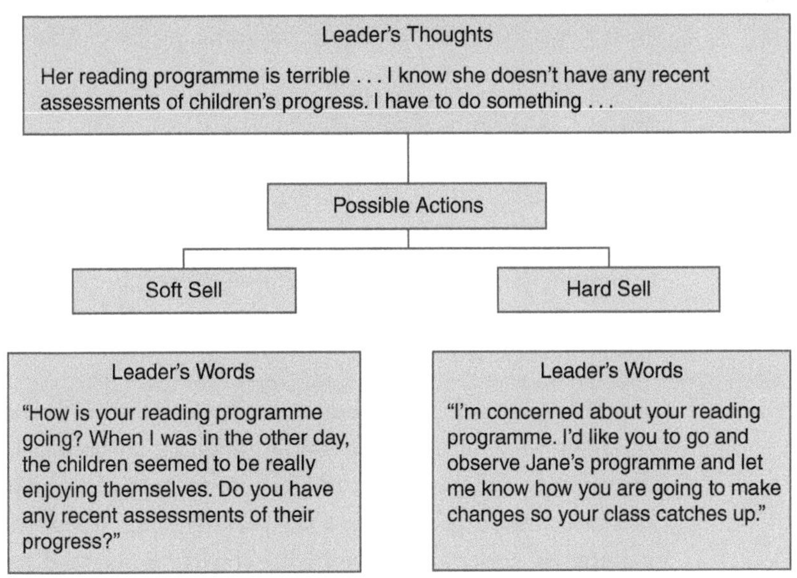

Source: Robinson (2011).

anticipates. In the soft-sell approach, he gives priority to the relationship by beginning with a leading question, hiding his own negative evaluation of the programme, and providing what Bridges (1992) calls "ceremonial congratulations" about children's enjoyment.

In the hard-sell approach, he gives priority to the task and sacrifices the relationship by declaring his concern and issuing instructions about what to do. Both versions of Model 1 are ineffective, because they fail to achieve the twin goals of building or maintaining respectful relationships while progressing the problem-solving.

If leaders come under sufficient pressure to address the problem, they may switch from their indirect soft-sell strategies to a more direct hard-sell approach, but this approach risks damaging the relationship. Although the hard-sell strategy is more likely to result in the recipients getting the message, it is also likely to provoke defensiveness, resentment, and in some cases, legitimate grievance.

Both the soft-sell and hard-sell versions of Model 1 are controlling. In the soft-sell version, leaders maintain control by not disclosing their own views while guiding others toward them with suggestions and leading questions. In the hard-sell version, leaders disclose their views but protect them from scrutiny by the force of their expression and the shutting down of discussion.

Argyris's (1982) research with hundreds of male and female members of both public and private sector organisations has shown that whether people employ a soft- or hard-sell strategy, they assume the validity of their views, just as the leader did about the quality of his teacher's reading programme.

When leaders take a closed-minded stance, they are then faced with the challenge of persuading others to their point of view while minimizing negative emotional reactions. It is leaders' assumption of the validity of their views, combined with the desire to minimise upset, that creates the task-relationship dilemma, because seeking to persuade others of one's own views without genuine openness to the views of others is deeply disrespectful.

The task-relationship dilemma is a powerful obstacle to leaders doing the right work in the right way. In addition to preventing effective conversations about perceived poor performance, the dilemma can bias the causal inquiry that is a key part of CCPS. In our research programme on leaders' problem-solving conversations, we noted that talk about the causes of the problems under discussion was rare. Most of the conversations moved swiftly from naming the problem (Stage 1) to suggesting or asking for solution strategies (Stage 4).

I wondered whether the rarity of causal talk was because leaders seldom thought about causes, or whether it signified reluctance to disclose their causal reasoning. We tested these two possibilities in a subsequent quantitative study of the conversations of forty-three educational leaders in which we systematically compared how those leaders thought about their nominated problem and how they talked about it with the person concerned (Sinnema et al., 2013).

We discovered that these leaders did indeed have plenty of ideas about the causes of the problem, but they seldom disclosed their ideas in their conversation with the person involved. One reason for the nondisclosure was their belief that in order to be supportive to the person whose teaching performance or behaviour was under discussion, they should provide support, which they understood as swiftly offering solution strategies. This belief does not, however, rule out some prior discussion of problem cause.

A more compelling reason for the low frequency of causal talk was avoidance of discussion of leaders' belief that aspects of teacher behaviour or performance might have contributed to the problem under discussion. For example, leaders were much more likely to disclose their belief that a student's background or attitudes caused her poor attendance than to disclose their belief that the teacher's relationships with the student contributed to her absence.

The reason for the nondisclosure, as confirmed in our qualitative studies of the problem-solving conversations of senior and middle leaders, was their fear of negative emotion—of triggering upset or conflict. In most cases, the result was either no discussion of causes or a biased discussion of only those causes that could be disclosed without fear of upset. In summary, when leaders experienced a dilemma between maintaining their relationships or progressing the problem-solving, they typically privileged the relationship, resulting in very limited discussion of the likely school-based causes of the problem under discussion.

When leaders experienced a dilemma between maintaining their relationships or progressing the problem-solving, they typically privileged the relationship, resulting in very limited discussion of the likely school-based causes of the problem under discussion.

So far, I have discussed how the task-relationship dilemma impedes effective management of teacher underperformance and can lead to biased analyses of the causes of students' difficulties. A third possible consequence of the dilemma is limited effectiveness of professional learning communities. One of the intended benefits of such communities is access to diverse ideas and points of view and thus more opportunities for critique and better-quality practice.

Research suggests, however, that educators seldom engage in the intended critical talk and that, once again, the reason is the task-relationship dilemma. In a book on instructional rounds, the authors describe how hard it is to shift a teacher culture characterised by the maxim "If you don't have anything nice to say don't say anything at all" (City et al., 2009, p. 76). Leaders need to model how to get beyond the "Land of Nice" so that team and network meetings become true learning opportunities rather than pleasant but unproductive occasions.

Nowhere is the ability to offer respectful critique more important than in formal and informal teacher evaluation. There is considerable evidence that, whether associated with high- or low-stakes consequences, teacher evaluation has negligible effects on the practice of the evaluated teachers (Firestone, 2014; Murphy et al., 2013).

One major reason is the reluctance of leaders to give negative feedback—a reluctance that produces a considerable mismatch between principals' private evaluation of the proportion of their teachers who are unsatisfactory and their formal evaluations of those same teachers (Kraft & Gilmour, 2017). Major reform efforts in the United States have assumed that a key reason for the mismatch is the difficulty in providing rigorous evidence of the alleged unsatisfactory performance of some teachers (Firestone, 2014). An evaluation of these reforms has shown that, despite substantial investment in a suite of validated evaluation tools, the proportion of teachers receiving a less-than-satisfactory rating has barely changed (Kraft & Gilmour, 2017).

The causes of the discrepancy between principals' private and formal evaluations of their teachers reach far deeper than technical measurement problems. There is considerable evidence that many leaders struggle with communicating and discussing negative feedback even under benign conditions, such as in a confidential and safe workshop (Sinnema et al., 2013). They unwittingly treat their feedback as true instead of fallible and as complete instead of partial, and this construction creates a dilemma between pursuing the problem and maintaining the relationship. Unless pressured to do otherwise, most leaders respond to the dilemma by protecting the relationship and withholding or minimising their critical evaluation. It is this dynamic that partially explains the discrepancy between some leaders' private and formal evaluations of their teaching staff.

Model 2: Productive Approaches to the Task-Relationship Dilemma

The task-relationship dilemma can be avoided or transcended by thinking in ways that enable rather than prevent the integration of good relationships with high-quality problem-solving. For an example of what this looks like, let's return to the scenario portrayed in Figure 11.2 in which the leader was caught in the task-relationship dilemma (Table 11.1). The leader avoids the dilemma with more virtuous thinking that integrates high concern for the task (ensuring the quality of teaching) and high concern for the relationship (being more open-minded and respectful). Analytic virtues of truth-seeking, integrated with a more respectful stance, resolve the problem of having to choose between relational and task goals.

Table 11.1 Virtuous Thoughts and Actions That Reframe the Task-Relationship Dilemma

LEADER'S THOUGHTS	LEADER'S WORDS	ANALYSIS
When I came into the class, I was shocked to see the book levels being used. I suspect the students are well behind where they should be. I must talk to Joanne about how to check this.	"When I came into your class the other day, I got the impression from the book levels being used that many of your students were well behind where I would expect them to be. So I thought I should tell you that and check it against your understanding of their current and expected levels."	• The leader's concerns are disclosed. • The grounds for the concerns are disclosed. • The leader believes his concern needs to be checked rather than assumed to be valid.

The leader has the same concerns as before, but they are reframed in a manner that enables their respectful disclosure without the need to soften, minimise, or edit out rudeness. The task-relationship dilemma is avoided because the concern is disclosed in a way that neither prejudges the situation nor protects the staff member from the possibility that change might be needed.

Provided that the leader continues to disclose, check, listen, and coconstruct the evaluation of the programme and any changes to it, the result should be a teacher who feels challenged yet respected and who trusts that her leader has been honest. The leader's thoughts do not create an impossible choice between tackling the educational issue and damaging the relationship.

The leader in Table 11.1 has initiated Stage 1 of CCPS through a fluid integration of problem-solving and interpersonal virtues. Analytic problem-solving virtues are evident in the way the leader clearly discloses his concern along with the grounds on which they are based. The open-minded stance of the leader is also evident in his desire to check his evaluation against that of the teacher.

Several interpersonal virtues are woven into his problem-solving. First, leadership virtues are seen in the fact that he takes his duty to ensure the quality of teaching and learning seriously enough to raise the issue with the teacher—a step that may have required interpersonal courage. Second, integrity is evident in the close match between what he thinks and what he says. Third, respect for the teacher is evident in his recognition that he needs to check his evaluation with that of the teacher—as a starting point for a coconstructed and evidence-based determination of whether there is a problem to be solved.

By this point, you may have noticed a common thread in any successful approach to the task-relationship dilemma: communication skills. To effectively integrate virtues and resolve difficult challenges, educational leaders will need to cultivate and employ communication skills in virtuous ways. Figure 11.3 provides a visual overview of how leadership, problem-solving, and interpersonal virtues are integrated in the context of CCPS. At its heart are the clusters and categories of problem-solving and interpersonal virtues that motivate three broad communication skills—advocacy, inquiry, and listening—that are deployed across all five stages of CCPS. If used in virtuous ways, these skills enable leaders to speak with integrity while respecting others and having the courage to be honest yet empathic. In the next section, I distinguish between virtuous and nonvirtuous uses of these three communication skills. It is the leader's motivation that makes the difference.

Applying Virtues to Communication

The fluidity and context-specific nature of problem-solving meetings and conversations means there are no rules for how to be effective—only guidance to be gained from a deep understanding of virtues and how they enable virtuous thought and action. Here I endeavour to provide such guidance through discussion of how virtues inform three key communication skills:

- Advocacy
- Inquiry
- Listening

Figure 11.3 The Integration of Virtues Within CCPS

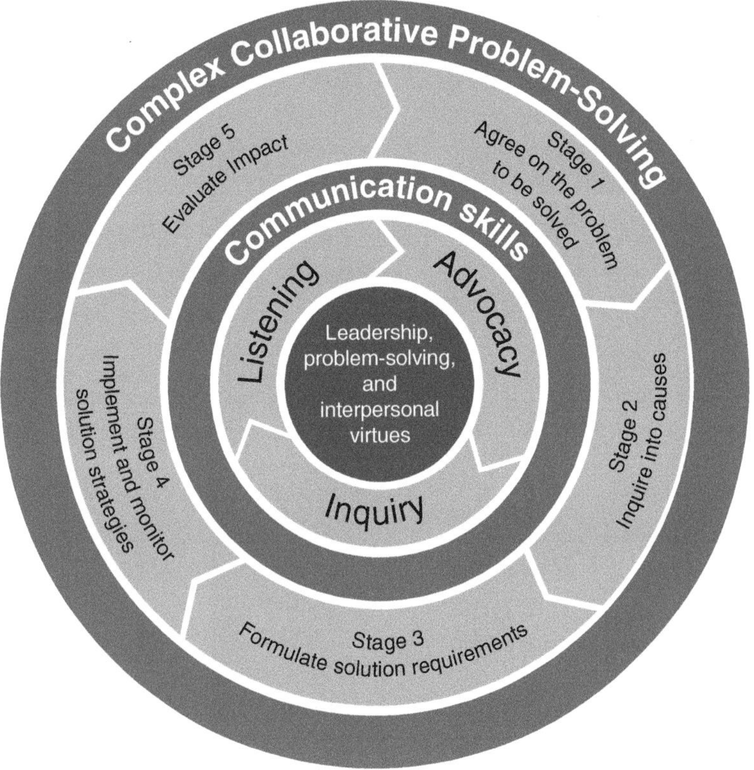

The fluidity and context-specific nature of problem-solving meetings and conversations means there are no rules for how to be effective—only guidance to be gained from a deep understanding of virtues and how they enable virtuous thought and action.

I begin by defining each skill and then showing how particular combinations of the three, informed by virtuous motives, enable leaders to integrate high concern for the task and high concern for relationships.

Advocacy. To advocate is to express one's own views by making statements about one's perceptions, beliefs, evaluations, reasons, or feelings. The views can be about oneself, other persons, the situation, or the problem at hand. By advocating their views, leaders provide a window into what they are thinking and feeling and thus enable others to know rather than guess their stance on a particular issue.

In the context of CCPS, advocacy includes statements about what is believed to be problematic and about its causes, solution requirements, and possible solution strategies. The contrast between virtuous and nonvirtuous advocacy highlights how they are distinguished by the motives that drive them (Table 11.2).

Table 11.2 Virtuous and Nonvirtuous Uses of Advocacy, Inquiry, and Listening Skills

SKILL	VIRTUOUS USES	NONVIRTUOUS USES
1. Advocacy	Disclosing all relevant beliefs as partial and open to challenge Respectfully disclosing relevant feelings about oneself and others Providing specific grounds for disclosed beliefs and feelings (reasons, evidence, and examples)	Withholding beliefs and feelings that may evoke negative emotions Disclosing contestable beliefs as if they are self-evident and obvious Repetitive advocacy (persuasion) Speaking in abstractions without giving clear reasons, evidence, or examples of what is meant
2. Inquiry • to understand others' thinking • to check reaction	Respecting others by making clear what one wants to know and why (focused inquiry) Asking genuine questions—i.e., those to which one doesn't already know the answer Providing the reasons for one's questions Inquiring by pausing and creating space for others' views Seeking feedback about others' reactions to one's own views Inquiring for any doubts and disagreements Seeking information that may disconfirm one's views	Protecting oneself or others by inviting discussion of the general topic rather than the specific concern Protecting oneself by asking leading questions instead of disclosing one's own views Controlling others by asking questions without giving reasons for the inquiry Terminating inquiry on the basis of unilateral decisions about what is acceptable to others Checking for agreement and overlooking or discouraging doubts and disagreement
3. Listening	Listening with a strategic focus Listening to all relevant views Summarising for clarity when issues are complex or contested Checking accuracy of one's understanding Avoiding interruption unless the need to interrupt is discussable Expressing genuine gratitude for what has been learned about others' views	Listening indiscriminately—to the neglect of role responsibilities Listening selectively based on prejudgment of the likely worth of people's contributions Not summarising because one has been thinking of what to say next Providing a selective summary that omits information that could derail one's agenda Interrupting repeatedly

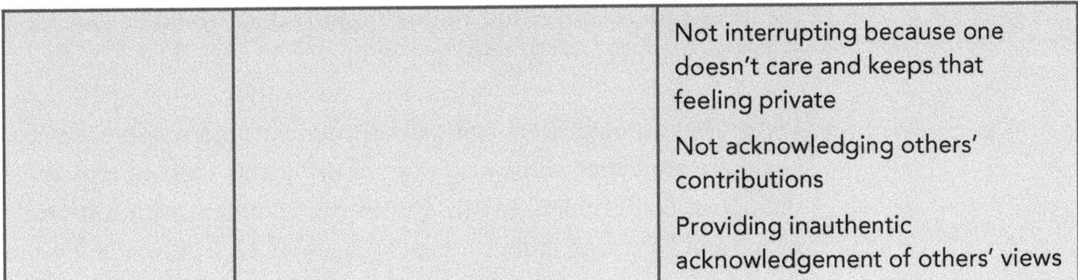

		Not interrupting because one doesn't care and keeps that feeling private Not acknowledging others' contributions Providing inauthentic acknowledgement of others' views

Leaders who are open-minded, courageous, and respectful disclose relevant beliefs because they are able to frame them in ways that avoid the task-relationship dilemma. They express them as their own point of view rather than as the reality, and they provide the grounds for their beliefs because they want to be understood and to enable others to check the quality of their thinking.

Inquiry. The second skill of inquiry is used to learn about others' thinking and to gain reactions to one's own thinking. While inquiry is most obvious in asking questions, one can inquire by pausing or through nonverbal behaviour such as a raised eyebrow.

Virtuous inquiry is genuine; that is, the only questions asked are those for which the leader does not already have an answer in mind. The questions of virtuous leaders are motivated by curiosity and empathy as they seek to understand others on their own terms and to gain frank feedback about their own views.

Virtuous inquiry is genuine; that is, the only questions asked are those for which the leader does not already have an answer in mind.

Virtuous leaders give reasons for their questions so others trust their intentions and don't feel quizzed or led to a particular point of view by a series of leading questions, such as, "Don't you think that you should . . . ?" or "Wouldn't you agree that . . . ?" The genuineness of their inquiries and their truth-seeking and open-minded stance are motivated by their desire to seek rather than claim the truth.

Providing reasons for one's questions is critical when repeated probe questions are required, as is often the case when attempting to understand another's tacit theory of action (see Chapter 8) or when someone is fearful of speaking up. In the latter case, integrity in the disclosure of the reasons for one's questions and empathy for the other's difficulty in answering them will help build the required trust.

Inquiry that is focused and clear helps to integrate task and relationship goals, because it is respectful to signal the intended purpose of the inquiry and seek tacit or explicit agreement on its pursuit. Once the purpose is agreed on, all parties can take responsibility for keeping the focus and using the time more efficiently than would be the case if the focus was unclear (Robinson, 1995).

Listening. It might seem strange to list nonvirtuous uses of listening, but there are better and worse ways of using this third interpersonal skill (Rice & Burbules, 2010). The entries "listening with a strategic focus" and "listening indiscriminately" in Table 11.2 draw attention to the way virtuous educational leaders make strategic choices about what to listen to—choices that are guided by the responsibilities of their role.

Virtuous leaders do not listen to gossip, except to discover whether it is a problem that needs to be addressed; they do not act as counsellors to their staff except to make agreed referrals to employee support services; they do not continue to listen to community members whom they perceive as inappropriately interfering in the running of the school instead of discussing the issue with them.

For those problems that are relevant to their role, virtuous educational leaders solicit and listen in an inclusive way to all contributions, including to the views of those who seem less supportive of their position. They encourage doubts and disagreements by communicating that they want to listen. Their desire to do so is motivated by respect and a genuine belief that their own understanding is fallible, incomplete, and likely to be enriched by exploring others' views.

The evidence that we have listened comes from others telling us we have done so—not from our own declarations. The virtuous listener concentrates on what others are saying, summarises what they think they have heard, and checks for accuracy by pausing or asking if they have understood. The skill of providing accurate summaries during and after meetings and conversations builds trust. This is especially true when teachers have previously experienced their leaders as talking over them in an attempt to persuade them what to do.

The skill of providing accurate summaries is relevant to strategic as well as interpersonal virtues. When conversations and meetings stray across multiple topics, accurate summaries that describe or pull together the various strands of the discussion enable participants to confirm the original focus or make a transparent decision to change it.

In our analyses of recordings of dozens of conversations and meetings, it is rare to find behavioural evidence of listening in the form of summaries or even paraphrasing (Le Fevre & Robinson, 2015). The explanation is found in the motivations that drive nonvirtuous listening (Table 11.2). Rather than paying attention, too often educational leaders are contemplating what they will say next in reply to the anticipated or actual disagreement of the other person. Distracted in this manner, they cannot recall what the other person said well enough to attempt a summary. When they do attempt a summary, we have found, leaders who are in persuasion mode and seeking to win may omit those views that are in tension with their own.

Combinations of communication skills. Virtuous and nonvirtuous interpersonal behaviour, nested within CCPS, is expressed through combinations of the three communication skills of advocacy, inquiry, and listening. When leaders advocate strongly with too little inquiry, there will be little learning and people are likely to feel controlled or imposed upon (McArthur, 2014). On the other hand, when leaders repeatedly inquire about others' views without disclosing their own, they are likely to generate suspicion and mistrust.

Table 11.3 contrasts some virtuous combinations that prevent the task-relationship dilemma with those that are likely to create it. All of the virtuous combinations include varieties of advocacy, inquiry, and listening. For example, while the second combination is predominantly focused on inquiry, providing reasons for an inquiry is a type of advocacy, just as providing a summary is a type of advocacy.

Table 11.3 Virtuous and Nonvirtuous Combinations of Advocacy, Inquiry, and Listening Skills

	VIRTUOUS COMBINATIONS	NONVIRTUOUS COMBINATIONS
1.	Advocate point of view *and* provide grounds (reasons, examples, illustrations) *and* inquire for reaction if needed *and* listen (summarise)	Advocate repeatedly without providing clear grounds for one's point of view Advocate repeatedly with grounds but with no or limited checking for reaction Initial advocacy followed by a unilateral decision to give in or give up
2.	Inquire *and* provide genuine reasons for the inquiry *and* listen (provide accurate summary) and repeat if needed	Ask unclear or clear questions without providing the real reasons for the inquiry Inquire repeatedly, with or without reasons and with no or limited summary of the response to the inquiry
3.	Listen (summarise), inquire for accuracy, and repeat until others confirm the accuracy of the summary	Summarise selectively to highlight confirming and downplay disconfirming or distracting points of view Summarise without inquiry for accuracy, followed by more advocacy that assumes understanding

Multiple virtues are likely to be at play in any of the combinations, depending on the stage of collaborative problem-solving. For example, courage, respect, and truth-seeking may be required to use the first combination to open up a difficult issue in Stage 1 of CCPS. Considerable empathy and interpersonal respect may be needed to use the second combination in Stage 2 of CCPS to inquire in virtuous ways into a defensive teacher's theory of action. Strategic virtues are key across both these combinations to establish and maintain a shared focus. Imaginative virtues and respect for the worthy interests of all parties are needed for the back-and-forth across all three combinations that is usually required to formulate and integrate an acceptable set of solution requirements.

While my intention in providing Tables 11.2 and 11.3 is to provide guidance on how to use and combine communications skills in virtuous ways, I stress that there are no rules about how to be a virtuous educational leader. Learning to be more virtuous requires a deep understanding of the virtues, context-specific practice, and evidence-informed reflection on that practice. It is the flexible, context-specific integration of virtuous skills that distinguishes leaders who do the right work in the right ways.

SUMMARY

Leadership requires simultaneous attention to the task or problem, the relationships required to progress the task, and to self-management. Managing the self requires activating virtuous internal motives and emotions and inhibiting any default interpersonal vices that threaten to take hold. Leaders do this leadership work the right way when they operate in virtuous ways at all three levels at once. In many situations, however, leaders struggle to weave these three strands together, because they experience a dilemma between progressing the problem-solving and maintaining relationships with the adults involved. This task-relationship dilemma is not inevitable. Rather, it is the consequence of ubiquitous analytic and interpersonal vices that are manifest in our desire to win and be in control—motives that produce a range of highly skilled "soft-sell" or "hard sell" controlling strategies. It is the assumption of validity, combined with the desire to minimise upset, that creates the task-relationship dilemma, because seeking to persuade others of the validity of one's own views without genuine openness to the views of others is deeply disrespectful.

The task-relationship dilemma explains some of the ineffectiveness of teacher evaluation, the limited causal inquiry into the links between teaching and students' learning, and the paucity of critical evaluation in teacher professional learning communities. Leaders with strong problem-solving and interpersonal virtues are able to treat their views as fallible rather than as the truth and treat others as people with whom they can inquire and learn rather than as objects of persuasion. When they do this, leaders can integrate their problem-solving and interpersonal virtues and thus avoid the task-relationship dilemma.

Virtuous use of these communication skills—advocacy, inquiry, and listening—is key to the avoidance of the task-relationship dilemma. The chapter concludes with illustrations of virtuous and nonvirtuous use of these skills.

REFLECTION AND ACTION

1. Do you sometimes experience a tension between leading improvement of teaching and learning (the task) and maintaining relationships? When you experience that tension, do you give greater emphasis to the task or to relationships? Why? What are the consequences of your choice?
2. Do you recognise the soft-sell and hard-sell versions of Model 1? How do you feel when you are on the receiving end of each version?
3. Discuss the advice provided in this chapter about how you could prevent or transform the task-relationship dilemma. Try out the advice and give one another feedback.
4. Virtuous inquiry is genuine—that is, the only questions that are asked are those for which the leader does not already have an answer in mind. Use a recording or detailed notes of a meeting or conversation to review the types of questions you ask. How often are your questions genuine, and how often are they leading? What thoughts and motives trigger your use of each type?

Being Virtuous in Tough Spots 12

In my leadership workshops, I am frequently challenged by leaders who are sceptical about the possibility of being virtuous in situations that they have experienced as challenging. Rather than debate the possibilities in the abstract, I inquire into the details of the situation and then ask them if they would be willing to show me what they do by acting out the situation with a suitable partner. If they agree, we gain some shared behavioural evidence and then work together to test the leader's conclusion that "it wouldn't work." The conclusion we typically draw after multiple rounds of practice is that whether or not it is possible is largely dependent on the leader's skill.

In this chapter, I show how it is possible to be virtuous in tough situations—situations that educational leaders experience as posing a dilemma between progressing the task and maintaining their relationships. I provide examples of three such situations—fostering accurate reporting, maintaining collegial accountability, and providing respectful critique—and discuss how virtuous motives and skills enable both task and relational goals to be achieved in each situation.

Fostering Accurate Reporting

It is often difficult for school leaders to gain accurate reports about what is happening in situations about which they have no firsthand information. The larger their school, the more they depend on other leaders to provide accurate reports about what is happening for parents, teachers, and students. When they feel they are not getting sufficient information or that the accuracy of their teacher's reports is questionable, leaders sometimes find it difficult to probe those reports without communicating mistrust. The leader who is knowledgeable and skilled in the integration of analytic and interpersonal virtues is able to model accurate reporting and respectfully require others to do the same.

Accurate reporting is not something that just happens. Deliberate acts of facilitation are needed to build a team culture in which members are constantly alert to the importance of thinking and talking in ways that increase the validity of their claims.

The interpersonal behaviours involved include providing or asking for examples that illustrate one's claims; giving or requesting the reasons for particular views; challenging apparent exaggeration or overgeneralisation; checking how educational jargon is understood, and deliberately seeking instances that might disconfirm important claims. Figure 12.1, an elaborated version of the ladder of inference (Figures 8.1 and 8.2), provides examples of questions leaders can ask to help colleagues interrupt and check the accuracy of their inferences.

Figure 12.1 Questions to Help Others Build a Stronger Ladder

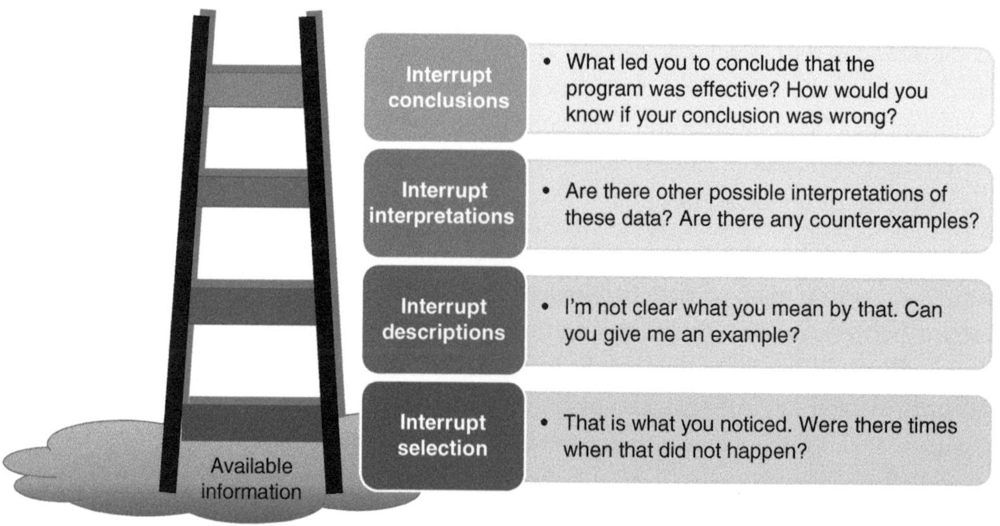

Source: Robinson (2011).

Some of these behaviours are used by the principal in the meeting excerpt included in Table 12.1. This principal was first introduced in Chapter 10 to illustrate the integrity with which he explained why he had called a meeting about teachers' progress in implementing the new Norwegian national curriculum. In this subsequent excerpt, we see how he encourages a culture of accurate reporting through a combination of analytic and interpersonal virtues.

The speech of the principal and year level leaders is analysed in Table 12.1 to indicate how he repeatedly challenged the abstract and unsubstantiated claims of the year level leaders by seeking the evidence on which they were based.

Table 12.1 A Principal's Analytic and Interpersonal Virtues Foster Accurate Reporting

SPEAKER	MEETING EXCERPT	ANALYSIS
Principal	You told me that you had some difficulties with the teachers. The deep learning was okay, but now you have some difficulties. What kind of difficulties?	Summarises earlier report of leader Seeks more detail about the reported difficulties
Year 9 leader	I think it's that the teachers think it's too much right now, and there has not been enough time to understand what the curriculum really says. So I think it could be both that some teachers are resistant to the new things and that I don't know how to lead them, because I have some who say this is okay and some who say we can just keep on the way we did things before.	Provides more detail and two possible explanations for teachers' response to new curriculum Trusts leader enough to disclose own possible leadership difficulties
Principal	How do you experience that resistance?	Seeks information about leader's feelings
Year 9 leader	It's like they don't want to try new things in the classroom in their subject.	Suggests possible reason for teachers' reaction without giving evidence on which the reason is based
Principal	Don't want to try? Do they tell you that they don't want to, or . . . ?	Seeks more specific evidence for claim that teachers "don't want to try"
Year 9 leader	I can't see any evidence in the classroom, and they just do as they always have done.	Indicates claim is based on observation of what teachers do
Principal	Okay. So that's one difficulty. But you also said something about time.	Seeks clarification of the second reported difficulty
Year 9 leader	Yes, they tell me that they find it hard because they have to read a lot. There's a lot of text in the new curriculum, and they don't understand everything that it says and how it would influence their practice. So I think maybe they need more time to really go deep into what it says, and maybe they can reflect on what is important for them.	Provides an argument about the need for time to reflect on the reading
Principal	So they don't try to do the teaching in another way, and they don't have time, and they don't understand the readings?	Summarises three possible explanations for teachers' limited progress and checks

(Continued)

Table 12.1 (Continued)

SPEAKER	MEETING EXCERPT	ANALYSIS
Year 9 leader	Yes.	Confirms accuracy of summary
Principal	Do you recognise that in the 10th grade?	Checks whether the Year 9 report applies to the 10th-grade teachers
Year 10 leader	No, not at all. I think this is not a democracy. It sounds to me like the teachers in ninth grade think they have the choice, but they don't. So we just have to move on, I think. Move on quickly with this new curriculum.	Attributes choice to Year 9 teachers without checking validity of claim
Principal	Yes. And they do?	Seeks evidence about what 10th-grade teachers do
Year 10 leader	Yes, everyone.	Provides no evidence for claim
Principal	And they have the time, and they understand everything they read?	Tests whether hypothesised difficulties of Year 9 teachers apply to Year 10 teachers
Year 10 leader	I think so, yes.	Claims difficulties do not apply, with no evidence provided
Principal	You think so?	Challenges unsubstantiated claim
Year 10 leader	Yes.	Asserts claim again with no evidence
Principal	How do you see it?	Challenges unsubstantiated claim for a second time
Year 10 leader	Well, I hear it in the discussions. They plan together, and I can tell that they are on the right track, because these themes [from the new curriculum] are there often in discussions. I think we are ready to move on.	Provides some evidence

Source: Robinson (2020).

The principal's analytic virtues are evident in his insistence that his team leaders communicate the grounds on which they have reached their conclusions about the progress of their teachers in implementing the new national curriculum. They are also evident in the way he keeps track of and systematically tests the validity of three possible explanations of the teachers' limited progress. But while such analytic virtues are crucial for building a culture of accurate reporting, interpersonal virtues are also needed to minimise the evaluative and conformity pressures that come with such report-back processes (Wageman & Fisher, 2014). In this team situation, feelings of being evaluated by the principal could reduce the willingness of the year-level leaders to communicate bad news about, for example, their teachers being opposed to the change or well behind in its implementation.

The principal's repeated probing does not alienate, because it is combined with interpersonal respect. His respect is seen in his careful listening, as evidenced in his repeated summaries, checking of what he has heard, and deferral of his own reaction. Furthermore, he is evenhanded in the way he holds his year-level leaders accountable for the accuracy of their reports, because the Year 10 leader, who reports good progress, is held accountable in the same way as the Year 9 leader, who reports little progress.

Authority figures can reduce evaluative pressure and feelings of surveillance if their questions are motivated by genuine curiosity about the degree of progress being made and by their commitment to learning with and supporting their subordinates. It is the combination of analytic and interpersonal virtues that enables leaders to avoid the task-relationship dilemma, which, in this example, would be experienced as a choice between gaining more accurate information (task) and making their teachers feel uncomfortable (relationship).

When leaders model and hold everyone accountable for accurate reporting, motivated by a desire to learn rather than shame or punish, they will develop team cultures in which accuracy is a shared expectation and collective responsibility.

When leaders model and hold everyone accountable for accurate reporting, motivated by a desire to learn rather than shame or punish, they will develop team cultures in which accuracy is a shared expectation and collective responsibility.

Building Collegial Accountability

One of the dynamics that erodes teachers' trust in their leaders is unwillingness to hold others to account for breaching collective agreements, whether those agreements are formalised in written policies or more informally communicated in shared understandings of collective decisions. Teamwork is undermined as teachers observe colleagues who appear to be putting their own interests above the wishes and decisions of the team and doing so with impunity.

Ideally, accountability for such behaviour is exercised by any member of the collective and not only by its formal leader. Teachers with or without a formal leadership position can exercise the sort of leadership that is key to a true sense of collective accountability. Unfortunately, such leadership is only too rare, because many teachers have experienced little such collegial accountability themselves and cannot envisage how to take such steps without unacceptable damage to their relationships.

In Table 12.2, I show how a principal (Sue) integrates problem-solving and interpersonal virtues to address the repeated lateness of a colleague (Bob) to the senior leaders' team meetings, which are scheduled to start at 3:15 p.m.

Table 12.2 A Principal's Dialogue Builds a Culture of Collegial Accountability

SPEAKER	CONVERSATION	ANALYSIS
Sue (Principal)	Bob, I've noticed that you've been arriving late to our team meetings this past month and so am wondering about your commitment to and engagement in these meetings. At one meeting you were about half an hour late, and for the others you arrived 5 to 10 minutes after we had begun. I want to understand what that's about and get your reaction to my concerns.	The combination of clear disclosure of her concern, along with the grounds for the concern and inquiry for reaction, reflects Sue's intent to be clear, focused, and respectful.
Bob	Well, I don't see a problem. I know I arrived at about 3:45 one day because I had issues with after-school childcare for my daughter, but I have been at meetings by 3:25 at the latest all the other weeks. That's not late.	Bob does not see a problem, so there is not yet agreement that there is a problem to be solved (Stage 1 of CCPS). The focus now needs to be on understanding the differing conclusions each has reached about whether Bob is late.
Sue	If I heard you correctly, you don't consider 3:25 to be late for our meeting.	Sue's open-minded attitude enables her to be curious rather than dismissive of Bob's claim.
Bob	Yes, that's right.	Bob's confirmation indicates that Sue has been respectful by listening to his contrary viewpoint.
Sue	For me that is late, because I understood we'd agreed to a 3:15 start and the other team members are present at that time. Can you tell me why you think 3:25 isn't late?	Sue explains the meaning she gives to a 3:25 arrival, with reasons. She inquires for Bob's reaction.
Bob	Well, I know it's officially a 3:15 start, but they always seem to start with "what's on top" and warm fuzzy stuff and then get on to the proper agenda at about 3:30. So I make sure I'm there in plenty of time before then.	Bob gives his reasons for arriving at 3:25 and explains why he thinks that is not late.

Sue	Ah . . . thanks for explaining that—I can see how that makes sense for you. So I've learnt two things—firstly, that you think that the first 10 minutes of our meetings aren't very worthwhile, and secondly, you don't think you're late because you make sure you're there before the important stuff happens.	Sue acknowledges the new information from Bob and provides a summary of what she has learned from him.
Bob	Yes. Exactly.	Bob confirms the accuracy of Sue's summary.
Sue	Okay, Bob, I'd like us to check with the rest of the team about the usefulness of that first ten minutes. However, to my mind we made a team agreement about the start time, and it undermines the team if people decide to ignore our agreements. If we revise it, then I believe this needs to be a team decision. [Pause]	Sue suggests testing whether other team members have views similar to Bob's. Sue critically evaluates Bob's justification for being late by advocating her own view with reasons.
Bob	Okay, that is fair enough. I'll put my concern on next week's agenda.	Agreement is reached on a next step.

Source: Leading by Learning and Evaluation Associates Ltd.

This brief example provides a clear illustration of how leadership involves working simultaneously across multiple task and relational dimensions of a situation. At the level of the task, the principal (Sue) is aware that she does not yet have agreement that Bob's lateness is a problem to be solved. In exploring why Bob believes he has not been late, Sue learns of a second possible problem, which is the usefulness of the first 10 minutes of the leadership team meeting. A third related problem is Bob's unilateral decision that he can ignore agreed protocols about when the meeting starts because he has privately decided that the first 10 minutes are not useful.

At the level of relationships, Sue wants to maintain Bob's trust by being curious rather than judgmental about his lateness and maintain the confidence of the rest of the senior leadership team by competently addressing Bob's behaviour.

By confronting Bob's violation of the team's agreed start time and suggesting that the whole team discuss the extent to which they share Bob's views, Sue is promoting collective accountability for the success of their meetings. If she had, for example, instructed Bob to come on time, she would have reinforced a belief that, as principal and the person with the most formal authority, it is her responsibility to ensure agreements are kept and that meetings are productive. Instead, the whole team will be discussing whether they have a problem to solve and, if so, whether it is about Bob's lateness or the team's use of meeting time or both.

Sue's approach is indicative of several different virtues. Her strategic awareness enables her to see the connection between an apparently trivial violation and the bigger-picture value of collective accountability. It is her commitment to the latter and her understanding of how to promote it that stops her from assuming responsibility for "fixing" the problem by issuing a quick set of instructions to Bob to "make sure to be on time at the next meeting." Integrity is also at play if Sue is walking her talk of collective accountability.

Sue's analytic virtues are evident in her recognition that she and Bob are on two different ladders of inference. Faced with the same facts about the timing of his recent arrivals, Bob and Sue interpret them very differently—to Sue they mean lateness and to Bob they do not. Sue's reaction to this surprising disagreement is curiosity rather than impatience or frustration. She is open-minded enough to ask Bob directly how, given the facts of the matter, he concludes that he is not late. Her stance enables Bob's frank explanation and feedback about what it means to him to be late in this specific context.

If we knew more about Sue, we could possibly attribute additional virtues to her, such as courage. For example, if she was fearful of confronting colleagues who violate agreements but nevertheless did so, motivated by her determination to build a culture of collective accountability, then courage would be at play, in addition to her strategic and analytic virtues. Other interpersonal virtues such as respect and integrity are evident in her fluent combinations of advocacy of her point of view, provision of reasons, inquiry for Bob's reactions and thinking, and careful listening, as seen in her accurate summaries of his explanations.

Providing Critical Evaluation

I have already discussed how the task-relationship dilemma reduces the frequency and effectiveness of critical evaluation and hence of leaders' ability to improve concerning aspects of teaching and learning. The rarity of critique also significantly reduces the impact of in-school and between-school professional learning communities.

In this third example of being virtuous in tough situations, I provide guidance (Table 12.3) for how to avoid the task-relationship dilemma

Table 12.3 A Guide to Virtuous Critical Evaluation

STEPS
Before you speak, think about: 1. What exactly am I critical of? 2. Why am I critical of it? 3. Am I open to the possibility of being wrong? 4. Will skilful sharing of my critique contribute to our shared purpose?
When you speak: 5. Disclose the target of your critique (a claim, argument, or practice) and check whether your perception of what was said or done is accurate. 6. Disclose your critique of the target along with your reasons and/or evidence, without presuming its correctness. 7. Inquire into the reaction to your critique, listen, summarise the reaction, and check. 8. If needed, inquire into the reasons for any disagreement and repeat the listen, summarise, and check sequence. 9. Identify the precise points of any remaining disagreement and advocate, inquire, and listen until you have a shared understanding or an agreed way of testing the validity and importance of the remaining differences.

through context-specific integration of problem-solving and relationship virtues. As stressed throughout, virtues encompass feelings and thoughts as well as behaviours. The key to more frequent and productive critical evaluation is unlearning the nonvirtuous thinking and actions that prevent its fluent and respectful expression.

Before providing detailed guidance on how to formulate and express critique, let us be clear on what it is. To evaluate is to indicate worth or value—either positive or negative. To critically evaluate *in a virtuous way* is to notice and disclose something that is believed to be problematic and relevant, along with the grounds for the belief and inquiry into others' reactions. The virtuous features of this concept of critical evaluation are the judgment that what one has noticed is relevant to the shared purpose, the combination of disclosure of the critique with disclosure of the grounds, and the openness to others' reactions. An open-minded attitude is signalled by the phrase "believed to be problematic" (or something similar), a phrase that implies the possibility of being wrong or, at least, of having differing views.

To critically evaluate *in a virtuous way* is to notice and disclose something that is believed to be problematic and relevant, along with the grounds for the belief and inquiry into others' reactions.

The target of critical evaluation can be a claim that is believed to inaccurate (e.g., "Gemma is making great progress in her reading"), an argument that is believed to be faulty (e.g., "We have to adopt this innovation because all our neighbouring schools have"), or particular leadership or teaching practices (e.g., a teacher who delays her reading programme because she believes her children don't have the necessary prereading skills).

For those who are not confident about the virtuousness of their critique, confidence can be gained by reflecting, before they speak, on the first four steps in Table 12.3. With increased confidence and skill, those steps will be taken in real time with little delay between formulation and expression of the critique.

I have included the first two steps because I have learned through facilitating many workshops that educators often express their critique so vaguely and indirectly that their listeners cannot understand what they are critical of and why. Step 4 is a check on relevance—a check that, on occasions of real uncertainty, may need to be made publicly as well as privately. Steps 5–9 are motivated by truth-seeking rather than truth-claiming—by the sincere conviction that the critique may need to be modified or withdrawn altogether.

In the following example of virtuous critical evaluation (Table 12.4), a team leader (Sony) talks with one of his teachers (Richie) about his written planning. The analysis in the right-hand column references the steps in Table 12.3 and the combinations of virtuous interpersonal behaviours they require.

Table 12.4 A Team Leader Provides Virtuous Critical Evaluation

THOUGHTS OF TEAM LEADER (SONY)	CONVERSATION	ANALYSIS
I need to explain my concern about the missing aspects of his planning and check that we had the same understanding of the agreement about planning requirements.	Sony: Richie, since our team meeting two weeks ago, the planning that you've submitted hasn't, in my view, shown the detail that I thought we had agreed as a team is necessary for ensuring quality learning for the students. I can see you've indicated the activities each group are doing but not the learning intentions and potential success criteria. So I want to check your understanding of what we agreed to about planning	The target of the critique (written planning) is clear—Step 5 The grounds for the critique are clear—Step 6 Inquiry for Richie's reaction indicating the possibility

	requirements and get your reaction to what I've said. Richie: Well, Sony, you're right. We did agree our planning should include learning intentions and criteria, and I do plan these things, but I don't see the point of writing all of that down in our planning books.	of differing understandings—Step 7
This is new information to me. I wasn't aware that he did not see value in written planning.	Sony: So you do plan in the detail that we agreed as a team, but you don't write it down because you don't see value in doing so . . . Sony: Given I don't believe you've previously raised an issue with written planning, I'm curious to know why you don't see value in doing so. Can you help me understand your reluctance? Richie: Well, like I said, I just think it's a waste of time. Sony: So it's a waste of time? Richie: Yeah. I plan really carefully in my head. I don't have time to write it all down in a fancy template that I won't use. Sony: So it's about the time to write it. Any other reason? Richie: Well, I'm experienced and know what I'm doing, and so I like to be flexible.	Summarises and checks Richie's reaction—Step 7 Sony inquires into the reasons for the disagreement—Step 8 Paraphrases as a way of encouraging Richie to say more—Step 8 Paraphrases as a way of encouraging Richie to say more—Step 8
Teacher and team leader explore the issue of flexibility, and Sony then provides a summary of what he has heard about why Richie is reluctant to meet all the written planning requirements. . . . The conversation continues with Sony suggesting where he and Richie agree and disagree.		
I like his focus on planning with the students and can understand some of his frustration. I do, however, need him to meet team and school requirements for written planning, because I need to have access to it to ensure continuity for learners in the event of teacher illness or a teacher leaving.	Sony: Thanks for sharing that. There are some things I see a little bit differently and things I agree with, so I would like to explain that now and get your reaction. Firstly, I like the way you are involving students in the planning because it does help to engage them in the lessons, and I can now see why more written planning would seem constraining. However, using the planning book is a school requirement, so we have a common format for recording what learning is planned for any class. If a teacher becomes ill or leaves, we need to be able to easily access what's in the teacher's head so that the students' learning isn't compromised. To be honest, I think we	Identifies the precise points of agreement and disagreement, providing educational grounds for what she can and cannot accept—Step 9

(Continued)

Table 12.4 (Continued)

THOUGHTS OF TEAM LEADER (SONY)	CONVERSATION	ANALYSIS
	both think planning is important—our point of difference may be how it is recorded and why. What's your reaction to that?	Step 7
	Richie: Yes, I can understand that, and I appreciate that you understand that I DO plan, even if it's focused on planning with the students. I am really reluctant to write things twice, though—it's so inefficient.	
Efficiency is important, so how can I make this work for us both?	Sony: I agree efficiency is important. So what I would like to do now is work with you to figure out a way to meet my requirement for written planning in a way that meets your need for efficiency and flexibility to plan with students. Are you okay to do that?	
	Richie: Yes, that sounds okay.	

Source: Leading by Learning and Evaluation Associates Ltd.

This conversation can also be read through the lens of collaborative complex problem-solving (CCPS), with the team leader systematically and iteratively working through its stages. Much of the conversation is taken up gaining agreement that there is a problem with Richie's written planning (Table 4.1, Stage 1), and that agreement is not reached until a great deal of inquiry has been conducted into what he is doing and not doing and why. Sony's repeated probing and summarising encourages Richie to trust that his team leader is curious rather than judgmental and thus to talk more.

The result is that Sony learns a great deal about Richie's theory of action for written planning, including the beliefs and motivations that explain his approach (Table 4.1, Stage 2). In Sony's eyes, Richie's convictions about efficiency, flexibility, and collaborative planning have educational merit, but so do his own convictions about the need for a consistent record of planned teaching across every class. Since both parties agree on the importance of all these solution requirements, they can bring their imaginative virtues to bear in formulating solution strategies that, as far as possible, integrate them all (Table 4.1, Stage 3).

System, school, and team leaders usually want to create cultures in which educators learn from one another by sharing and critiquing their practice. While there may be a lot of sharing, there is far less public critique. The paucity of public critique is sometimes explained by leaders' self-handicapping beliefs about their limited knowledge and experience, the boundaries of their role, and whether critique is appropriate in a given context. More commonly, however, leaders appeal to the task-relationship dilemma to explain the rarity of face-to-face critique.

It is hoped that the guide to virtuous face-to-face critique provided in this section will enable educators to build cultures where critical evaluation is seen as an essential part of learning how to do the work while building trust.

SUMMARY

Three situations in which leaders frequently find it difficult to be virtuous were analysed to show why the difficulties arise and how they can be overcome through a combination of problem-solving and interpersonal virtues.

Leaders, especially those in large schools, have to rely on the accuracy of the reports they receive from their staff. In many contexts, a culture of accurate reporting has to be deliberately fostered, because staff have developed habits of selective reporting, making unsubstantiated claims, and exaggeration. When fostering greater accuracy requires repeated inquiries and requests for evidence, leaders often experience a dilemma between gaining more accurate information (task) and making their teachers feel uncomfortable (relationship). Leaders can avoid the dilemma by integrating analytic (truth-seeking) and interpersonal virtues through careful listening and summarising (respect) and curiosity about what is really happening and why (empathy).

A second situation in which leaders can experience the task-relationship dilemma is in holding others to account for maintaining formal or informal agreements. When such agreements are violated with impunity, trust in the leader is diminished and collective responsibility is eroded. Leaders with strategic virtues see the connection between the possible violation and the mutually accountable culture they seek to develop. Their analytic virtues enable them to test rather than assume that the violation has occurred, and if it did, their interpersonal virtues make them curious about why.

Providing a critical evaluation constitutes a third situation in which leaders can experience a dilemma between pursuing the task (providing the critique) and maintaining their relationships. The dilemma arises because, convinced of the validity of their critique, they fear its communication will damage their relationships. When educational leaders feel forced to choose between protecting the relationship or providing the feedback, they typically choose the former.

To help leaders avoid the task-relationship dilemma, the chapter provides a nine-step guide to more virtuous critical evaluation that is informed by relevant problem-solving and interpersonal virtues.

REFLECTION AND ACTION

1. In your school or team, is there a culture of collegial accountability, or is accountability to collective decisions seen as the formal leader's responsibility? What are the implications of each of these accountability cultures?
2. Reflect on your recent experience of a professional learning community. Do its members provide respectful critique of each other's practice, or does it operate more as a "Land of Nice"? What are the consequences of how it operates for the learning of its members?
3. In your team, review Table 12.3 and discuss how to use the guide to increase the frequency of virtuous critical evaluation.

Virtuous Leadership of Educational Improvement 13

A Case Study[1]

In this chapter, I show how all the components required to do the right work the right way come together in the leadership of school improvement. In contrast to the previous shorter examples, this case of school improvement describes how multiple system- and school leaders worked together to address the long-standing attendance problem at Vauxhall Secondary College[2] in Victoria, Australia. (In the Victorian system, system leaders are those whose professional responsibilities go beyond an individual school.)

While no one leader was perfect, their combined virtues were sufficient to enable them to make significant progress in resolving the problem. The leadership virtues of the system leader and of one school leader in particular created the urgency needed to put and keep the problem on the agenda. The strong problem-solving virtues of the system leader, particularly her deep knowledge of the five stages of CCPS, provided the structure needed to keep the work progressing in a thorough and systematic fashion. Nested within the problem-solving structure was a collaborative and inclusive process characterised by multiple problem-solving and interpersonal virtues as well as the occasional vice.

While no one leader was perfect, their combined virtues were sufficient to enable them to make significant progress in resolving the problem. The leadership virtues of the system leader and of one school leader in particular created the urgency needed to put and keep the problem on the agenda.

[1] This chapter is a revised version of the case report originally commissioned by the Department of Education and Training, Victoria, Australia. I am deeply grateful to the leaders, teachers, and staff at Vauxhall School, for without their cooperation and active participation, this case study could not have been completed. Particular thanks are due to the system leader (SEIL) serving Vauxhall Secondary College, as her efforts provided the inspiration for this case. I also gratefully acknowledge my collaboration with Jacqui Patuawa in the design and delivery of the Collaborative Complex Problem Solving (CCPS) programme.

[2] The names of the school and its leaders are pseudonyms.

The Problem: Attendance at Vauxhall Secondary College

Vauxhall Secondary College (VSC) is a coeducational Years 7–12 state school that serves a semirural community of 14,000 made up of tradespeople operating their own businesses, young professional families, commuters, and retirees. The school is classified, on the basis of family education and occupation, as of medium socioeconomic status.

At the time this case was completed, the school had 1,200 students served by 105 teachers, 26 of whom were newly appointed. There was also a new senior leadership team comprising the principal and two assistant principals. The school was, in the words of the principal, "in a rebuilding mode."

Attendance had been a problem at VSC for many years. In its final report on the most recent external review of the college, the review panel noted that absence in the previous four years had increased to a level that was well above the absence rates of similar schools.

The panel believed that the relatively high absence rates at VSC could explain the decline in Year (Grade) 11 and Year 12 students gaining the senior secondary school qualification (Victorian Certificate of Education; VCE) that provides a pathway into apprenticeships and tertiary study. The increase in absence was also associated with a decline over the same period in the college's results in standardised assessments of numeracy and literacy (NAPLAN).

The review panel linked the attendance problem to students' attitudes about attendance and to poorly understood and inconsistently applied procedures for managing attendance. It recommended that the college analyse the absence data, develop actions to change attitudes about attendance, and revise policies and processes to improve attendance rates.

When asked to describe what had been done in response to these recommendations, the previous principal, who was now retired, explained that, although structural changes had been made that shifted responsibilities for attendance to different staff roles, problems of variable practice and accountability had not been addressed. He wrote,

> We weren't clear enough on the expectation for follow-up on absences, and we never tackled the accountability issue with mentor teachers either. Again, variation in practice from staff meant the problem worsened. There was more than enough to focus on, and we were spread thin . . . we just couldn't do all the work we needed to. And attendance—while we returned

> to it every month—was never any one person's portfolio—so it lacked leadership.

The previous principal had heard enough about the school's new approach to improving attendance to make a disarmingly honest comparison with what had been done under his leadership. Under his leadership, he explained, "the general approach was a policy- and compliance-based one. And I guess this is the fundamental difference with the causal inquiry approach underway now—instead of seeking compliance, you're seeking understanding."

The catalyst for tackling the problem once again was a yearlong statewide programme on collaborative complex problem-solving (CCPS) for system leaders. While the majority of the participants were senior educational improvement leaders (SEILs), some of their area directors also attended the workshops. In Victoria, the primary responsibility of a SEIL is to support the leaders of the twenty or so schools they oversee in taking the most effective and evidence-based approaches to improvement.

The purpose of the programme was to teach participants to use the five-stage model of CCPS, described in detail in Chapter 4, to solve a long-standing and important problem in one of their schools. The model was extensively described and illustrated, and participants were coached on how to use it to solve their selected school improvement problem. A CCPS template for summarising progress through the five stages was provided to course participants.

The intent, in addition to resolving the selected problem, was that participants would gain sufficient confidence in the theory and practice of CCPS to use it after completion of the yearlong programme in the resolution of other complex school improvement problems. Consolidation and transfer of participants' learning to new problems were fostered by having them collaborate between sessions in their office-based teams and work together on their chosen problems during the sessions. The VSC case was chosen for this report both because it constituted one of the more thorough cases conducted during the programme and because a case about attendance has wide application to differing school types.

The Leaders: Roles and Contributions

Three leaders played key roles in improving attendance at VSC. Magda Swanson, the SEIL for VSC, introduced CCPS to the school and was very deliberate about teaching it to the school's senior and middle leaders. The principal, Sam Buxton, authorised the work and delegated its leadership within the school to Keith Richardson, the assistant principal.

Magda had a strong sense of responsibility for improving students' attendance and achievement at the school. Once she began the CCPS programme, she thought, *I'm ready to do this because we have got to do something.*

Magda had been working in her role as SEIL in the network to which the college belonged for two years prior to the start of the case and had developed a relationship with its leaders during the 10 months she had been supporting middle leaders to improve Year 9 literacy results. Three months into the attendance project, she was transferred to another school network. Although she was able to negotiate continued responsibility for supporting the college's efforts to improve attendance, she no longer had any formal responsibility for the college, which was now overseen by a different SEIL.

From that point on, her continued work at VSC was done in addition to the full load of new schools she had been assigned from her new network. She continued with the additional work because it was important to her to persevere. As she said, "if I'm going to do something, I'm going to do it, and I want to get the best out of it." Her perseverance was motivated by her strong leadership virtues, manifest in her desire to do her duty as an educator, and because she cared. She explained, "I get as much pleasure out of seeing their attendance going up as probably what Sam does. I'm invested in my school's success. That's it."

Magda brought strong analytic virtues to her work at VSC, one aspect of which was her capability in using data. When asked where she had learned these skills, she explained,

> I think I've always probably been a leader who's used data. I've probably always tried to use data as a conversation starter. So I've always tracked my students, my kids at risk, and the high-achieving kids. As a principal in a school, I tracked all the kids who were 12 months behind in their learning. . . . I had a folder with all their individual learning plans there, and their teachers would come in and talk about the different kids if I asked. I also tracked the kids one year above. They had to have individual learning plans, and then I tracked their formative and summative test results in numeracy and literacy and correlated everything.

As we shall see, her skill in using data enabled her, in collaboration with the assistant principal, to build a deep understanding of the nature and causes of the attendance problem at VSC.

Sam, the principal of VSC, had been at the school for twenty years and risen through the ranks from an initial appointment as lead teacher to assistant principal and then principal. He described his responsibilities for solving the attendance problem in largely symbolic terms because he had delegated leadership of the problem-solving to the assistant principal. It was his job, he explained, to ensure attendance was front and centre on the agenda and in his conversations with teachers and the community.

He also saw himself in an accountability role in which it was his job to speak with teachers about any performance issues. He was much happier having those conversations since doing a course on trust building, which had prompted a shift from his controlling style to one in which he did much more listening.

Keith took up his appointment as assistant principal in January, the same month that the school's annual plan, which specified new targets for student attendance, academic achievement, and qualifications, was signed off. Keith brought knowledge and skills to VSC that made him well suited to lead the push to improve attendance.

First, he had taught in a school in England where a new team of senior leaders had come together and taken the school into the top ten most improved English schools twice in the five years he was at the school. From that experience he knew improvement was possible, as well as something of what was required from leaders to drive it.

Second, Keith brought expectations of attendance that were considerably higher than those held by many VSC teachers and parents. His expectations reflected his experience as a teacher in England, where the expectation was that attendance would be in the 90% range. As he put it, "I was acutely aware of the attendance difference, I suppose, between what I'd experienced in England and what I experienced here [in two public schools in Victoria]."

Furthermore, he had been held accountable in England for meeting those expectations, not only by the national inspection agency (OFSTED) but also by his year-level coordinator, who would ask questions about the follow-up he was doing as a mentor and about how he was liaising with well-being staff on behalf of absent students. In addition, there were weekly meetings where teachers would discuss student absence and well-being and make follow-up plans.

A third asset Keith brought to his attendance role was that he enjoyed data analysis and would use his ninety-minute train journey to school to

> just sit with my laptop and just strip data and muck around with it and do stuff. And I started to look at the patterns in what was happening, and not make any conclusions, but just get that data, really big data. With 1,200 kids, five lessons a day, five days a week, we're talking about tens of thousands of data points. I think it's actually 30,000 data points a week. . . . So, I looked at it by period, I looked at it by gender, I looked at it by year group, and discovered patterns.

A fourth asset that he brought to the role was his deep understanding as a math teacher of the educational consequences of missing lessons. As he explained,

> I've been a maths and science teacher, and especially in maths, it's a very foundational subject. So if you miss a block, you can't step onto the next level sort of thing. So I know the harm it [absence] causes, and the disengagement that it then reinforces, in that [students think], "I've missed this, I've missed that. Now I've come back into class and now I can't engage at all. So am I going to be engaged when I come back? No. I'm going to miss more, I'm going to miss more." And how it becomes maybe a destructive cycle . . . I'd seen that.

The Method: Using CCPS to Improve Attendance

In this section, the case narrative is told through the five stages of CCPS (Tables 13.1 through 13.5). The right-hand side of each section lists the behavioural indicators associated with each stage, and cross-reference numbers in the narrative show instances where they have been used. Many of the indicators integrate problem-solving and interpersonal virtues in recognition of the need for a structured and collaborative approach. For example, most of the indicators included in the first stage of CCPS make direct or indirect reference to such interpersonal virtues as respect, integrity (honesty), and frankness. The complexity and messiness of this real case means that evidence for every indicator is not always present, that the indicators may occur out of sequence, and that they may recur as earlier steps are revisited. For more on the theory and practice of CCPS, see Chapter 4.

Table 13.1 Stage 1: Agree on the Problem to Be Solved (Problem Identification)

CASE NARRATIVE	CCPS INDICATORS
Several factors came together at VSC to create a strong and urgent demand to solve the attendance problem. First, at a system level, there were now sophisticated longitudinal and comparative attendance databases available to every Victorian school, and there were mandated processes, such as strategic and annual planning, for using the data for the purpose of school improvement. The recently completed review of VSC had used these data to note the attendance problem and made its resolution a priority in the schools' three-year strategic plan [1.1]. Second, Magda's offer to help the school with its attendance problem was welcomed by the principal because she already had a good relationship with the school, and Sam was attracted by her view that a systematic problem-solving process could help senior leaders be more successful [1.2]. Third, an inclusive and honest series of data-based meetings were held to discuss the scope and seriousness of the attendance problem. After gaining the principal's commitment, Keith and Magda led a meeting with the senior leaders at which they used multiple data sets to emphasise the scope and urgency of the problem [1.1, 1.2]. Across the whole school, the average number of days absent in the previous school year had been 32.1.[3] In Years 11 and 12, the average equivalent full-time student days of absence had been 39.9 and 30.7, respectively. The seriousness of the absence problem was communicated by contrasting these absence rates with those of 11 other secondary colleges serving similar communities across the state. Average absence rates at VSC were higher than those of all 11 comparable schools [1.1, 1.2]. Magda also communicated the seriousness of the problem by suggesting that the high level of absence was linked to the performance of Vauxhall's Year 11 and 12 students in the statewide VCE [1.3]. Only 2% of eligible students at VSC had achieved a high score in English, compared to 9% of eligible students in 11 comparison schools. The senior leadership team agreed that the absence rate was an urgent and important problem and expressed their commitment to working together to solve it [1.5, 1.6]. While Magda and Keith were frank about the nature and seriousness of the problem, they avoided blame and built trust by describing a coherent approach to solving the problem, communicating their own commitment, and inviting all present to join them in the effort [1.1, 1.2]. Instead of relying on the	When leaders believe particular student outcomes are problematic, they 1.1 clearly and respectfully describe the outcomes they consider problematic (which students, which outcomes). 1.2 are honest and nonblaming about the seriousness of the problem as they see it. 1.3 give specific reasons and/or evidence to explain why they think the student outcomes are problematic. 1.4 ask for frank feedback on whether others agree the outcomes are problematic. 1.5 establish sufficient agreement with those involved about the scope and urgency of the student outcome problem. 1.6 establish sufficient agreement with those involved about whether to begin a collaborative problem-solving process.

(Continued)

[3] All attendance data in this case study were drawn by Magda from the official interactive data displays, known as Panorama reports, that provide a range of performance data to every Victorian school.

Table 13.1 (Continued)

CASE NARRATIVE	CCPS INDICATORS
external demand of system leaders to solve the problem, Magda and Keith's clear and evidence-based approach resulted in the initial commitment of a critical mass of staff. Staff's knowledge of the problem and commitment to solving it was strengthened by Keith's decision to display up-to-date weekly attendance data on the staff room walls and to invite teachers to detect patterns in the data [1.1, 1.4]. He reports, "After roughly a term of displaying this data, there were a couple of patterns that started to come out. We started to see that there were higher absences towards the end of the day and higher absences towards the end of a week. The phrase I used was, 'We have a culture where we check out early. We finish early'. . . . and that was a repeated pattern, week on week, for the whole of the term." Keith was very conscious of the need for a deliberate and collaborative problem-solving process. He explained his approach to teachers this way: "So, without actually shoving [the problem] down anyone's throat or coming to any conclusions or trying to be just solution driven—'Right, what are we going to do to fix this?'—I just said, 'Here's the data, here's the data,' and I did that week on week for Term 1, and we started to see some patterns. And staff were coming up to me informally and saying, 'Hey, I've noticed this.'" [1.4]. By sharing the data "week on week," Keith built trust by demonstrating his own level of commitment to solving the problem. He explains, "All the work I was doing with the data was as much about me showing I'm prepared to do extra work that I don't think anyone else has done here before, by stripping these data out of the system, displaying it in the staff room, and opening up the conversation. And they saw it wasn't just a flash in the pan and thought, 'He hasn't done it for a couple of weeks and then walked away from it. He did it for the whole term. He did it every week for the whole term. They [school leaders] are not giving up on it. This is a thing.'" Keith also included parents in this first stage of problem-solving by publishing an article in the March school newsletter that talked about attendance and showed the percentage of absence by day of the week and by period. The focus on attendance was also communicated to Year 7 parents by Sam and Keith at an information evening held in Week 1. The result of this inclusive and evidence-based process was that leaders, teachers, and parents were informed about the nature and seriousness of the problem, were made aware that improved attendance was firmly on the agenda, and expressed their willingness to set out on a collaborative problem-solving process.	

Table 13.2 Stage 2: Inquire Into Causes

CASE NARRATIVE	CCPS INDICATORS
Given the long history of failed attempts to solve the attendance problem, Magda urged the college's leaders to inquire into the causes of the problem before trying any more "solutions." The inquiry process began with Keith holding a teacher forum at which he sought explanations for the attendance problem [2.2]. Teachers attributed the problem to 15 possible causes, the majority of which were about the management of attendance. This theme covered weaknesses in how attendance was recorded, tracked, and followed up; how features of the school schedule, such as the positioning of free periods and the holding of special events, led to major drops in attendance; and how limited communication with parents about attendance might have contributed to the problem. The second causal theme proposed by teachers was student well-being, including sickness, sense of safety at school, and poor relationships with teachers. A small third group of teacher-nominated causes described limited parental strategies for supporting students' schooling and the taking of family holidays during school time [2.3]. At a second meeting with the full school leadership team of 12 senior and middle leaders, Magda suggested 12 additional causes that were quite different from those provided at the earlier forum, because they challenged leaders and teachers to consider their own unwitting contributions to the problem [2.1]. For leaders, she raised the possibility that there had been a lack of consistent messaging about the links between students' attendance and their academic success [2.1]. For teachers, she suggested that limited capability in presenting lessons that were engaging and met the learning needs of low-attendance students might have a causal role. She also suggested that capability in managing challenging behaviour was a causal possibility, for the absence of challenging students might be a relief to some of their teachers [2.1]. Since teachers believed many of the causes of students' absence were located in students themselves and in their families' circumstances, Magda suggested that such beliefs had led them to see themselves as having little influence over the problem. She also suggested that long-standing community perceptions about attendance and parental apathy in explaining their child's absence were possible contributors to the problem [2.1]. Although the school leadership team agreed that Magda's proposed causes were all possibilities, rather than presume their	When there is an agreed demand that a student outcome problem be solved, leaders 2.1 disclose their own beliefs about possible causes of the problem. 2.2 invite others' beliefs about the possible causes. 2.3 listen carefully to others' beliefs about the causes, especially at points of disagreement. 2.4 engage in collaborative discussion and preliminary evaluation of the suggested causes to identify those that are worth investigating further. 2.5 agree on an inquiry process and timeline to create/find relevant evidence to test the remaining most likely classroom- and school-based causes. 2.6 implement the inquiry process. 2.7 organise and lead team discussion of what the evidence suggests about the validity of each hypothesis and about new hypotheses.

(Continued)

Table 13.2 (Continued)

CASE NARRATIVE	CCPS INDICATORS
validity, the group made a plan to test their causal beliefs by asking all parents and students for their views about attendance [2.4, 2.5]. Students were asked questions about their reasons for coming to school, reasons for missing school, and knowledge of aspects of the college's attendance procedures. Students were also asked who noticed their absence and what would help them get to school on time [2.6]. While the discussion to date had made teachers well aware of the technical limitations of the college's attendance management systems, the survey shed new light on how the need for students to be active participants in those systems had been overlooked. For example, 93% of students were unaware of what triggered a letter to parents for unexplained absences, and 49% did not know if the college contacted their family when they were absent. It seemed that although attendance procedures were designed to influence student behaviour, students themselves were somewhat ignorant of how those procedures worked. As well as confirming the role of weak attendance management, the survey results suggested possible links between students' attendance and their engagement with their lessons and their teachers. When students were asked to choose their top reasons for coming to school, 60% of their selections were for "the importance of their education" while only 3% of their top reasons were for "my classes are interesting." In short, while students were motivated by the general idea of being educated, what was happening in their classes was not contributing to that motivation. The role of teacher-student relationships in student absence was suggested by students' answers to the question about who noticed when they were absent. The groups they saw as most likely to notice were their parents and friends, followed by their teachers. The group they saw as least likely to notice was staff with specialist student welfare responsibilities. From the parent survey, staff learned more about parental attitudes towards absence, with 75% of parents nominating 100% or 95% attendance as an acceptable level and 22% agreeing that "it's OK to take a day off now and then." Some also commented about the importance of taking family holidays, even if they were taken during school time. Approximately 10% of parents reported needing help to support their child in attending school and that there were issues at home that prevented their child from attending regularly on time [2.6].	2.8 repeat the above steps until a sufficiently agreed evidence-based analysis of cause is reached.

Once Keith and Magda had processed the survey data, they met with the full leadership team to share the results, update them on progress, and get their feedback [2.7]. Magda summarised progress, as she did after every major meeting and phone call, by updating the problem-solving template and sharing it with Keith and the principal. In addition, Keith shared the data sets he had developed to track attendance at VSC with the leaders of another secondary college and coached them in how to obtain similar data sets and undertake parent and student surveys. In summary, the inquiry process confirmed three broad causes of the attendance problem. First, limitations in attendance management were likely contributors, not only because they prevented accurate and timely tracking of attendance but also because students had limited knowledge of and active involvement with those procedures. Second, although the student survey did not directly assess students' engagement with teachers and their classes, it yielded sufficient evidence about their reasons for coming to school and about who noticed their absence to suggest that this second group of causal factors had some validity. Regarding the third group of causal possibilities, parental attitudes, there was some limited evidence to suggest that the attitude of a minority of parents might contribute to low attendance [2.7].	

Table 13.3 Stage 3: Formulate Solution Requirements

CASE NARRATIVE	CCPS INDICATORS
Since the inquiry led by Magda and Keith had revealed three groups of cause, solutions needed to be found that addressed each group. Once again, Magda made the problem-solving process explicit by explaining to teachers why it was important to formulate solution requirements before settling on actual solutions [3.1]. She saw solution requirements as "the litmus test you run all the solutions through" before deciding which to adopt. If, she explained, the cause of a student learning problem was ignorance and boredom, then a suitable solution should meet the two requirements of increasing students' knowledge and increasing their engagement [3.3]. Her repeated description of "probable" causes reinforced the need for an open-minded stance while hypotheses were still being tested. In CCPS, the most important solution requirement is the goal to be achieved; the remaining requirements support goal	When there are agreed likely school-based causes of the student outcome problem, leaders 3.1 invite nominations of solution requirements. 3.2 ensure that the student outcome goal is listed as one key requirement. 3.3 ensure that additional requirements that directly address the

(Continued)

Table 13.3 (Continued)

CASE NARRATIVE	CCPS INDICATORS
achievement and are discerned from the causal inquiry and practical considerations such as available time and money. VSC's most recent strategic plan included the goal of improving attendance such that in four years' time, absence across Years 7–12 would have reduced from 28.3 days to 18. The target for the first year of implementation of the plan was a modest reduction of average absent days for students in Years 7–12 from 28 to 25 days or less [3.2]. After validating the main causes of the attendance problem, Magda and Keith led teachers in determining, for each of the three groups of cause, what was required if this goal was to be met [3.1, 3.3]. The final list of nine solution requirements, in addition to the goal, was then recorded on the problem-solving template as follows [3.3, 3.4]: Attendance Management 1. Systems to report, track, and follow up on absences are clearly defined, and roles are made clear. 2. Leadership communicates clear expectations of student attendance within the school and the community and celebrates/rewards positive attendance rates. 3. All staff own the issue of the school's high student absence and work on the improvement strategy within their learning teams. 4. Students with chronic absences are case managed by the school. Student Engagement With Teachers and Teaching 5. Teachers are accountable for planning for teaching that is evidence informed, differentiated, and engaging. 6. Teachers know the importance of relationships with students in addressing absences. 7. Students have stronger educational pathways. 8. The college is a stable and safe learning environment for all. 9. Students are engaged in personal points of interest throughout their college life. Parental Attitudes No requirements were set specifically to address parental knowledge of and attitudes towards attendance, apart from the reference in requirement #2 to communicating clear expectations	causes are nominated (e.g., if a cause of math outcomes is that students have not been taught discipline-specific vocabulary, one criterion must be that any new approach must include a focus on how to teach this). 3.4 include any resource constraints on the solution (e.g., time, money, access to relevant expertise). 3.5 revise and invite reflection on the adequacy of the whole set of requirements and on how tensions between them could be reduced. 3.6 propose, invite, and discuss solution strategies that best satisfy the *set* of requirements. 3.7 summarise and check agreement on why certain solution strategies have been ruled in and others ruled out.

about attendance to parents. Much later in the problem-solving process, as described in a later section of this case report, the importance of giving greater attention to parents' knowledge of and attitudes towards attendance became apparent. With the nine solution requirements in mind, Keith and Magda led the full leadership team in suggesting solution strategies that met these requirements [3.6]. The instructions that guided the leadership team in this activity included suggestions about some of the virtuous communication skills that promote successful CCPS: *It is important to:* • *Disclose your views about how to solve the problem and why you think it will work* • *Inquire into others' ideas about solutions and why they think those ideas will work* • *Critically evaluate the match of the suggested solutions to the solution requirements* • *Establish common ground about how to solve the problem* Magda foreshadowed the work to come by including in her last slide: • *Remember this is a big piece of work that will be complex to address given the identified causes.* • *Carefully thought-out implementation plans for each of the solution strategies will need to be completed, including ways to "know thy impact."* These instructions provide a further example of how Magda integrated relevant aspects of her problem-solving and interpersonal virtues. She didn't have time at that stage, nor did she have permission, to teach the staff about interpersonal virtues. Nevertheless, she cued them, through these instructions, to complete the activity by using some of the virtuous communication skills discussed in Chapter 11, such as disclosing one's own point of view, giving reasons, and inquiring into others' points of view. Magda encouraged teachers to use the school's already completed annual plan as a starting point for suggesting solution strategies, but she warned that, since these strategies had been formulated in a separate planning process that did not include rigorous causal inquiry into the attendance problem, each strategy should be carefully evaluated against the solution requirements [3.6].	

Table 13.4 Stage 4: Implement and Monitor Solution Strategies

CASE NARRATIVE	CCPS INDICATORS
Keith introduced several strategies designed to improve the management of attendance. The before-school Friday briefing meetings attended by all staff were replaced by meetings between mentors and their year-level teams [4.1]. He provided weekly attendance data for each of these teams on Thursday night so that these meetings could focus on the level of attendance, progress made, and students who needed follow-up [4.3]. These data-based meetings were a direct response to the students' survey feedback that had indicated that their friends were more likely to notice their absence than their teachers. As Keith put it, "now the teacher does notice, and now they're having conversations. . . . And there's communication and it's really fair, and it's all transparent. There's no underhand message. . . . It's a well-being conversation. 'What can we do to help you? I've noticed you haven't been here. What can we do to help?' We've started having those kind of conversations" [4.4, 4.5]. For the next four months, Keith introduced additional attendance management strategies, including frequent messages at assemblies about why attendance was important. He also introduced real-time and highly public monitoring of the impact of the solution strategies by using a thermometer display of attendance levels for Years 7–9 and an associated attendance competition between student mentor groups with public congratulations and prizes for winners [4.3, 4.4]. For the first time, the school rewarded and celebrated attendance rather than only noting and punishing absence. Strategies for Year 10–12 students included letters to students about the consequences of their absence for award of qualifications and repositioning of their free periods when absence had been high. At all year levels, systems for timely recording and use of data about lateness and absence from lessons were improved. School policies on student attendance and progression were also reviewed. Finally, in the area of attendance management, the college took a proactive stance for the first time by gathering attendance data from feeder primary schools to identify Year 7 students who might need early intervention to prevent a continuation of poor attendance [4.1]. While Keith's efforts were thorough in improving attendance management practices, the causal analysis and last five solution	When there are agreed solution strategies, leaders 4.1 develop action plans for their implementation (what, who, when, etc.). 4.2 identify implementation indicators to monitor the quality of implementation of the solution strategies. 4.3 plan how the data on implementation of the solutions will be collected, used, and reviewed. 4.4 plan how progress towards the goal will be monitored. 4.5 integrate discussion of implementation and outcome data into meeting routines.

requirements (5–9) indicated that the attendance problem was also linked to student engagement with teaching and teacher-student relationships. Improvement was sought in these aspects by gaining staff agreement with a schoolwide instructional model that had been foreshadowed in the school's strategic plan and been under development by the school's Teaching and Learning team for several months. The purpose of the model was to increase the consistency of teaching practice by providing an explicit standard of quality. Without an explicit and agreed standard, it was impossible to develop a stronger culture of collective responsibility and accountability for quality teaching [4.2]. Nor was it fair to hold people to account for not meeting a standard that had not been made explicit. Implementation of the new instructional model was supported by providing training for leaders of teacher professional learning communities so they could facilitate rich conversations about teaching and learning [4.5]. In the initial brainstorm about the causes of the attendance problems, teachers had emphasised attendance management processes and student and family attitudes and circumstances. It was Magda who had brought forward the possibility of causes related to teaching and teacher-student relationships. Senior leaders attempted to strengthen the link between student experiences of teaching, engagement, and attendance by giving more weight to student voices. Teachers were required to include the results of student surveys taken at the end of each unit of work in their professional learning plan [4.3]. For some teachers, these student voice data, where students described three areas of strength and three areas that needed improvement in the teaching of the unit, proved very confronting. The intention was that teachers would discuss the data with their students [4.3] and that, as a result, as Keith explained, students would "feel hopefully more connected, more engaged, more invested in their learning, because they have a voice in their learning." While the student voice data were confidential to each teacher, they were aggregated by learning domain, which enabled senior leaders to see which departments needed more support [4.3]. By keeping the data confidential at the level of individual teachers, however, there was a risk that those who most needed help would fail to access it. When challenged about this, Keith replied that, at least in his own professional development group, the people with bad feedback were the first in his office saying, "I'm really concerned about this. What can I do?" The reported teacher reactions suggested that, at least for this group, the compulsory use of student voice data had not reduced teachers' trust in their leaders.	

(Continued)

Table 13.4 (Continued)

CASE NARRATIVE	CCPS INDICATORS
A few solution strategies were designed to address parents' role in the attendance problem. Keith sent messages to families communicating the school's expectations of attendance until the last day of school. By doing this, Keith intended to disrupt the school culture of winding down teaching in the last two to three weeks of Term 4. He explained, "That is the expectation, and I'm not going to waver from that, because my experience is that I've always set myself a standard, and the standard is teaching up until the end of the term. And yeah, you get a few activity days, I get that, a bit of fun and celebration at the end of the year. But in the same respect, you're teaching until the end. Even as far as what a lesson looks like. You're not just sticking a movie on and saying you're doing your job, babysitting. That's not acceptable. We're teaching until the end. I think that's just my own standard." Throughout Stage 4, Magda and Keith kept in constant touch, with Keith sharing his strategies and Magda monitoring their impacts on attendance by regularly checking the DET software [4.4]. In these discussions she constantly referred back to the degree of alignment between Keith's solution strategies and the solution requirements. Keith was well aware that some requirements had not yet received sufficient attention.	

The New Challenge: Addressing an Unanticipated Obstacle

School improvement problems are complex because their structure is revealed through successive iterations between and within each of the five stages. Complex problem-solving is seldom a linear process. Regardless of the thoroughness of the causal inquiry stage—and Stage 2 of CCPS was very thorough at VSC—the introduction of solution strategies at Stage 3 often reveals more about the forces maintaining the status quo. That is what happened in Term 4 at VSC.

When Sam asked Keith to construct the programme for the last few weeks of school, there was little to guide him, as the previous assistant principal had left the school without handing over her knowledge or documentation. All Keith knew was that an alternative programme comprising a variety of activities was run instead of the regular timetable.

Keith saw this as problematic because attendance figures in the last two weeks of school were typically even worse than for the rest of the year, and student results suggested that high-quality opportunities to learn the school curriculum were needed throughout the school year. For Keith, teaching until the end of the year was a matter of principle.

When staff realised there would be no alternative programme, "there was an absolute explosion," with a few teachers from the senior school directing written and verbal vitriol at Keith for taking "the time they had earned at the end of the year" away from them. Some of those teachers had interpreted Keith's request for teachers in each learning domain to collaborate in covering classes as implying that they were doing nothing, were lazy, and were not valued. Keith had made this request because he was conscious of complaints about the inequitable workload at the end of the year between teachers of senior students, who had completed all their teaching, and junior school teachers, who were still marking exams, writing reports, and teaching some classes.

The strength of the reaction of some teachers is easier to understand when put in the context of a school culture that had, until the last few years, "actively discouraged kids from coming to school for the last three weeks." This year there would be many more students at school than usual because Keith had communicated the importance of student attendance till the last day of school in a message to all parents.

The response of the senior leaders to the vitriol was respectful, clear, and student centred. Sam reported receiving "some extraordinary emails, which we wrote back to. We wrote back to everyone about it, saying, 'The slight is something that you've read into this. There was no slight here. We're looking for people to act in a considered and collegial way. He [Keith] gave you an option: you can do this [organise your teaching loads] within your groups, or I can put it together and I'll tell you. You tell me what you want to do.' So actually, it was really good. It was a transparent, robust conversation with the whole staff."

The swift reaction of some teachers should have alerted senior leaders to the need to slow down and return to Stage 1 of the CCPS process to test whether teachers accepted that the alternative programme was problematic. Keith did not do so, because in his mind he already had staff commitment to solving the attendance problem and thus their commitment to addressing all its causes, including any end-of-year activities that families interpreted as relatively unimportant and therefore as legitimating their early departure on holiday.

But it was far from clear that this connection had been made by teachers in the senior school. Their agreement to the problem-solving process was done in ignorance of its implications for the alternative programme, because no one, including Keith himself, had made that connection. For teachers, solving the attendance problem was one thing, suspending the alternative programme quite another.

Keith acknowledged that his communication about the alternative programme could have been better and described himself as working hard in that area. He gave as an example an email he had sent the day before in which he had been open about the possible limitations of his own behaviour. "If you think I haven't done the right thing, then I'm sorry about that. I'll give you reasons why I did take that action, and I'll work harder to improve my practice in that area."

The new approach to the end of the school year was but one example of what Sam described as the shift to a more student-centred school culture where there was a keener sense that "moments matter, that the time we have them here is really important. And I don't think that was appreciated or understood." The last three weeks of school were made to matter more by running a Step Up programme for the Year 10 and 11 students in which students began their next year's courses. This strategy, which parents and students "were happy with," began to change community views about the educational value of the last few weeks of school at VSC.

Table 13.5 Stage 5: Evaluate Impact

CASE NARRATIVE	CCPS INDICATORS
Magda and Keith tracked the impact of the CCPS process on attendance at VSC by using the state-provided online attendance data to compare absence rates before, during, and after the intervention [5.1, 5.2]. By comparing yearlong attendance rates at two different December dates, they were able to estimate the extent to which the replacement of the alternative programme had had an impact on attendance in the last three weeks of school. Their disaggregation of the data by year level also allowed them to establish the shifts made by different student groups and determine whether those shifts had been sustained in the following year [5.3].	Leaders establish indicators for evaluating impact on student outcomes. They 5.1 plan how progress towards student outcome goals will be evaluated. 5.2 integrate collection of attendance data into management routines.

To understand more about the impact of the college's new attendance strategies on students, Magda conducted separate focus groups with eleven Year 10 students (three focus groups) and seven Year 8 students (two focus groups) [5.3]. Nine of the eleven Year 10 students had been chronically absent in the prior year (defined in Victoria as absent for 30 days or more), and all were on track in late September to reduce their annual absence days by between 50% and 75%. After explaining the purpose of the focus group, Magda showed each Year 10 student their Years 7–9 attendance data and asked for their reaction. About half "had no idea" that their absence had been so high, and the rest, while vague about the number of days they had been absent, were not surprised by the data. They were aware of a major shift in teachers' management of attendance, commenting that, "Teachers are now more on to you being at school. Rolls are being marked more and better." When these Year 10 students were asked why they were now missing far less school, they referenced preparation for national qualifications (VCE), subject choices, and new academic priorities. But underlying these reasons was a shift in the way they exercised their autonomy. Whereas previously they had chosen to skip classes with teachers they disliked, begin their holidays a week earlier than the official dates, stay at home when feeling a bit unwell, or miss school to participate in various sports tournaments, they now exercised choices with educational goals and consequences in mind. They were beginning to experience how greater attendance led to better marks and less academic stress, with these positive benefits in turn increasing their motivation to achieve their qualification and tertiary entry goals. A key trigger for this positive dynamic was their ability as Year 10 students to choose some of their subjects. It was not specific teacher practices that changed their attitude but rather the ability to choose their subjects and be taught by teachers they liked [5.3]. The seven students in Magda's Year 8 focus groups had been absent for between 11 and 25.5 days in the preceding year. As for their older counterparts, they either had no idea or only a vague notion of how many days they had been absent in Year 7. When asked why their attendance had increased, they described how the incentives and competition Keith had organised through the junior school assembly motivated them to come to school so as not to let down their peers. As one put it, "there is a little more pressure to attend now with the thermometer, and mentor teachers are checking up a lot more on unexplained absences."	5.3 draw and discuss data-based conclusions about the extent of improvement, for which students, in which classes, and possible reasons why.

(Continued)

Table 13.5 (Continued)

CASE NARRATIVE	CCPS INDICATORS
Like the Year 10 students, these Year 8 students attributed much of the shift to what amounted to improved self-management. They were now "getting more used to school and homework" and "establishing better habits and routines." Also like the Year 10 students, they described what amounted to a positive cycle of greater attendance leading to better test scores, more confidence, and therefore more desire to be at school. For some, their better self-management extended to managing sickness and mental health issues differently, because they saw that rather than personal issues being a reason to not go to school, going to school could "get their mind on other things"[5.3].	
Improved attendance rates had, in the opinion of senior leaders, contributed to teachers' greater sense of efficacy. As Sam explained, "I think, like I said, the power of what we've done with attendance is really palpable, and will ripple out in terms of teachers' belief that we can make a difference to data. And pride in that." He reflected on how interest in attendance across the school "grew and grew" and "had an impact, because suddenly it was important for us all to talk about it, and it became an item of culture in the school" [5.3].	

Reflections on the Success of CCPS at Vauxhall Secondary College

Table 13.6 indicates that in the year prior to the intervention, there was chronic average absence (defined as 30 or more days per year) at all levels except Year 7. By the beginning of December, after consistently working on the attendance problem for nine months, the intervention had led to a drop of average absence days at each year level by between 2.7 days at Year 7 and 12.4 at Year 8. The challenge of reversing the culture of sporadic attendance in the last three weeks remained, however, for despite replacing the alternative programme, absence increased in the last three weeks of school by an average of 4.5 days for Year 8, 7.6 days for Year 9, and 5.6 for Year 10 students.

Of even more significance than the gains made during the year of the CCPS intervention is evidence that the school continued to substantially improve its attendance rates in the following year. This suggests that the approach taken by school and system leaders to solving the long-standing attendance problem had shifted the beliefs and practices

Table 13.6 Average Number of Days Absent at VSC by Year Level

	PRIOR TO CCPS INTERVENTION	DURING CCPS INTERVENTION		FOLLOW-UP ONE YEAR LATER
YEAR LEVEL	YEAR TO DECEMBER 20	YEAR TO DECEMBER 1	YEAR TO DECEMBER 20	YEAR TO DECEMBER 20
7	22.3	19.6	19.6	14.7
8	31.7	19.3	23.8	21.2
9	39.4	29.2	36.8	24.7
10	31.8	26.9	32.5	28.7
11	39.9	VCE exam period[4]	34.0	27.7
12	30.7	VCE exam period	29.5	27.4
All years	32.1		28.7	23.5

[4] A comparison between December 1 and December 20 for Year 11 and Year 12 students is not possible because they are not at school during the VCE exam period. In Australia the school year begins in February and ends in early December.

of leaders, teachers, students, and parents in ways that had created a school culture where attendance mattered because it shaped the learning opportunities, well-being, and future of every student.

A complex problem has multiple strands, each of which is tightly linked to the others such that solving any one strand requires attention to its relationship with the others. This was certainly the case at Vauxhall Secondary College. While the whole problem had to be kept in mind, it was practically impossible to tackle it all at once, and that is why each of the three strands of the attendance problem—attendance management, the quality of teaching and teacher-student relationships, and community expectations and attitudes—had to be addressed somewhat separately. In doing so, it was critical, however, that leaders maintained a strategic approach by paying attention to how all three strands worked together to create and sustain the whole problem. For example, while considerable improvement had been made in the management strand of the problem, senior leaders knew that increased attendance would not lead to sustained student engagement and growth in achievement unless students' greater attendance enabled them to experience consistently high-quality teaching. That is why time and effort were put into the new instructional framework and into gaining and using students' feedback about how they

A complex problem has multiple strands, each of which is tightly linked to the others such that solving any one strand requires attention to its relationship with the others.

experienced their lessons. But there was a lot more work to be done before the fifth solution requirement—"Teachers are accountable for planning for teaching that is evidence informed, differentiated, and engaging"—could be met.

When asked at the end of the year if teachers now made stronger connections between attendance and their own teaching and relationships with students—connections that were specified in the sixth solution requirement—Keith commented, "I don't know if they'd make that strong link at the moment." At every stage of the problem-solving process, the contribution of teaching and teacher-student relationships had been less salient in staff discussion than the management of attendance.

It made sense that the school initially concentrated on attendance management, so it could get greater clarity about the scope of the problem and accurate data about the impact of its improvement strategies. But the improvement is not likely to be sustained, nor to bring educational benefits in terms of better results and qualification rates, until many more students report that interesting and engaging lessons are a primary motivator for them coming to school. That should be the next stage of the problem-solving process.

Reflections on the Contributions of Leaders' Virtues to the Success of CCPS at VSC

At the outset of the case, I described some of the relevant virtues, including knowledge, motives, and skills, that Magda, Sam, and Keith brought to the process of solving the attendance problem at VSC. This section reports their reflections on what they learned during the year-long process, including what they have still to learn and how they have shared their learning with others inside and outside the college. It also includes my own reflections on how virtues enabled their progress and how the occasional vice limited it.

Magda's Learning

When reflecting on what she had learned from using the CCPS approach at VSC, Magda contrasted her previous approach to school improvement as a SEIL—get the data, decide the focus, and then set up a small school improvement team to drive the change—with her new more inclusive and analytic approach. It was not just that she had greater analytic and collaborative skills; her skills were more virtuous because she now had a strong and internalised rationale for using and improving them. She believed that by being more analytic and collaborative, there was a far greater chance of challenging and changing the theories of action that sustained the practices that contributed to the improvement problem:

> When I think about theories of action—what we never did was challenge those. It was a classic bypass model in the past, done from our own best intentions as leaders. But we didn't really get to the core of why people were holding so tight to those long-held beliefs. And we didn't challenge them, through what we knew and learnt and what the data were saying. We just kind of went, 'Well, okay, we're going to stack this on top, and it'll be fine.' When in fact, we know that it's not.

She described how the combination of high levels of collaboration and deep causal inquiry had transformed the way she worked as a SEIL in her other schools. It was now more focused and less "scattergun." Her office colleague, who had been less confident in taking up the approach until he saw the success that Magda was having, described the contrast between the typical SEIL approach to school improvement and CCPS in very similar terms:

> Our approaches have tended to be, "Here's a problem. Let's throw solutions at it." But the idea is, let's stop that automatic response of solution strategies and actually undertake the time to do a causal enquiry, to determine our hunches, unpack them, test them through evidence. So that we can actually get down to the nitty gritty of what are the underlying causes around this identified problem.

When Magda was challenged by colleagues who questioned why she was so intensively focused on attendance when the school needed to improve in several additional areas, her answer was grounded in her strong strategic virtues. She explained,

> Ultimately, a SEIL has to pick an area that is going to have a domino effect on other areas. You've got to strategically look at what you're going to focus on. I could have focused on Year 12 VCE English, but if the kids aren't there, if the kids don't actually access that teaching, then we're back to square one. So that's what leads you back to, "Well, what's the root cause?"

Magda was sufficiently committed to her new learning that she not only completed a yearlong case in a school for which she no longer had any formal responsibility, but she did it in the context of office colleagues who had far lower commitment to CCPS than her own. When Magda arrived at the first CCPS workshop, she came with three male colleagues with whom she had collaborated, as requested by the programme designers, to select a common set of problems that they would each pursue in one of their allocated schools. One of her three colleagues moved to a different role, leaving only two as participants in the programme, and for those two, "things seemed to fizzle out."

Why was Magda able to transform her usual approach to school improvement while her two colleagues, who had experienced exactly the same learning opportunities and office context, were unable to do so? What motivated her to make those choices?

There is no doubt that Magda's leadership virtues were strong. She was strongly committed to educational purposes and saw it as her duty to help improve schools that were failing their students. When she saw the data about student achievement and attendance levels at four secondary colleges in the geographical area served by her office, her reaction was, "We have to do something." But the motivation to "do something" does not explain why she turned from driving improvement through early specification of solutions to a process that required prior collaborative causal inquiry.

She speculated that the difficulty for her colleagues in making this shift was the inevitable uncertainty and loss of control that comes with a causal inquiry approach. The typical "Here are the solutions" approach to improvement does not work when your solutions should reflect what you have learned about the deep causal drivers of the problem. In Magda's words, this was true "because you can't go in with the end in mind. As much as we'd kind of like to, you've got to be open to learn." In saying this, Magda was highlighting the importance of tolerating uncertainty, of having a low need for closure, and of being open-minded about what the data might reveal.

A second factor that may explain Magda's greater willingness to experiment with collaborative problem-solving is that she was less experienced with the approach typically taken by SEILs to school improvement than her colleagues. Their greater experience meant they held more ingrained theories of action about how to do their school improvement work. She explained that her colleagues had experienced a lot of "Here's an initiative. Make sure it's in schools. Lot of top-down stuff. That's what they're used to." In contrast, she described the "magic" of teachers collectively naming what they think is wrong and why, and how that process motivates them to get involved in testing their beliefs.

Magda's commitment to being an educational leader, in its strong sense of educating others, was apparent throughout the yearlong problem-solving process at VSC. She taught others by providing principled rationales for each step of the CCPS approach, seeking consent and collaboration at every step, and making the process very concrete through her modelling and feedback.

Magda's leadership virtues, as seen in her willingness to lead by offering her ideas and her support, were apparent in contexts that went well beyond VSC. She saw her role as inducting and enabling other leaders to solve the many student outcome problems that were apparent in their data. From an early stage, she had shared her learning and expertise with her network and office colleagues:

> I've done another problem-solving process with [another school] and it's so easy now because they've already been through it once. They named the cause and wanted to carry on through the process. And that's what I want. I want people like Keith to do their own causal enquiry around "Why are the staff absences so hard?" I want one of my other schools to do their own causal enquiry around "Why has there been a decrease in the maths data when it was chugging along so well? What's happened for it to go down?" That's what this is about—it's training schools to be able to do it themselves. We're not the lifesavers every time there's a problem with data. They have to be able to do it themselves.

Magda's efforts to share the approach she was using with office colleagues and school leaders in her network appeared to be paying off. Magda described how the language of causal inquiry became more common:

> To hear people start using the language . . . they talk about schools wanting to find out what are the causes of the problem. It's the language that's coming into SEIL talk when we're talking about schools now. It's quite empowering. And even the area director, she says it gets into the 'wicked problems.' That's really good language.

Her enthusiasm about the approach, combined with her willingness to share her VSC strategies and attendance data with office colleagues, inspired them to give it a go themselves.

Sam's Learning

Given that Sam delegated most of the work of improving attendance to his assistant principal, there is far less to say about what Sam learned through the CCPS process. He believed, however, that he had learned more effective problem-solving strategies and, in broad terms, accurately described the links between CCPS and the analytic virtues involved in testing and improving the quality of a leader's thinking:

> [CCPS] is really great because it stops you from knee-jerking solutions, which won't be effective, and it means you spend some time really thinking about the complexities and the different possible influences on the problem. And it actually means that you get a deeper knowledge of your organisation and your community because of that. Again, it's about improving the quality of your thinking.

Keith's Learning

In reflecting on what he had learned about school improvement during the yearlong attendance project (Table 13.7), Keith's first thoughts were about integrity—about doing what was promised even when it proved difficult.

Table 13.7 Interview Extract 1

Keith	So, yeah, energy and drive are really important. Consistency of process as well, that you don't waver. . . . It's just being consistent every single week. Never not doing it. Like maybe on a Thursday when I've had something on and I haven't delivered the data, I've made sure I was in early on the Friday to make sure the data were there ready for that meeting.
Viviane	You said you're going to do it, so you do it. That's sort of walking the talk.
Keith	Absolutely, yeah. I'm very, very big on that, and my leadership style is that and giving the tools to support the staff do the work. And the tool in this case is the data.

As discussed in Chapter 6, leadership is about empowering others so they learn and can help to sustain and embed improvement. When I asked Keith about the sustainability of his single-handed leadership of the absence initiative, he acknowledged he had not set up a school improvement team because he thought he had the skills and time to do it himself. Furthermore, it was important to him to learn the work himself before asking others to do it.

He was aware, though, that his single-handed leadership of the new attendance strategies was not sustainable and that his leadership in the following year needed to be different. Table 13.8 is how he anticipated he could hand over the weekly analysis of the attendance data to the year-level coordinators:

Table 13.8 Interview Extract 2

Keith	And even like the way I collect the data on a Thursday night, I could easily show the year-level coordinator. From day one next year, say, "The expectation is that you strip the data out of the system on a Thursday night." I know it takes less than four minutes to strip it out, rearrange it, put it into the tables, colour code the 100 percenters, colour code the less [inaudible] percenters, and send it to the staff. I know it takes less than four minutes each week.
Viviane	For people who have your skill.
Keith	But it's not difficult. But yeah, it takes me just under 20 minutes to do all six, or just under 20 minutes actually. If I just spread that around, I've just got half an hour back every week, and it's much more self-sustaining.

I challenged Keith's certainty and precision about the amount of time the task required because I was concerned that his considerable knowledge and skill in mathematics and data analysis could reduce his empathy for any year-level leaders who were less confident and capable than he was. He needed to be open to the possibility that his predictions about what the handover would involve could be mistaken. Handover could require active mentoring, not just communicating expectations.

Keith also reflected on his use of the problem-solving process he had been taught by Magda. He drew an analogy between the causal inquiry stage of problem-solving and hypothesis testing:

> I'm a science teacher from all my years. It's made it into a more hypothesis testing process. It's become a kind of science project, which I enjoy, and it makes sense to me, and it's my thinking process. So, yeah, it's been the template for it, and the support for it.

Like Magda and Sam, Keith described how he had used the process to interrupt the "quick fix" that had happened in so many of his conversations with staff and parents.

> It's really supported me in recent conversations. I sat in this office recently, and I was working with a year-level coordinator and two parents. And as the parents were listing their problems, he [the year level coordinator] was almost immediately bouncing back solutions. And I said, "Just wait. Let's just hear what's happening here first."

The school's new leaders were motivated by internalised standards of good practice that led them to evaluate the current situation as unacceptable.

Keith was now sufficiently expert in the theory and practice of CCPS to transfer his learning from a yearlong school improvement project to brief conversations about more everyday problems.

SUMMARY

This case illustrates how the leadership, problem-solving, and interpersonal virtues of school and system leaders contributed to the success of a school improvement effort. Leaders did the right work by finally addressing the attendance problem that reduced students' opportunities for deep learning by approximately 30% . While no one leader was perfect, they did the right work the right way, using their combined virtues to make significant progress in resolving the problem.

Leadership virtues were evident in the sense of duty and responsibility that two new leaders brought to the effort. While school leaders were accountable to an external review panel, such accountability had failed to make a difference to past attendance rates. The school's new leaders were motivated by internalised standards of good practice that led them to evaluate the current situation as unacceptable. They were also confident, based on their knowledge and prior experience, that they could, in collaboration with teachers, close the gap between the current and desired attendance rates. The system leader in particular embraced her role as leader of other leaders, explicitly teaching the rationale and skills required to systematically work through the CCPS process.

A cluster of problem-solving virtues enabled the leaders to interrupt the school's prior "quick fix" problem-solving strategies and model and teach the more deliberate and systematic inquiry process required for CCPS. Strategic virtues were evident in the leaders' ability to provide compelling educational arguments about why attendance should be given priority and to maintain the focus on resolving it for the intervention year and beyond.

Analytic virtues were evident in the systematic inquiry process the leaders designed, the purpose of which was not only to find the causes of absence but also, in so doing, to test the validity of teachers' long-held beliefs about its causes. Analytic virtues were also seen in the constant use of data to monitor progress and make the required adjustments—virtues that were greatly enabled by sophisticated online databases that the state took responsibility for providing to all its educational leaders.

Imaginative virtues were evident in the way leaders modelled attention to the set of solution requirements and made constant reference to them when evaluating suggested solution strategies.

The case includes multiple manifestations of leaders' interpersonal virtues. Courage and integrity were seen in the direct, clear, and evidence-based way the two leaders communicated the seriousness and importance of the absence problem. Empathy was also apparent in the nonblaming manner in which these messages were communicated and in the ability of the system leader to learn from students themselves about the reasons for their absence.

Respect for teachers and families underpinned the highly collaborative problem-solving process. That collaboration broke down, however, as the assistant principal attempted to maintain improved attendance in the face of an unanticipated suspension of the regular timetable in the final weeks of the school year. Ensuring high-quality teaching throughout the year was on the agenda for the next round of CCPS.

REFLECTION AND ACTION

1. Discuss a recent school improvement project you have been involved in. How did the process leaders took compare with the five-stage CCPS process undertaken by Keith and Magda?
   a. Were you clear about the specific teaching and learning problem you were trying to solve? (Stage 1)
   b. Did you inquire into the school-based causes of the problem before introducing solution strategies such as new programmes? (Stage 2)
   c. Did you agree on a set of solution requirements before discussing what the "fix" would be? (Stage 3)
   d. How systematically did you monitor implementation of your solution strategies? (Stage 4)
   e. What evidence did you have of the impact of your efforts on the original teaching and learning problem? (Stage 5)
2. Discuss the reasons for any gaps between the CCPS model and the approach taken by the leaders of the improvement project you discussed.
3. What shifts need to be made to ensure greater success in future projects?

CONCLUSION

Conclusion 14

In this final chapter I address some of the questions that I have been asked by colleagues and practitioners while writing this book. I hope that my answers to their questions reinforce some of my key messages and elaborate on how educational leaders can learn to be more virtuous.

1. *You have devoted a whole chapter to discussion of the purposes of education. Do you think that this should be given more emphasis in leadership development?*

   Yes, I do, because pursuit of the proper purposes of education constitutes the right work for educational leaders. Deep knowledge of educational purposes enables leaders to make strategic choices about how to spend their time, and to question mandates and activities that distract from those purposes.

   With deep understanding of the proper purposes, leaders can detect ways in which those purposes are being undermined or misunderstood. For example, in some high schools, the autonomy purpose is misunderstood as giving senior students considerable choice about what to study and when and where to study. But true autonomy, in the educational sense, requires more than giving students choice. In addition, it requires that students have enough knowledge to make informed choices and enough self-mastery to pursue their choices despite doubts and setbacks (Winch, 2002). Only when those three conditions are met is the purpose of developing self-regulated autonomous persons likely to be achieved.

2. *There are several chapters on the science of teaching and learning. Do you want to see more emphasis on that science in leadership development?*

   Yes, I do, because the science of teaching and learning tells us how students learn and how to teach in ways that promote the sort of deep learning that is required by modern curricula. This knowledge provides important guidance on how to achieve the proper purposes of education. Since much of this science is recent, it should not be assumed that leaders are sufficiently familiar with it to use it as a standard against which they can evaluate and improve teaching and learning in their contexts. Research is needed on just how knowledgeable leaders are about this science.

3. *Doing the right work the right way sounds very prescriptive. Is it?*

It is the ethical duty of educational leaders to pursue the proper purposes of education, and the science of learning and teaching should be at the heart of how they perform their role.

Yes, it is prescriptive, because all members of professional bodies are expected to be ethical, and ethics is by definition prescriptive. It is the ethical duty of educational leaders to pursue the proper purposes of education, and the science of learning and teaching should be at the heart of how they perform their role. That is what I call doing the right work. It is also prescriptive because I want them to do the right work in the right way—that is, in a virtuous way. Beyond those two broad principles (do one's duty and do it in virtuous ways), there is little prescription, because virtuous practice is responsive to context. The details of virtuous practice are not specifiable in advance of knowledge of contextual requirements. That is why I have provided a detailed account of what context is and of the steps involved in taking context into account. Leaders are compelled at every step to think for themselves about what the circumstances demand (Aristotle/Thomson, 2004).

4. *Is being a virtuous educational leader the same thing as being a virtuous person?*

This question is hotly debated by philosophers (Swanton, 2016). My view is that being a good person and being a good leader are completely compatible, but they are not the same thing. In my discussion of virtues (Chapter 6), I argue that virtues need to be tailored to the requirements of the role. For example, while the virtues of a good person include empathy, the empathy of educational leaders is tailored to the specific requirements of the role. Their empathy is manifest in their nonjudgmental inquiries into their colleagues' experience of their work and in their sincere attempts to help them meet their professional aspirations. In doing so, they may become aware of personal issues that are preventing a teacher from carrying out their professional responsibilities, but their empathy should not lead them to become the counsellor of such staff or to sacrifice the interests of the students of such teachers. That is just one example of how the basic empathy of a good person is tailored to the requirements of the role of educational leader.

5. *What type of leadership development would be required to develop more virtuous educational leaders?*

   Since the general characteristics of effective professional development for educators have been discussed in Chapter 3, I confine my answer to the particular features required for the development of virtue.

   a. The first requirement is a greater focus on leadership character in the selection, induction, and development of educational leaders. Before such a focus can be established, system leaders need to answer the question "What sort of persons do we want our educational leaders to be?" I have answered this question by arguing for the leadership, problem-solving, and interpersonal virtues that I believe are central to excellent performance of the role. A stronger focus on character implies considerable emphasis on the motives and reasoning of leaders in addition to their knowledge and skills.

   b. A second requirement is deep knowledge of what virtues are in general, and of those specific virtues that are relevant to the role. Deep knowledge, combined with practical wisdom, enables leaders to discern how to be virtuous and responsive to the particular requirements of a situation.

   c. A third requirement is personal commitment to being a better leader—a commitment that is fostered by reflection and safe discussion of the gap between the leader I currently am and the leader I should be. The gap can be closed by setting "be" goals that are explicit about increasing relevant virtues and reducing the associated vices, and by pursuing "do" goals that are linked to the "be" goals. (Chapter 5).

   d. A fourth requirement is a strong focus on the reasons for leaders' actions. This focus develops virtue because virtuous leaders do things for the right reasons, and articulation of reasons is a prerequisite for the evaluation of actions. For educational leaders, right reasons are nearly always linked to students' learning and well-being. Skill is needed, therefore, in articulating and evaluating the educational reasons for decisions. In my experience, lack of relevant educational knowledge and habitual reference to policy and regulation are key reasons why educational leaders fail to provide educational grounds for their decisions. And since one cannot be virtuous without relevant knowledge, gaining such knowledge is an integral part of virtue development.

e. Since virtues are evident in practice, a fifth requirement for learning to be more virtuous is rich opportunities to practise followed by evidence-based reflection. The relevant evidence is the thoughts and motivations that produced the behaviour of the leader in the specific situation. That is why I have included so many excerpts of leaders' speech and thoughts in this book. Without those two types of evidence, this would be a book about virtues rather than a book about how to be more virtuous.

f. Examination of the context that surrounds specific leadership practices is a sixth requirement. The excellence of a leader's response cannot be evaluated without knowing the context, for it is the excellence of the integration of contextual requirements that determines the virtuousness of the leader's response. When professional learning opportunities address leaders' on-the-job challenges, participants can describe how they have understood and responded to those contextual requirements and, if needed, rethink their interpretations and responses.

The excellence of a leader's response cannot be evaluated without knowing the context, for it is the excellence of the integration of contextual requirements that determines the virtuousness of the leader's response.

6. *Is becoming more virtuous as a leader a matter of individual development? What about the systems and organisations in which leaders work? What role does institutional and organisational culture play in shaping character?*

   While I have acknowledged throughout that individually virtuous leaders need virtue-enhancing institutional cultures in order to thrive, I have devoted little space to how such cultures are developed. My hope is that others will be inspired by this book to take up the challenge of describing such cultures and, more importantly, of articulating a theory and practice of how to transform virtue-inhibiting cultures into virtue-enhancing ones. There is something of a chicken-and-egg problem involved here, for individual leaders who lack the requisite virtues will not be able to envisage, let alone enact, virtue-enhancing reforms. On the other hand, expecting leaders to develop virtuous practice in virtue-inhibiting cultures can be a bridge too far.

   A way out of the conundrum, as is so often the case, is to avoid abstract debate about individual versus system influences and go back to specifics. The Vauxhall school case (Chapter 13) is an example of how sufficiently virtuous individuals can transform a culture that was defensive with respect to the long-standing problem of poor attendance and achievement. Despite a culture of blame, nonlearning, and pessimism about improvement, leaders were able to model and build a new nondefensive learning culture through a combination of their own character and powerful problem-solving strategies. If leaders cannot or will not challenge virtue-inhibiting cultures, then who will?

Perhaps the most important requirement in taking up this transformative challenge is that of virtuous courage. In virtue-inhibiting cultures, there are often strong implicit or explicit prohibitions on certain types of critique. Underperformance of teachers is not discussable except in the car park; fear of being culturally inappropriate silences those who want to question what is being done in the name of equity; fear of being further stereotyped silences teachers who repeatedly find themselves unsupported in their championing of marginalised students; and conflict-averse leaders sacrifice student well-being and learning because they fear damaging relationship with colleagues. Challenging such cultures requires all the virtuous courage a leader can muster. But the good news is that with greater skill comes greater ability to envisage and enact virtuous ways of challenging such cultures.

7. *How do you know whether or not you are a virtuous leader?*

It can be very hard to judge one's own character, and while a colleague's perceptions are likely to be more accurate than one's self-evaluation, they too may prove inaccurate. So, what to do? For myself, I don't think generalised evaluations of overall leadership character are very useful. There are so many different virtues manifested in so many different ways across so many different contexts that overall judgments provide little guidance about what, if anything, needs to improve.

Rather than focus on overall virtuousness, it is more fruitful for leaders to focus on the situations in which they suspect they have not been virtuous. I can often identify those situations from my negative emotional reactions—from my feelings of defensiveness, impatience, frustration, or disappointment in the ways I have treated others. I can then reflect on how I thought about and behaved in those situations. Why was I feeling defensive, and how did that feeling influence what I did or did not say? Having identified my defensive reasoning and behaviour, I can then reframe my thinking so I can be more open to others' views rather than defend myself against them.

With repeated analysis of specific nonvirtuous responses, leaders' overall virtuousness is likely to increase as they become more knowledgeable about virtues and more skilled in thinking and acting in virtuous ways across a wider range of situations. In short, virtuous character develops by reflecting on why our behaviour has fallen short and striving to do better next time. Perhaps the key to being a more virtuous educational leader is really wanting to be so.

Perhaps the key to being a more virtuous educational leader is really wanting to be so.

References

Absolum, M. (2006). *Clarity in the classroom.* Hodder Education.

Allen, D., Roegman, R., & Hatch, T. (2015). Investigating discourses for administrators' learning within instructional rounds. *Educational Management Administration & Leadership, 44*(5), 837–852. https://doi.org/10.1177/1741143215574507

Annas, J. (2011). *Intelligent virtue.* Oxford University Press.

Argyris, C. (1976). Theories of action that inhibit individual learning. *American Psychologist, 31*(9), 638–654. https://doi.org/10.1037/0003-066X.31.9.638

Argyris, C. (1982). *Reasoning, learning and action: Individual and organizational.* Jossey-Bass.

Argyris, C. (1990). *Overcoming organizational defenses: Facilitating organizational learning.* Boston, MA: Allyn and Bacon.

Argyris, C. (2003). A life full of learning. *Organization Studies, 24*(7), 1178–1192. https://doi.org/10.1177/01708406030247009

Argyris, C., & Schon, D. A. (1974). *Theory in practice: Increasing professional effectiveness.* Jossey-Bass.

Argyris, C., & Schon, D. A. (1996). *Organizational learning II: Theory, method and practice.* Addison Wesley.

Aristotle. (2004). *The Nicomachean ethics* (J. A. K. Thomson, Trans.). Penguin Books. (Original work published ca. 350 BCE)

Australian Institute for Teaching and School Leadership. (2014). *Australian professional standard for principals and leadership profiles.* Education Services Australia.

Bargh, J. A., Gollwitzer, P., & Oettingen, G. (2010). Motivation. In S. T. Fiske, D. T. Gilbert, & G. Lindzey (Eds.), *Handbook of social psychology* (5th ed., Vol. 1, pp. 268–316). John Wiley and Sons.

Becker, M. C., & Lazaric, N. (Eds.). (2009). *Organizational routines: Advancing empirical research.* Edward Elgar.

Berliner, D. C. (1987). Simple views of effective teaching and a simple theory of classroom instruction. In D. Berliner & B. Rosenshine (Ed.), *Talks to teachers* (pp. 93–110). Random House.

Berliner, D. C. (1990). What's all the fuss about instructional time? http://courses.ed.asu.edu/berliner/readings/fuss/fuss.htm

Biesta, G. (2009). Good education in an age of measurement: On the need to reconnect with the question of purpose in education. *Educational Assessment, Evaluation & Accountability, 21*(1), 33–46. https//doi.org/10.1007/s11092-008-9064-9

Biesta, G. J. (2020). Risking ourselves in education: Qualification, socialisation and subjectification revisited. *Educational Theory, 70*(1), 89–104.

Bransford, J. D., Brown, A. L., & Cocking, R. R. (Eds.). (2000). *How people learn: Brain, mind, experience, and school* (Expanded ed.). National Academy Press.

Bransford, J., Darling-Hammond, L., & LePage, P. (2005). Introduction. In L. Darling-Hammond & J. Bransford (Eds.), *Preparing teachers for a changing world* (pp. 1–39). Jossey-Bass.

Bridges, E. M. (1992). *The incompetent teacher* (Rev ed.). Falmer Press.

Bryk, A. S., & Schneider, B. L. (2002). *Trust in schools: A core resource for improvement.* Russell Sage Foundation.

Bryk, A. S., & Schneider, B. L. (2003). Trust in schools: A core resource for school reform. *Educational Leadership, 60*(6), 40.

Bush, T., Bell, L., & Middlewood, D. (Eds.). (2019). *Principles of educational leadership and management* (3rd ed.). SAGE.

Cameron, M., & Lovett, S. (2015). Sustaining the commitment and realising the potential of highly promising teachers. *Teachers and Teaching, 21*(2), 150–163.

Campbell, J. P. (2013). Leadership, the old, the new and the timeless: A commentary. In M. G. Rumsey (Ed.), *The Oxford handbook of leadership* (pp. 401–419). Oxford University Press.

City, E. A., Elmore, R. F., Fiarman, S. E., & Teitel, L. (2009). *Instructional rounds in education.* Harvard Education Press.

Ciulla, J. B. (2004). Ethics and leadership effectiveness. In J. Antonakis, A. T. Cianciolo, & R. J. Sternberg (Eds.), *The nature of leadership* (pp. 302–327). Sage.

Ciulla, J. B. (2012). Ethics and effectiveness: The nature of good leadership In D. V. Day & J. Antonakis (Eds.), *The nature of leadership* (2nd ed., pp. 508–542). Sage

Clarke, T. (2020). Children's wellbeing and their academic achievement: The dangerous discourse of "trade-offs" in education. *Theory and Research in Education, 18*(3), 263–294. https://doi.org/10.1177/1477878520980197

Cohen, D. K., & Mehta, J. D. (2017). Why reform sometimes succeeds: Understanding the conditions that produce reforms that last. *American Educational Research Journal, 0*(0), 0002831217700078. https://doi.org/10.3102/0002831217700078

Darling-Hammond, L., Flook, L., Cook-Harvey, C., Barron, B., & Osher, D. (2019). Implications for educational practice of the science of learning and development. *Applied Developmental Science,* 1–44. https://doi.org/10.1080/10888691.2018.1537791

Datnow, A. (2000). Power and politics in the adoption of school reform models. *Educational Evaluation and Policy Analysis, 22*(4), 357–374. https://doi.org/10.3102/01623737022004357

Deans for Impact. (2015). *The science of learning.* Author.

Deci, E. L., Koestner, R., Ryan, R. M., & Cameron, J. (2001). Extrinsic rewards and intrinsic motivation in education: Reconsidered once again. *Review of Educational Research, 71*(1), 1–51.

De Dreu, C. K. W. (2010). Social conflict: The emergence and consequences of struggle and negotiation. In S. T. Fiske, D. T. Gilbert, & G. Lindzey (Eds.), *Handbook of social psychology* (5th ed., Vol. 2, pp. 983–1023). John Wiley.

Department for Education. (2014). *The national curriculum in England: Framework document.* Author. https://www.gov.uk/government/organisations/department-for-education

Desimone, L. M., & Garet, M. S. (2015). Best practices in teachers' professional development in the United States. *Psychology, Society, & Education, 7*(3), 252–263.

Dewey, J. (1922). *Human nature and conduct: An introduction to social psychology.* Henry Holt.

Dillon, R. S. (2021). Respect. In E. N. Zalta (Ed.), The Stanford encyclopedia of philosophy (Summer 2021 ed.). https://plato.stanford.edu/archives/sum2021/entries/respect/

Doyle, W. (1983). Academic work. *Review of Educational Research, 53*(2), 159–199.

Doyle, W. (1986). Classroom organization and management. In M. C. Wittrock (Ed.), *Handbook of research on teaching* (3rd ed., pp. 392–431). American Educational Research Association.

Doyle, W. (2006). Ecological approaches to classroom management. In C. S. Weinstein & C. M. Evertson (Eds.), *Handbook of classroom management: Research, practice and contemporary issues* (pp. 97–126). Routledge.

Dunning, D. (2012). Judgment and decision making. In S. T. Fiske & C. N. Macrae (Eds.), *The Sage handbook of social cognition* (pp. 251–272). Sage.

Elmore, R. F. (2004). *School reform from the inside out: Policy, practice, and performance.* Harvard Education Press.

Euwema, M. C., Van de Vliert, E., & Bakker, A. B. (2003). Substantive and relational effectiveness of organizational conflict behavior. *The International Journal of Conflict Management, 14*(2), 119–139.

Favero, N., Meier, K. J., & O'Toole, J. L. J. (2016). Goals, trust, participation, and feedback: Linking internal management with performance outcomes. *Journal of Public Administration Research and Theory, 26*(2), 327–343. https://doi.org/10.1093/jopart/muu044

Fay, B. (1987). *Critical social science: Liberation and its limits.* Cornell University Press.

Firestone, W. A. (2014). Teacher evaluation policy and conflicting theories of motivation. *Educational Researcher, 43*(2), 100–107.

Foot, P. (2002). *Virtues and vices and other essays in moral philosophy.* Oxford University Press.

Fulmer, S. M., & Turner, J. C. (2014). The perception and implementation of challenging instruction by middle school teachers. *Elementary School Journal, 114*(3), 303–326. https://doi.org/10.1086/674053

Gates, S. M., Baird, M. D., Master, B. K., & Chavez-Herrerias, E. (2019). *Principal pipelines: A feasible, affordable, and effective way for districts to improve schools.* RAND Corporation.

Gates, S. M., Kaufman, J. H., Doan, S., Tuma, A. P., & Kim, D. (2020). *Taking stock of principal pipelines: What public school districts report doing and what they want to do to improve school leadership.* RAND Corporation.

Goddard, R. D., Salloum, S. J., & Berebitsky, D. (2009). Trust as a mediator of the relationships between poverty, racial composition, and academic achievement: Evidence from Michigan's public elementary schools. *Educational Administration Quarterly, 45*(2), 292–311. https://doi.org/10.1177/0013161x08330503

Goldring, E., Grissom, J., Neumerski, C. M., Blissett, R., Murphy, J., & Porter, A. (2020). Increasing principals' time on instructional leadership: Exploring the SAM® process. [Instructional leadership]. *Journal of Educational Administration, 58*(1), 19–37. http://dx.doi.org/10.1108/JEA-07–2018–0131

Goud, N. H. (2005). Courage: Its nature and development. *The Journal of Humanistic Counseling, Education and Development, 44*(1), 102–116.

Graesser, A. C., Fiore, S. M., Greiff, S., Andrews-Todd, J., Foltz, P. W., & Hesse, F. (2018). Advancing the science of collaborative problem-solving. *Psychological Science in the Public Interest, 19*(2), 59–92.

Grainger, S., & Byres, J. (2010). *Do sweat the small stuff!!! A case study of one school's improvement journey.*

Grissom, J. A., & Loeb, S. (2011). Triangulating principal effectiveness. *American Educational Research Journal, 48*(5), 1091–1123. https://doi.org/10.3102/0002831211402663

Grissom, J. A., Loeb, S., & Master, B. (2013). Effective instructional time use for school leaders: Longitudinal evidence from observations of principals. *Educational Researcher, 42*(8), 433–444. https://doi.org/10.3102/0013189X13510020

Hallinger, P. (2005). Instructional leadership and the school principal: A passing fancy that refuses to fade away. *Leadership and Policy in Schools, 4*(3), 221–239.

Hamilton, A., Reeves, D., Clinton, J., & Hattie, J. (2022). *Building to impact.* Corwin.

Hammerness, K., Darling-Hammond, L., Bransford, J., Berliner, D. C., Cochran-Smith, M., McDonald, M., & Zeichner, K. (2005). How teachers learn and develop. In L. Darling-Hammond & J. Bransford (Eds.), *Preparing teachers for a changing world* (pp. 358–389). Jossey-Bass.

Hand, M. (2014). Aims, concept of. In D. C. Phillips (Ed.), *Encyclopedia of educational theory and philosophy* (Vol. 1, pp. 30–32). SAGE.

Hannah, S. T., Sweeney, P. J., & Lester, P. B. (2010). The courageous mind-set: A dynamic personality system approach to courage. In C. L. S. Pury & S. J. Lopez (Eds.), *The psychology of courage: Modern research on an ancient virtue* (pp. 125–148). American Psychological Association.

Hare, W. (2003). The ideal of open-mindedness and its place in education. *Journal of Thought, 38*(2), 3–10.

Hart, W., Albarracin, D., Eagly, A., Brechan, I., Lindberg, M. J., & Merrill, L. (2009). Feeling validated versus being correct: A meta-analysis of selective exposure of information. *Psychological Bulletin, 135*(4), 555–588.

Hatano, G., & Oura, Y. (2003). Commentary: Reconceptualizing school learning using insight from expertise research. *Educational Researcher, 32*(8), 26–29. https://doi.org/10.3102/0013189x032008026

Herman, J. (2014). Opportunity to learn. In R. Gunstone (Ed.), *Encyclopedia of Science Education* (pp. 1–4). Springer.

Higham, R., Earley, P., Coldwell, M., Stevens, A., & Brown, C. (2015). *New pathways into headship?* Retrieved from http://shura.shu.ac.uk/10832/1/RR332A_New_Pathways_into_Headship_2015.pdf

Hochbein, C., Mahone, A., & Vanderbeck, S. (2021). A systematic review of principal time use research. *Journal of Educational Administration, 59*(2), 215–232. https://doi.org/10.1108/JEA-09–2019–0163

Kahneman, D. (2011). *Thinking fast and slow.* Farrar, Straus and Giroux.

Kaya, M., & Erdem, C. (2021). Students' well-being and academic achievement: A meta-analysis study. *Child Indicators Research, 14*(5), 1743–1767. https://doi.org/10.1007/s12187–021–09821–4

Keltner, D., & Lerner, J. S. (2010). Emotion. In S. T. Fiske, D. T. Gilbert, & G. Lindzey (Eds.), *Handbook of social psychology* (Vol. 1, pp. 317–352). John Wiley and Sons.

Kraft, M. A., & Gilmour, A. F. (2017). Revisiting *The Widget Effect*: Teacher evaluation reforms and the distribution of teacher effectiveness. *Educational Researcher, 46*(5), 234–249. https://doi.org/10.3102/0013189X17718797

Kruglanski, A. W., & Sheveland, A. (2012). Thinkers' personalities: On individual differences in the processes of sense making. In S. T. Fiske & C. N. Macrae (Eds.), *The Sage handbook of social cognition* (pp. 474–495). Sage.

Latham, G. P., & Locke, E. A. (2006). Enhancing the benefits and overcoming the pitfalls of goal setting. *Organizational Dynamics, 35*(4), 332–340.

Latham, G. P., & Locke, E. A. (2007). New developments and directions for goal setting research. *European Psychologist, 12*(4), 290–300.

Lee, S. W. (2018). Pulling back the curtain: Revealing the cumulative importance of high-performing, highly qualified teachers on students' educational outcome. *Educational Evaluation and Policy Analysis, 40*(3), 359–381. https://doi.org/10.3102/0162373718769379

Le Fevre, D. M., & Robinson, V. M. J. (2015). The interpersonal challenges of instructional leadership: Principals' effectiveness in conversations about performance issues. *Educational Administration Quarterly, 51*(1), 58–95. https://doi.org/10.1177/0013161x13518218

Leithwood, K. A. (2012). *The Ontario leadership framework: With a discussion of the research foundations*. Retrieved from http://www.yrdsb.com/Careers/Documents/Ontario%20Leadership%20Framework.pdf

Lencioni, P. M. (2002). Make your values mean something. *Harvard Business Review, 80*(7), 113–117.

Lipshitz, R., Klein, G., Orasanu, J., & Salas, E. (2001). Taking stock of naturalistic decision making. *Journal of Behavioral Decision Making, 14*(5), 331–352. https://doi.org/10.1002/bdm.381

Louis, K. S., & Robinson, V. M. J. (2012). External mandates and instructional leadership: School leaders as mediating agents. *Journal of Educational Administration, 50*(5), 629–665. https://doi.org/10.1108/09578231211249853

MacAllister, J. (2016). What should educational institutions be for? *British Journal of Educational studies, 64*(3), 375–391. https://doi.org/10.1080/00071005.2015.1131811

MacIntyre, A., & Dunne, J. (2002). Alasdair MacIntyre on education: In dialogue with Joseph Dunne. *Journal of Philosophy of Education, 36*(1), 1–19. https://doi.org/10.1111/1467-9752.00256

Martin, R. (2009). *The opposable mind: Winning through integrative thinking*. Harvard Business Press.

Marzano, R. J., Waters, T., & McNulty, B. (2005). *School leadership that works: From research to results*. ASCD and McREL.

May, H., & Supovitz, J. A. (2011). The scope of principal efforts to improve instruction. *Educational Administration Quarterly, 47*(2), 332–352. https://doi.org/10.1177/0013161x10383411

May, W. F. (1994). The virtues in a professional setting. In K. Fulford, G. Gillett, & J. Soskice (Eds.), *Medicine and moral reasoning* (pp. 75–90). Cambridge University Press.

Mazutis, D., & Slawinski, N. (2008). Leading organizational learning through authentic dialogue. *Management Learning, 39*(4), 437.

McArthur, P. W. (2014). Advocacy and inquiry. In D. Coghlan & M. Brydon-Miller (Eds.), *The Sage encyclopedia of action research* (pp. 27–29). Sage.

McLelland, D. C., & Burnham, D. (1976). Power is the great motivator. *Harvard Business Review, 54*(2), 100–110.

Mestry, R. (2019). Resource management In T. Bush, L. Bell, & D. Middlewood (Eds.), *Principles of educational leadership and management* (3rd ed., pp. 149–164). Sage.

Meyer, F., Le Fevre, D. M., & Robinson, V. M. J. (2017). How leaders communicate their vulnerability: Implications for trust building. *International Journal of Educational Management, 31*(2), 221–235. https://doi.org/10.1108/IJEM-11–2015–0150

Miles, K. H., & Frank, S. (2008). *The strategic school: Making the most of people time and money*. Corwin.

Ministry of Education. (2018). *Statement of intent 2018–2023*. Available from https://www.education.govt.nz

Ministry of Education and Research. (2019). *Core curriculum: Values and principles for primary and secondary education*. Ministry of Education and Research. Available from https://www.regjeringen.no

Minor, E. C., Desimone, L., Caines, L. J., & Hochberg, E. D. (2016). Insights on how to shape teacher learning policy: The role of teacher content knowledge in explaining differential effects of professional development. *Education Policy Analysis Archives, 24*(61), 1–34.

Mintrop, H. (2012). Bridging accountability obligations, professional values and (perceived) student needs with integrity. *Journal of Educational Administration, 50*(5), 695–726. https://doi.org/10.1108/09578231211249871

Mintrop, R., & Zumpe, E. (2019). Solving real-life problems of practice and education leaders' school improvement mind-set. *American Journal of Education, 125*(3), 295–344. https://doi.org/10.1086/702733

Mintzberg, H. (2009). *Managing*. Berrett-Koehler.

Muijs, D., Kyriakides, L., van der Werf, G., Creemers, B., Timperley, H., & Earl, L. (2014). State of the art—Teacher effectiveness and professional learning. *School Effectiveness and School Improvement, 25*(2), 231–256. https://doi.org/10.1080/09243453.2014.885451

Mumford, M. D., Gibson, C., Giorgini, V., & Mecca, J. (2014). Leading for creativity: People, products and systems. In D. V. Day (Ed.), *The Oxford handbook of leadership and organizations* (pp. 757–782). Oxford University Press.

Murphy, J., Hallinger, P., & Heck, R. H. (2013). Leading via teacher evaluation: The case of the missing clothes? *Educational Researcher, 42*(6), 349–354. https://doi.org/10.3102/0013189x13499625

National Academies of Sciences, Engineering, and Medicine. (2018). *How people learn II: Learners, contexts, and cultures*. National Academies Press.

National Policy Board for Educational Administration. (2015). *Professional Standards for Educational Leaders 2015*. Author.

National Research Council. (2012). *Education for life and work: Developing transferable knowledge and skills in the 21st century*. National Academies Press.

Nelson, R. R. (2008). Factors affecting the power of technological paradigms. *Industrial and Corporate Change, 17*(3), 485–497.

Nickles, T. (1981). What is a problem that we might solve it? *Synthese, 47*(1), 85–118.

Nuthall, G. (2007). *The hidden lives of learners.* NZCER Press.

Nye, B., Konstantopoulos, S., & Hedges, L. V. (2004). How large are teacher effects? *Educational Evaluation and Policy Analysis, 26*, 237–257.

Oc, B. (2018). Contextual leadership: A systematic review of how contextual factors shape leadership and its outcomes. *Leadership Quarterly, 29*(1), 218–235. https://doi.org/10.1016/j.leaqua.2017.12.004

OECD. (2005). The definition and selection of key competencies: Executive summary. http://www.oecd.org

OECD. (2019a). *OECD future of education and skills 2030 (Concept note: Core foundations for 2030).* https://www.oecd.org/education/2030-project/contact/OECD_Learning_Compass_2030_Concept_Note_Series.pdf

OECD. (2019b). *OECD future of education and skills 2030: Transformative competencies for 2030.* https://www.oecd.org/education/2030-

Patall, E. A., Cooper, H., & Wynn, S. R. (2010). The effectiveness and relative importance of choice in the classroom. *Journal of Educational Psychology, 102*(4), 896–915.

Patuawa, J., Robinson, V., Sinnema, C. E. L., & Zhu, T. (2021). Addressing inequity and underachievement: Middle leaders' effectiveness in problem solving. *Leading and Managing, 27*(1), 51–78.

Peeters, A., Robinson, V., & Rubie-Davies, C. (2020). Theories in use that explain adolescent help seeking and avoidance in mathematics. *Journal of Educational Psychology, 112*(3), 533–550. https://doi:org/10.1037/edu0000423

Peterson, C., & Seligman, M. E. P. (2004). *Character strengths and virtues: A handbook and classification.* American Psychological Association and Oxford University Press.

Phillips, D. C. (1987). Validity in qualitative research: Why the worry about warrant will not wane. *Education and Urban Society, 20*(1), 9–24.

Pring, R. (2014). Leadership: Skilled manager or virtuous professional? In *Investing in our education: Leading, learning, researching and the doctorate* (Vol. 13, pp. 59–73). Emerald Group Publishing Limited.

Razer, M., & Friedman, V. J. (2017). *From exclusion to excellence: Building restorative relationships to create inclusive schools.* Sense.

Rice, S., & Burbules, N. C. (2010). Listening: A virtue account. *Teachers College Record, 112*(11), 2728–2742.

Richardson, H. S. (1990). Specifying norms as a way to resolve concrete ethical problems. *Philosophy & Public Affairs, 19*(4), 279–310.

Rivkin, S. G., Hanushek, E. A., & Kain, J. F. (2005). Teachers, schools, and academic achievement. *Econometrica, 72*(2), 417–458.

Robinson, V. (1993). *Problem-based methodology: Research for the improvement of practice.* Pergamon Press.

Robinson, V. M. J. (1995). Dialogue needs a point and purpose: Review essay. *Educational Theory, 45*(2), 235–249. https://doi.org/10.1111/j.1741–5446.1995.00235.x

Robinson, V. M. J. (2006). Putting education back into educational leadership. *Leading & Managing, 12*(1), 62–75.

Robinson, V. (2011). *Student-centered leadership.* Jossey-Bass.

Robinson, V. (2018). *Reduce change to increase improvement.* Corwin.

Robinson, V. (2020). Educational leadership and virtuous courage. *Leading and Managing, 25*(2), 1–13.

Robinson, V., Bendikson, L., McNaughton, S., Wilson, A., & Zhu, T. (2017). Joining the dots: The challenge of creating coherent school improvement. *Teachers College Record, 119*(8), 1–44.

Robinson, V. M. J., Le Fevre, D. M., & Sinnema, C. E. L. (Eds.). (2016). *Open to learning leadership: How to build trust while tackling tough issues.* Hawker Brownlow Education.

Robinson, V. M. J., Lloyd, C., & Rowe, K. J. (2008). The impact of leadership on student outcomes: An analysis of the differential effects of leadership type. *Educational Administration Quarterly, 44*(5), 635–674. https://doi.org/10.1177/0013161X08321509

Robinson, V., Meyer, F., Le Fevre, D., & Sinnema, C. E. L. (2020). The quality of leaders' problem-solving conversations: Truth seeking or truth claiming? *Leadership and Policy in Schools, 20*(4), 650–671.

Ryan, R. M., & Deci, E. L. (2000). Self-determination theory and the facilitation of intrinsic motivation, social development, and well-being. *American Psychologist, 55*(1), 68–78.

Schmidt, W. H., Burroughs, N. A., Zoido, P., & Houang, R. T. (2015). The role of schooling in perpetuating educational inequality: An international perspective. *Educational Researcher, 44*(7), 371–386. https://doi.org/10.3102/0013189x15603982

Schmoker, M. (2016). *Leading with focus: Elevating the essentials for school and district improvement.* ASCD.

Scriven, M. (1991). Beyond formative and summative evaluation. In M. W. McLaughlin & D. C. Phillips (Eds.), *Evaluation and education: At quarter century* (pp. 19–64). NSSE and University of Chicago Press.

Sebastian, J., Camburn, E. M., & Spillane, J. P. (2018). Portraits of principal practice: Time allocation and school principal work. *Educational Administration Quarterly, 54*(1), 47–84. https://doi.org/10.1177/0013161x17720978

Seijts, G. H., & Latham, G. P. (2012). Knowing when to set learning versus performance goals. *Organizational Dynamics, 41*(1), 1–6. https://doi.org/10.1016/j.orgdyn.2011.12.001

Shaked, H. (2019). Perceptual inhibitors of instructional leadership in Israeli principals. *School Leadership & Management, 39*(5), 519–536.

Simon, H. A. (1993). Decision-making: Rational, non-rational, and irrational. *Educational Administration Quarterly, 29*(3), 392–411.

Sinnema, C. E. L., Le Fevre, D., Robinson, V. M. J., & Pope, D. (2013). When others' performance just isn't good enough: Educational leaders' framing of concerns in private and public. *Leadership and Policy in Schools, 12*(4), 301–336. https://doi.org/10.1080/15700763.2013.857419

Slavin, B. (2020). The details matter. That's why proven tutoring programs work better than general guidelines. *Robert Slavin's Blog* (wordpress.com).

Sockett, H. (2009). Dispositions as virtues: The complexity of the construct. *Journal of Teacher Education, 60*(3), 291–303. https://doi.org/10.1177/0022487109335189

Sockett, H. (2012). *Knowledge and virtue in teaching and learning: The primacy of dispositions.* Routledge.

Soll, J. B., Milkman, K. L., & Payne, J. W. (2015). Outsmart your own biases. *Harvard Business Review, 93*(5), 64–71.

Spiegel, J. S. (2012). Open-mindedness and intellectual humility. *Theory and Research in Education, 10*(1), 27–38. https://doi.org/10.1177/1477878512437472

Spillane, J. P. (2013). The practice of leading and managing teaching in educational organisations. In OECD (Ed.), *Leadership for 21st century learning* (pp. 59–82). OECD Publishing.

Spillane, J. P., & Seashore Louis, K. (2002). School improvement process and practices: Professional learning for building instructional capacity. In J. Murphy (Ed.), *The educational leadership challenge: Redefining leadership for the 21st century* (pp. 83–104). University of Chicago Press.

Spillane, J. P., Camburn, E. M., Pustejovsky, J., Pareja, A. S., & Lewis, G. (2008). Taking a distributed perspective: Epistemological and methodological trade-offs in operationalizing the leader-plus aspect. *Journal of Educational Administration, 46*(2), 189–213. https://doi.org/10.1108/09578230810863262

State of Victoria, Department of Education and Training. (2019). *Amplify: Empowering students through voice, agency and leadership.* https://www.education.vic.gov.au/Documents/school/teachers/teachingresources/practice/Amplify.pdf

Steele, M. D., Johnson, K. R., Otten, S., Herbel-Eisenmann, B. A., & Carver, C. L. (2015). Improving instructional leadership through the development of leadership content knowledge. *Journal of Research on Leadership Education, 10*(2), 127–150. https://doi.org/10.1177/1942775115569353

Stein, M. K., & Nelson, B. S. (2003). Leadership content knowledge. *Educational Evaluation and Policy Analysis, 25*, 423–448.

Sun, J., & Leithwood, K. (2015). Direction-setting school leadership practices: A meta-analytical review of evidence about their influence. *School Effectiveness and School Improvement, 26*(4), 499–523.

Swanton, C. (2005). *Virtue ethics: A pluralistic view* (Paperback ed.). Oxford University Press.

Swanton, C. (2016). A virtue ethical theory of role ethics. *The Journal of Value Inquiry, 50*(4), 687–702. https://doi.org/10.1007/s10790–016–9582–5

Tekkumru Kisa, M., & Stein, M. K. (2015). Learning to see teaching in new ways: A foundation for maintaining cognitive demand. *American Educational Research Journal, 52*(1), 105–136. https://doi.org/10.3102/0002831214549452

Timperley, H. S. (2005). Distributed leadership: Developing theory from practice. *Journal of Curriculum Studies, 37*(4), 395–420. https://doi.org/10.1080/00220270500038545

Timperley, H. S. (2008). *Teacher professional learning and development* (Vol. 18). International Academy of Education and International Bureau of Education.

Timperley, H. S. (2011). Knowledge and the leadership of learning. *Leadership and Policy in Schools, 10*(2), 145–170. https://doi.org/10.1080/15700763.2011.557519

Tomlinson, C. A., & Murphy, M. (2018). The empathetic school. *Educational Leadership, 75*(6), 22–27.

Tschannen-Moran, M., & Gareis, C. R. (2015). Faculty trust in the principal: An essential ingredient in high-performing schools. *Journal of Educational Administration, 53*(1), 66–92. http://dx.doi.org/10.1108/JEA-02-2014–0024

Utdanningsdirektoratet. (n.d.). *National curriculum for knowledge promotion in primary and secondary education and training: The quality framework*. Available from https://www.udir.no

Van Gog, T., Kester, L., & Paas, F. (2011). Effects of concurrent monitoring on cognitive load and performance as a function of task complexity. *Applied Cognitive Psychology, 25*(4), 584–587. https://doi.org/10.1002/acp.1726

Wageman, R., & Fisher, C. (2014). Who's in charge here? The team leadership implications of authority structure. In D. Day (Ed.), *The Oxford handbook of leadership and organizations* (pp. 455–481). Oxford University Press.

Wang, M.-T., & Holcombe, R. (2010). Adolescents' perceptions of school environment, engagement, and academic achievement in middle school. *American Educational Research Journal, 47*(3), 633–662. https://doi.org/10.3102/0002831209361209

Welsh, D., Bush, J., Thiel, C., & Bonner, J. (2019). Reconceptualizing goal setting's dark side: The ethical consequences of learning versus outcome goals. *Organizational Behavior and Human Decision Processes, 150*, 14–27. https://doi.org/10.1016/j.obhdp.2018.11.001

Wildy, H., Pepper, C., & Guanzhong, L. (2011). Applying standards for leaders to the selection of secondary school principals. *Journal of Educational Administration, 49*(3), 276–291. https://doi.org/10.1108/09578231111129064

Wilson, A., Madjar, I., & McNaughton, S. (2016). Opportunity to learn about disciplinary literacy in senior secondary English classrooms in New Zealand. *The Curriculum Journal, 27*(2), 204–228.

Winch, C. (2002). The economic aims of education. *Journal of Philosophy of Education, 36*(1), 101–117. https://doi.org/10.1111/1467–9752.00262

Witziers, B., Bosker, R. J., & Krüger, M. L. (2003). Educational leadership and student achievement: The elusive search for an association. *Educational Administration Quarterly, 39*(3), 398–425.

Wolcott, H. F. (2003). *The man in the principal's office: An ethnography* (Updated ed.). AltaMira Press. (Original work published 1973)

Yeager, D. S., & Walton, G. M. (2011). Social-psychological interventions in education: They're not magic. *Review of Educational Research, 81*(2), 267–301. https://doi.org/10.3102/0034654311405999

Zaki, J., & Ochsner, K. (2016). Empathy. In L. Feldman Barrett, M. Lewis, & J. Haviland-Jones (Eds.), *Handbook of emotions* (4th ed., pp. 871–884). Guildford Press.

Index

CORWIN
A SAGE Publishing Company

Zeitfracht Medien GmbH
Ferdinand-Jühlke-Straße 7
99095 Erfurt, Deutschland
produktsicherheit@kolibri360.de